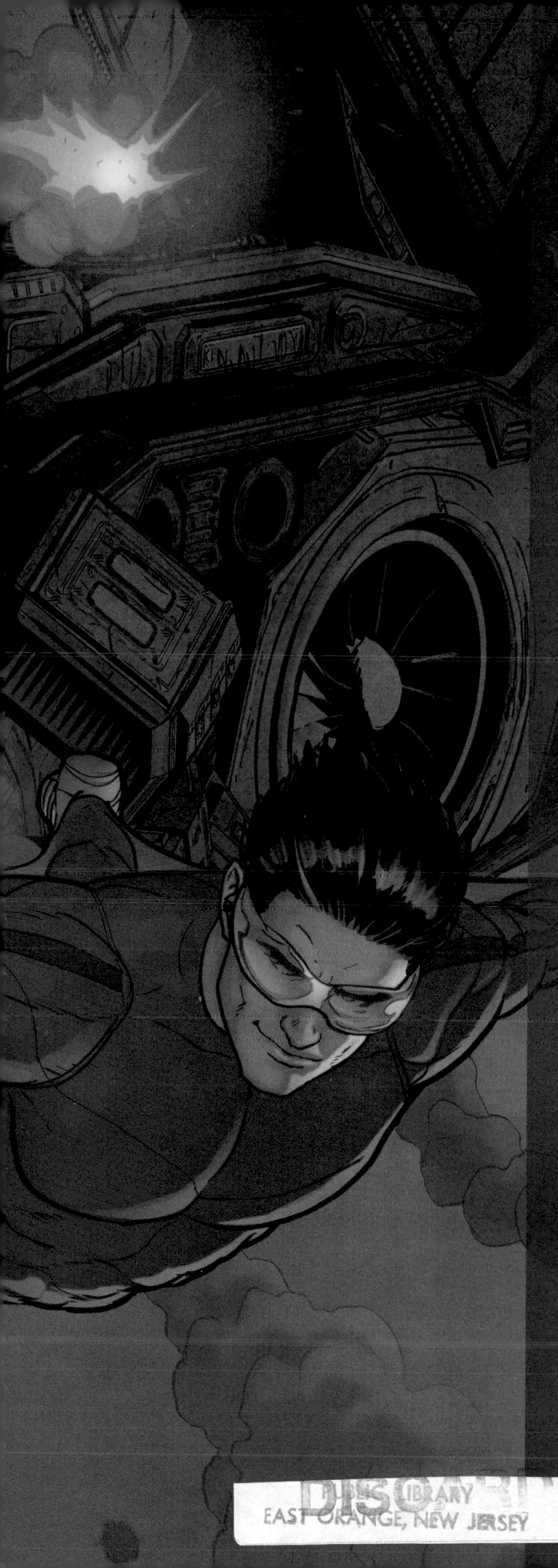

GRAYSON

VOLUME 1
AGENTS OF SPYRAL

WRITTEN BY
TIM SEELEY
TOM KING

ART BY
MIKEL JANÍN
STEPHEN MOONEY
GUILLERMO ORTEGO
JUAN CASTRO

INKS BY
JONATHAN GLAPION

COLOR BY
JEROMY COX

LETTERS BY
CARLOS M. MANGUAL

COLLECTION COVER ARTIST
ANDREW ROBINSON

BATMAN CREATED BY
BOB KANE

GRAYSON VOLUME 1: AGENTS OF SPYRAL

Published by DC Comics. Compilation Copyright © 2015 DC Comics. All Rights Reserved.
Originally published in single magazine form in GRAYSON 1-4, GRAYSON: FUTURES END 1, SECRET ORIGINS 8
Copyright © 2014 DC Comics. All Rights Reserved. All characters, their distinctive likenesses and related elements
featured in this publication are trademarks of DC Comics. The stories, characters and incidents featured in this publication
are entirely fictional. DC Comics does not read or accept unsolicited ideas, stories or artwork.

DC Comics, 2900 West Alameda Avenue, Burbank, CA 91505
Printed by RR Donnelley, Owensville, MO, USA. 12/11/15.
ISBN: 978-1-4012-5759-0
First Printing.

Library of Congress Cataloging-in-Publication Data

Seeley, Tim, author.
Grayson. Volume 1, Agents of Spyral / Tim Seeley, Mikel Janín.
pages cm. — (The New 52!)
ISBN 978-1-4012-5259-0
1. Graphic novels. I. Janín, Mikel, illustrator. II. Title. III. Title: Agents of Spyral.
PN6728.G723S44 2015
741.5'973—dc23
2015007188

i14189550

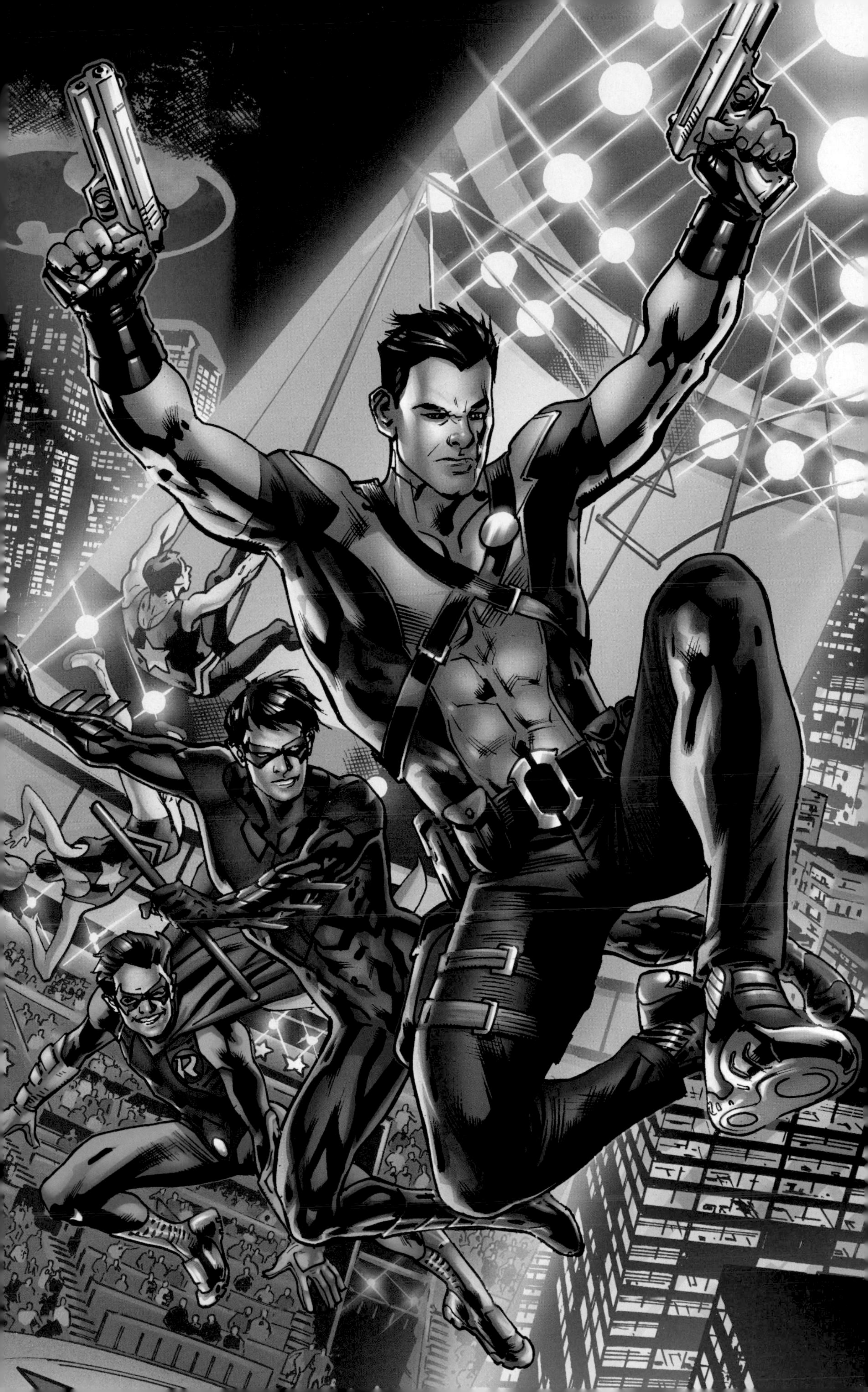

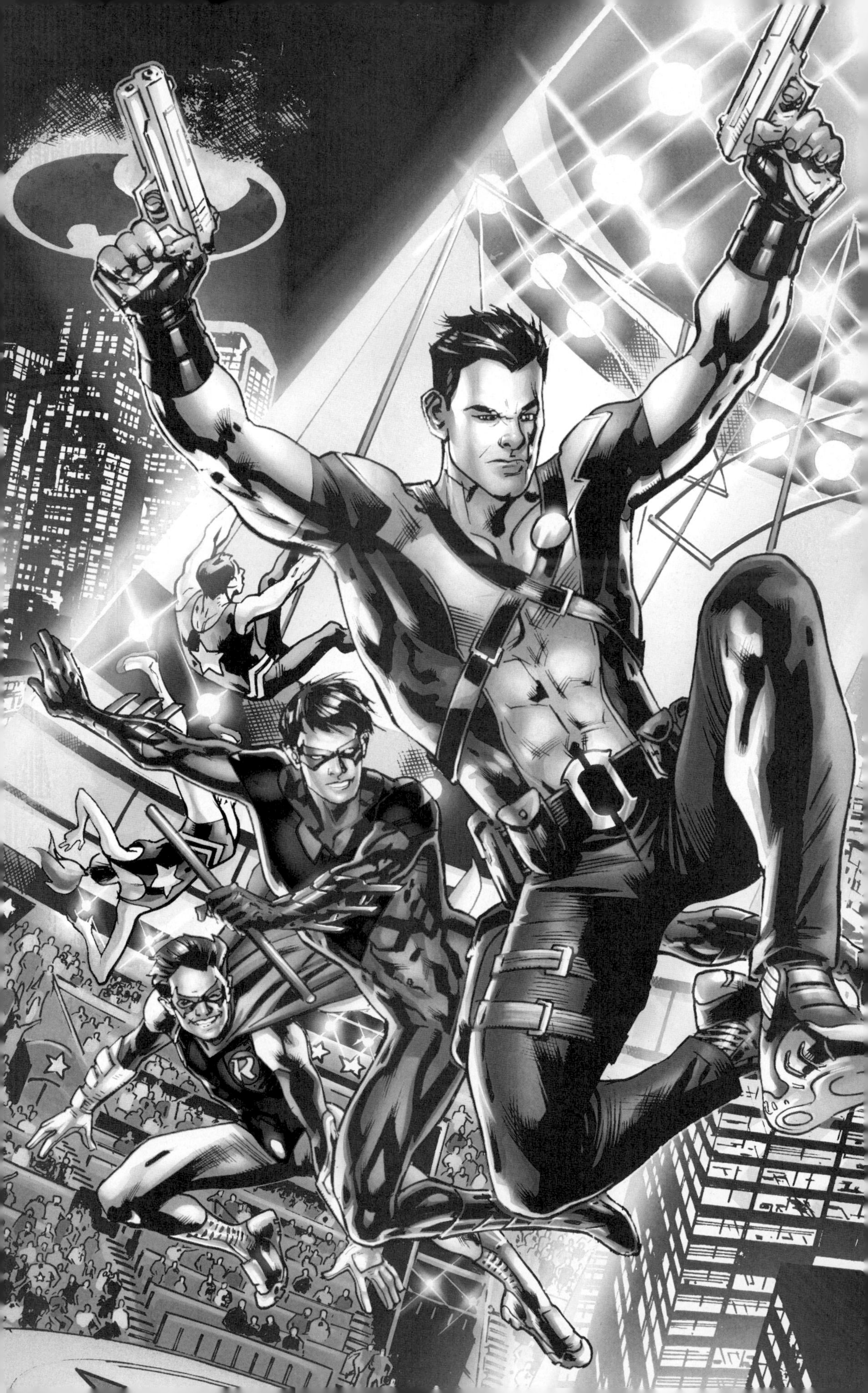

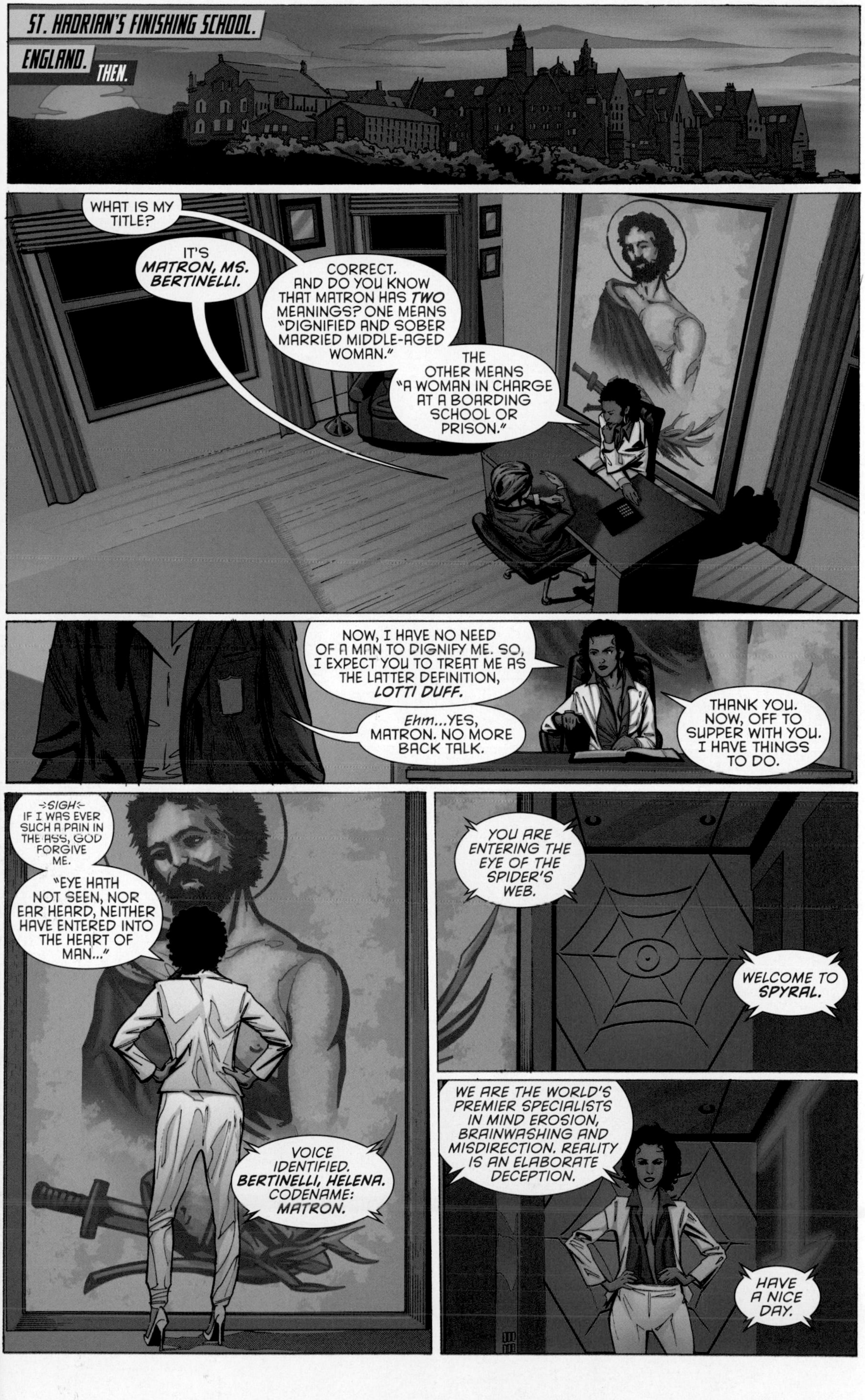

ST. HADRIAN'S FINISHING SCHOOL.
ENGLAND.
THEN.
WHAT IS MY TITLE?
IT'S MATRON, MS. BERTINELLI.
CORRECT. AND DO YOU KNOW THAT MATRON HAS TWO MEANINGS? ONE MEANS "DIGNIFIED AND SOBER MARRIED MIDDLE-AGED WOMAN."
THE OTHER MEANS "A WOMAN IN CHARGE AT A BOARDING SCHOOL OR PRISON."
NOW, I HAVE NO NEED OF A MAN TO DIGNIFY ME. SO, I EXPECT YOU TO TREAT ME AS THE LATTER DEFINITION, LOTTI DUFF.
Ehm...YES, MATRON. NO MORE BACK TALK.
THANK YOU. NOW, OFF TO SUPPER WITH YOU. I HAVE THINGS TO DO.
SIGH
IF I WAS EVER SUCH A PAIN IN THE ASS, GOD FORGIVE ME.
"EYE HATH NOT SEEN, NOR EAR HEARD, NEITHER HAVE ENTERED INTO THE HEART OF MAN..."
VOICE IDENTIFIED. BERTINELLI, HELENA. CODENAME: MATRON.
YOU ARE ENTERING THE EYE OF THE SPIDER'S WEB.
WELCOME TO SPYRAL.
WE ARE THE WORLD'S PREMIER SPECIALISTS IN MIND EROSION, BRAINWASHING AND MISDIRECTION. REALITY IS AN ELABORATE DECEPTION.
HAVE A NICE DAY.

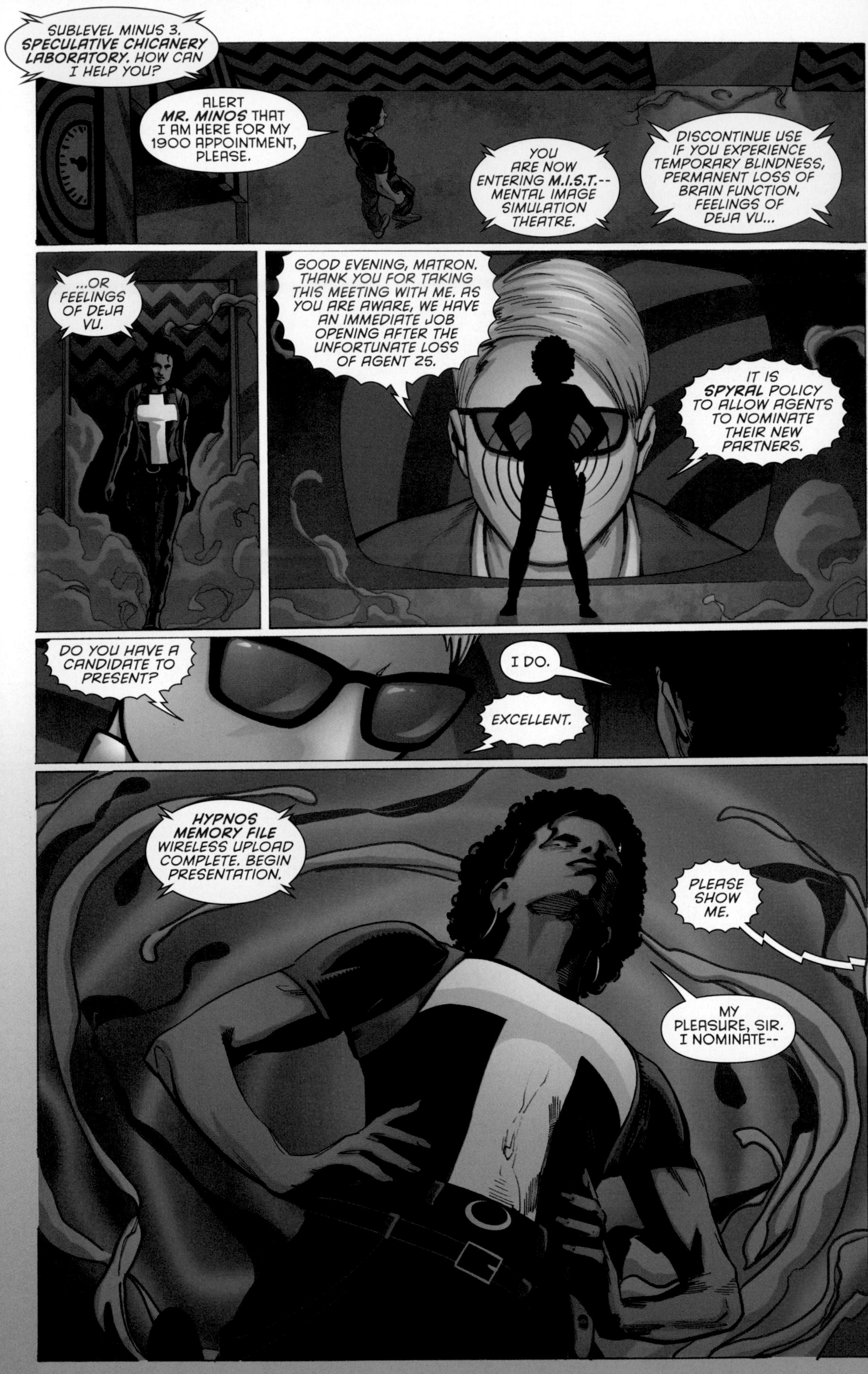
SUBLEVEL MINUS 3. SPECULATIVE CHICANERY LABORATORY. HOW CAN I HELP YOU?
ALERT MR. MINOS THAT I AM HERE FOR MY 1900 APPOINTMENT, PLEASE.
YOU ARE NOW ENTERING M.I.S.T.-- MENTAL IMAGE SIMULATION THEATRE.
DISCONTINUE USE IF YOU EXPERIENCE TEMPORARY BLINDNESS, PERMANENT LOSS OF BRAIN FUNCTION, FEELINGS OF DEJA VU...
...OR FEELINGS OF DEJA VU.
GOOD EVENING, MATRON. THANK YOU FOR TAKING THIS MEETING WITH ME. AS YOU ARE AWARE, WE HAVE AN IMMEDIATE JOB OPENING AFTER THE UNFORTUNATE LOSS OF AGENT 25.
IT IS SPYRAL POLICY TO ALLOW AGENTS TO NOMINATE THEIR NEW PARTNERS.
DO YOU HAVE A CANDIDATE TO PRESENT?
I DO.
EXCELLENT.
HYPNOS MEMORY FILE WIRELESS UPLOAD COMPLETE. BEGIN PRESENTATION.
PLEASE SHOW ME.
MY PLEASURE, SIR. I NOMINATE--

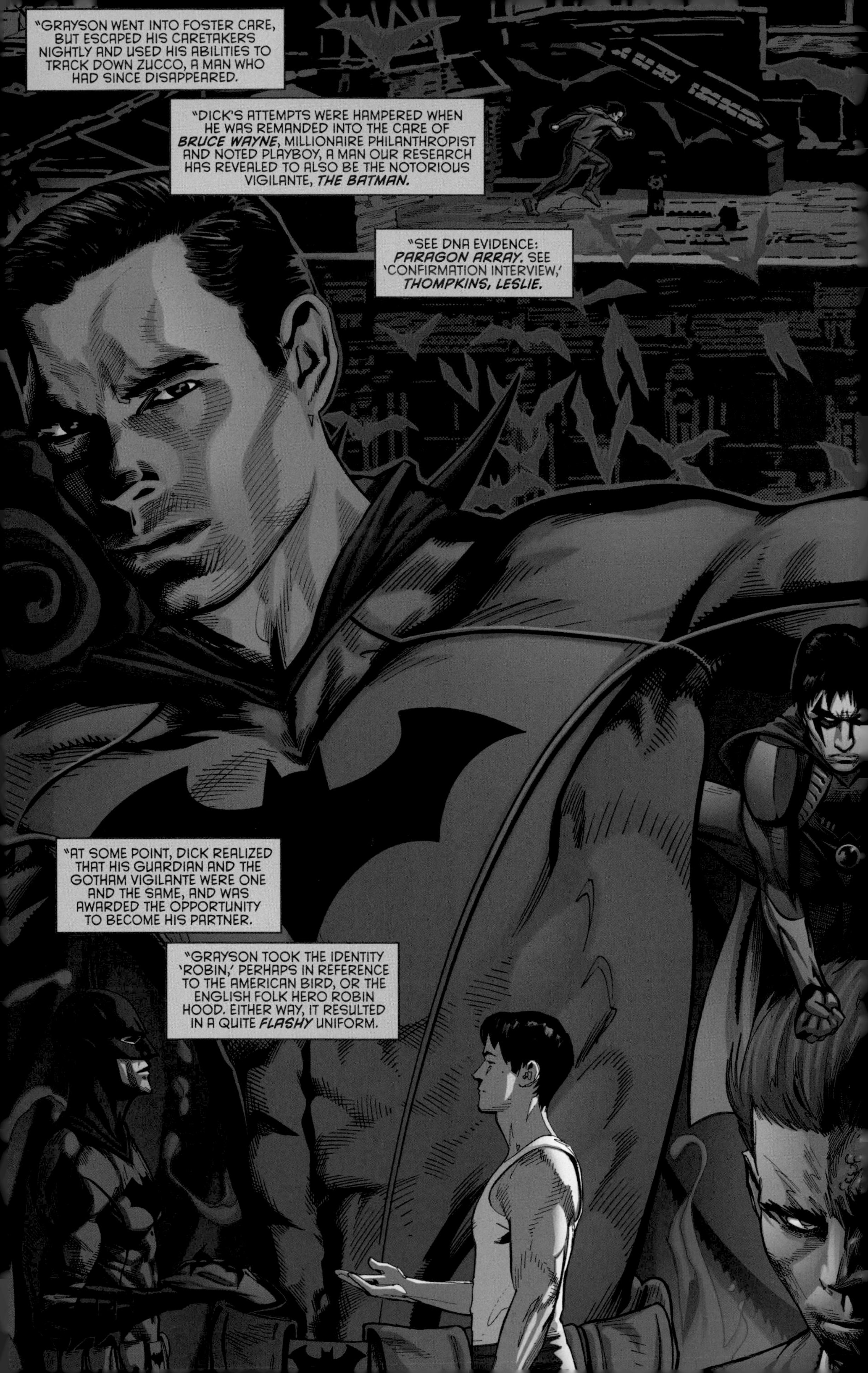
"GRAYSON WENT INTO FOSTER CARE, BUT ESCAPED HIS CARETAKERS NIGHTLY AND USED HIS ABILITIES TO TRACK DOWN ZUCCO, A MAN WHO HAD SINCE DISAPPEARED.
"DICK'S ATTEMPTS WERE HAMPERED WHEN HE WAS REMANDED INTO THE CARE OF *BRUCE WAYNE*, MILLIONAIRE PHILANTHROPIST AND NOTED PLAYBOY, A MAN OUR RESEARCH HAS REVEALED TO ALSO BE THE NOTORIOUS VIGILANTE, *THE BATMAN.*
"SEE DNA EVIDENCE: *PARAGON ARRAY.* SEE 'CONFIRMATION INTERVIEW,' *THOMPKINS, LESLIE.*
"AT SOME POINT, DICK REALIZED THAT HIS GUARDIAN AND THE GOTHAM VIGILANTE WERE ONE AND THE SAME, AND WAS AWARDED THE OPPORTUNITY TO BECOME HIS PARTNER.
"GRAYSON TOOK THE IDENTITY 'ROBIN,' PERHAPS IN REFERENCE TO THE AMERICAN BIRD, OR THE ENGLISH FOLK HERO ROBIN HOOD. EITHER WAY, IT RESULTED IN A QUITE *FLASHY* UNIFORM.

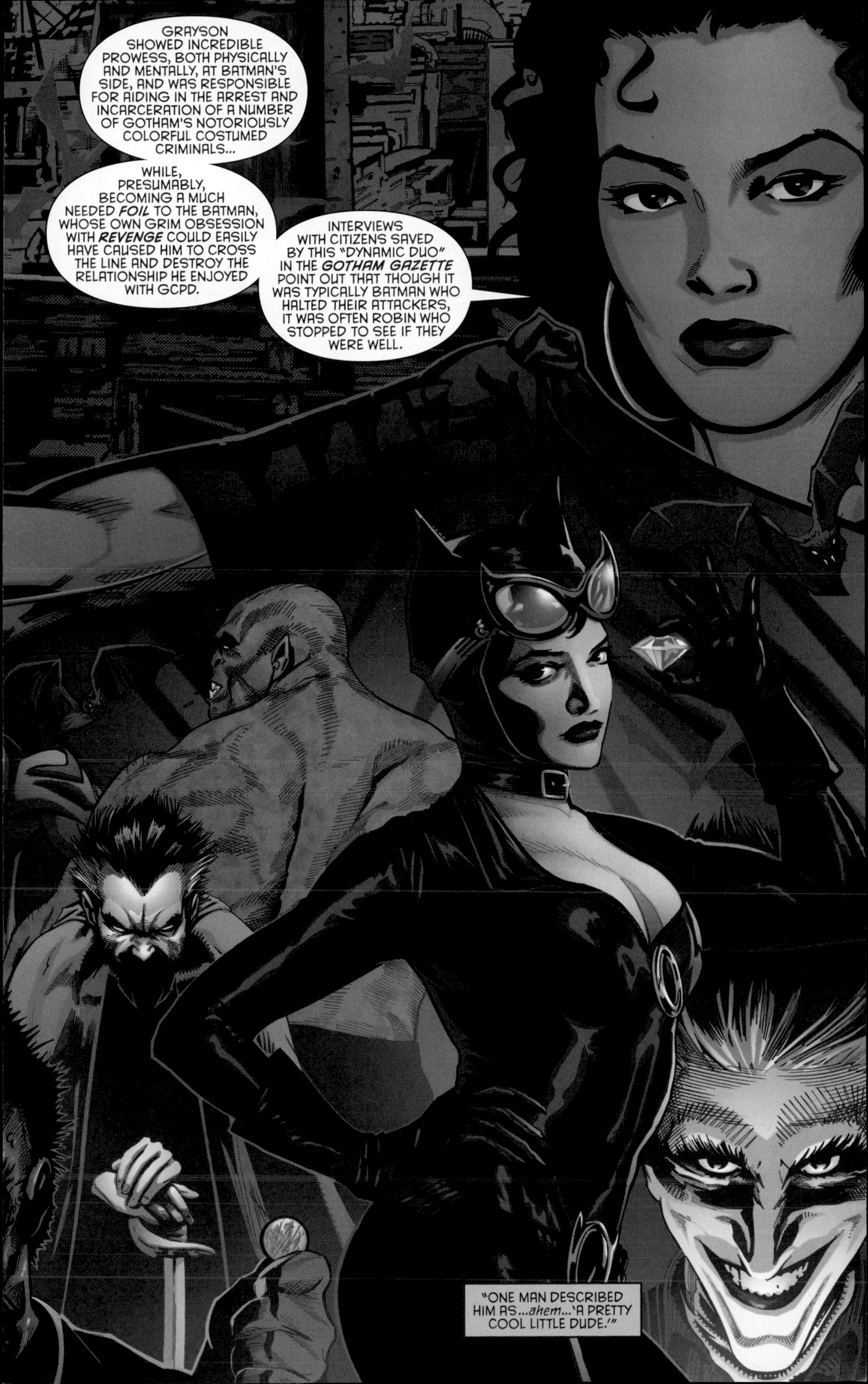
GRAYSON SHOWED INCREDIBLE PROWESS, BOTH PHYSICALLY AND MENTALLY, AT BATMAN'S SIDE, AND WAS RESPONSIBLE FOR AIDING IN THE ARREST AND INCARCERATION OF A NUMBER OF GOTHAM'S NOTORIOUSLY COLORFUL COSTUMED CRIMINALS...
WHILE, PRESUMABLY, BECOMING A MUCH NEEDED *FOIL* TO THE BATMAN, WHOSE OWN GRIM OBSESSION WITH *REVENGE* COULD EASILY HAVE CAUSED HIM TO CROSS THE LINE AND DESTROY THE RELATIONSHIP HE ENJOYED WITH GCPD.
INTERVIEWS WITH CITIZENS SAVED BY THIS "DYNAMIC DUO" IN THE *GOTHAM GAZETTE* POINT OUT THAT THOUGH IT WAS TYPICALLY BATMAN WHO HALTED THEIR ATTACKERS, IT WAS OFTEN ROBIN WHO STOPPED TO SEE IF THEY WERE WELL.
"ONE MAN DESCRIBED HIM AS...*ahem*...'A PRETTY COOL LITTLE DUDE.'"

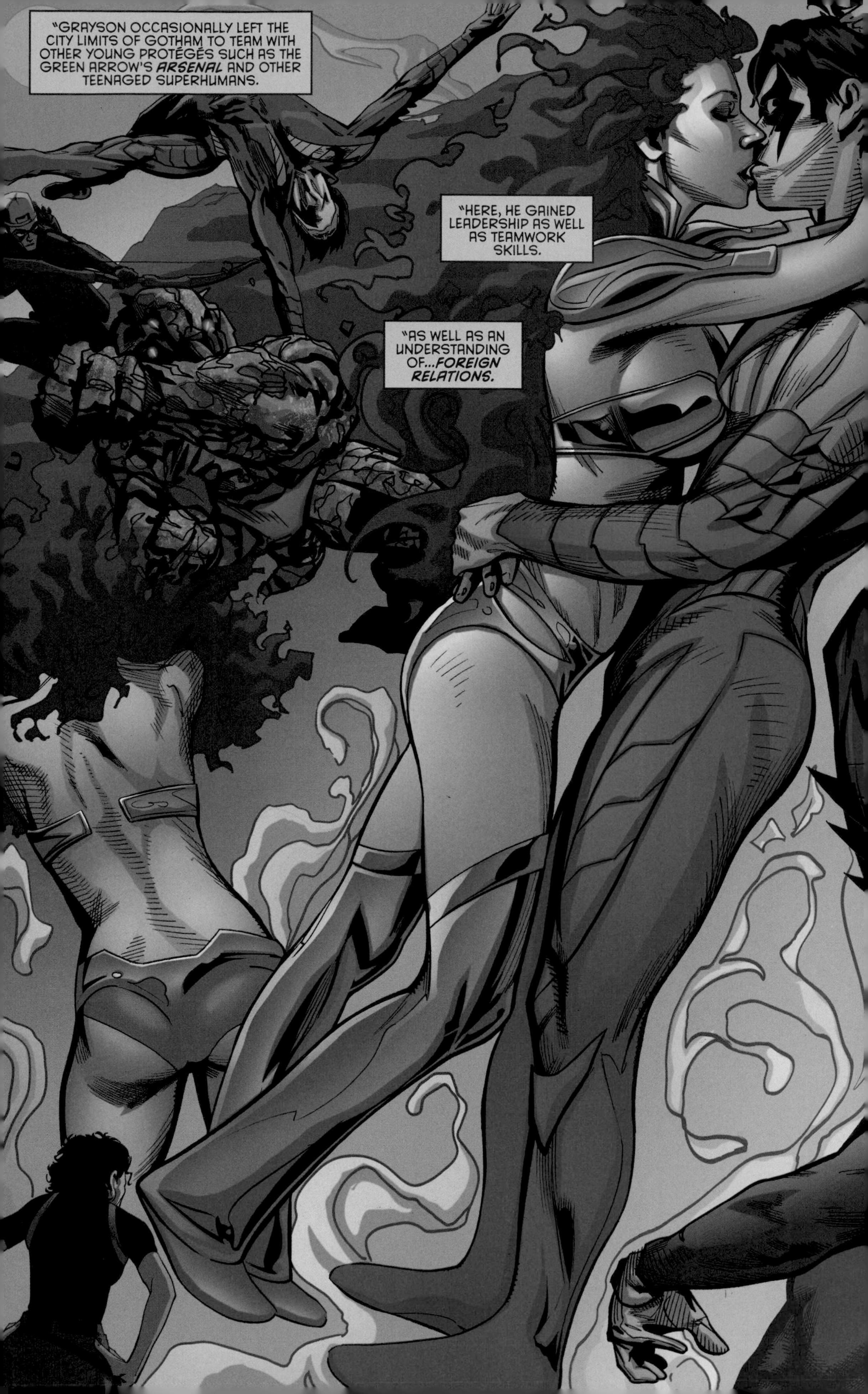

"GRAYSON OCCASIONALLY LEFT THE CITY LIMITS OF GOTHAM TO TEAM WITH OTHER YOUNG PROTÉGÉS SUCH AS THE GREEN ARROW'S *ARSENAL* AND OTHER TEENAGED SUPERHUMANS.
"HERE, HE GAINED LEADERSHIP AS WELL AS TEAMWORK SKILLS.
"AS WELL AS AN UNDERSTANDING OF...*FOREIGN RELATIONS.*

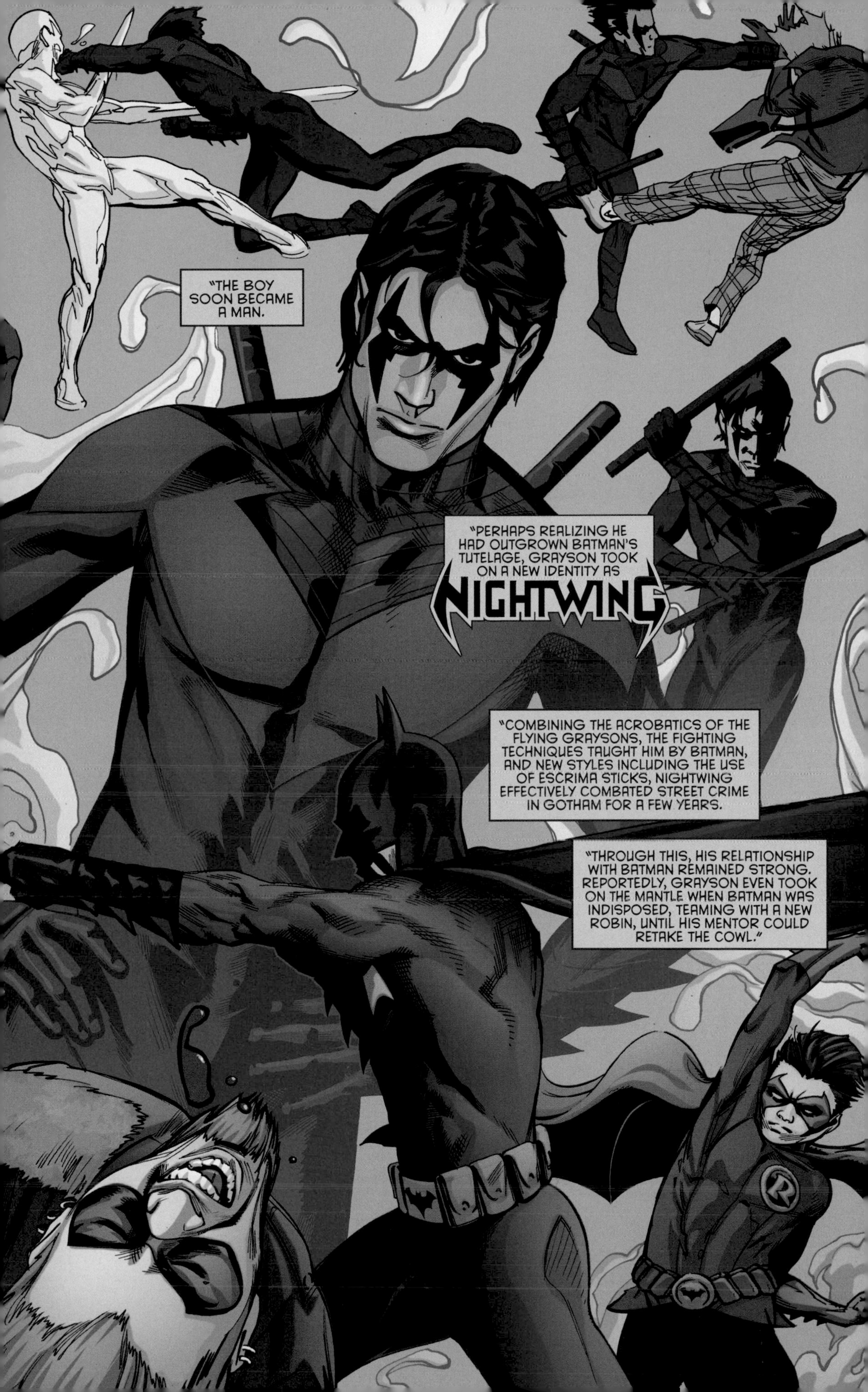
"THE BOY SOON BECAME A MAN.
"PERHAPS REALIZING HE HAD OUTGROWN BATMAN'S TUTELAGE, GRAYSON TOOK ON A NEW IDENTITY AS
NIGHTWING
"COMBINING THE ACROBATICS OF THE FLYING GRAYSONS, THE FIGHTING TECHNIQUES TAUGHT HIM BY BATMAN, AND NEW STYLES INCLUDING THE USE OF ESCRIMA STICKS, NIGHTWING EFFECTIVELY COMBATED STREET CRIME IN GOTHAM FOR A FEW YEARS.
"THROUGH THIS, HIS RELATIONSHIP WITH BATMAN REMAINED STRONG. REPORTEDLY, GRAYSON EVEN TOOK ON THE MANTLE WHEN BATMAN WAS INDISPOSED, TEAMING WITH A NEW ROBIN, UNTIL HIS MENTOR COULD RETAKE THE COWL."

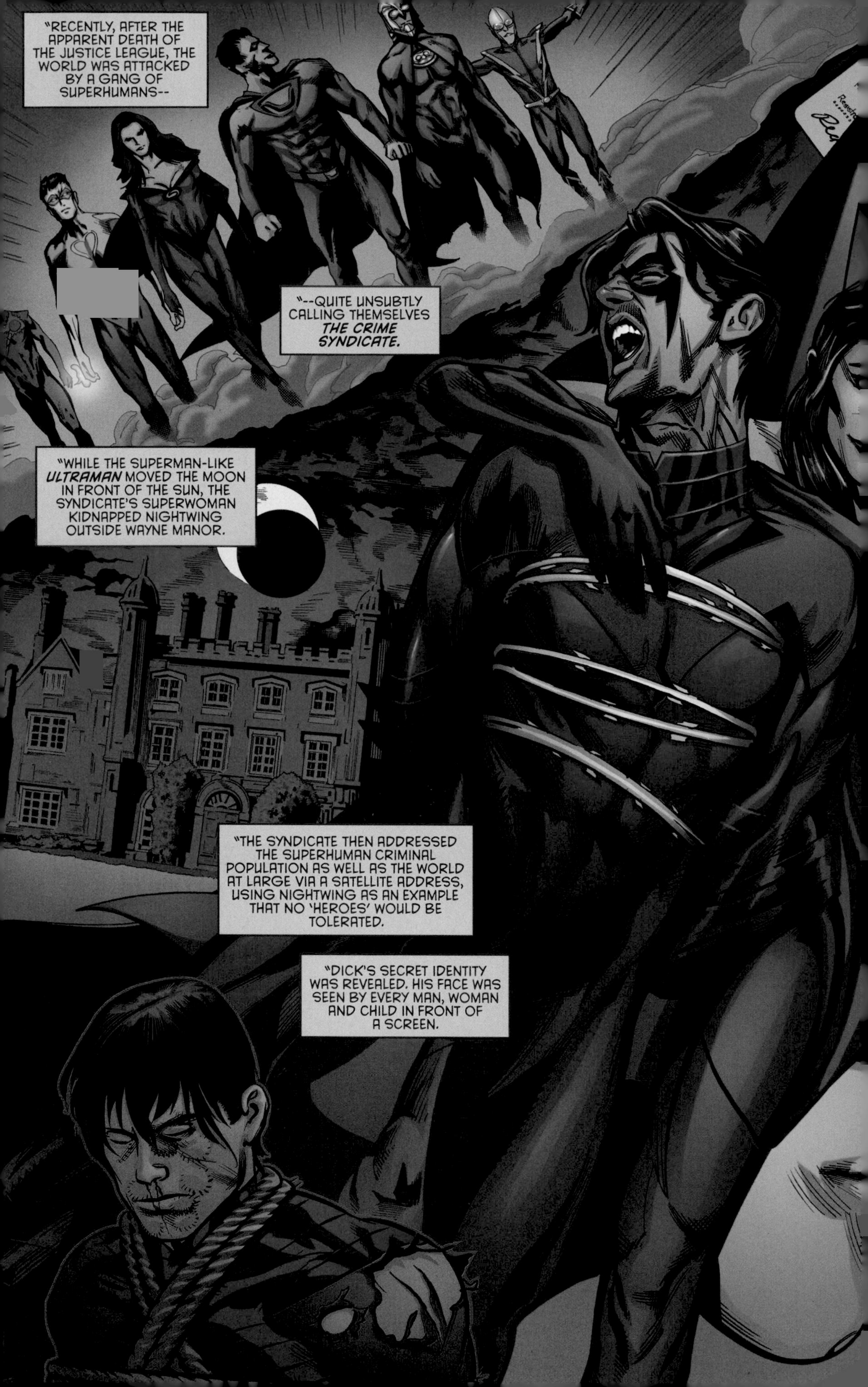
"RECENTLY, AFTER THE APPARENT DEATH OF THE JUSTICE LEAGUE, THE WORLD WAS ATTACKED BY A GANG OF SUPERHUMANS--
"--QUITE UNSUBTLY CALLING THEMSELVES THE CRIME SYNDICATE.
"WHILE THE SUPERMAN-LIKE ULTRAMAN MOVED THE MOON IN FRONT OF THE SUN, THE SYNDICATE'S SUPERWOMAN KIDNAPPED NIGHTWING OUTSIDE WAYNE MANOR.
"THE SYNDICATE THEN ADDRESSED THE SUPERHUMAN CRIMINAL POPULATION AS WELL AS THE WORLD AT LARGE VIA A SATELLITE ADDRESS, USING NIGHTWING AS AN EXAMPLE THAT NO 'HEROES' WOULD BE TOLERATED.
"DICK'S SECRET IDENTITY WAS REVEALED. HIS FACE WAS SEEN BY EVERY MAN, WOMAN AND CHILD IN FRONT OF A SCREEN.

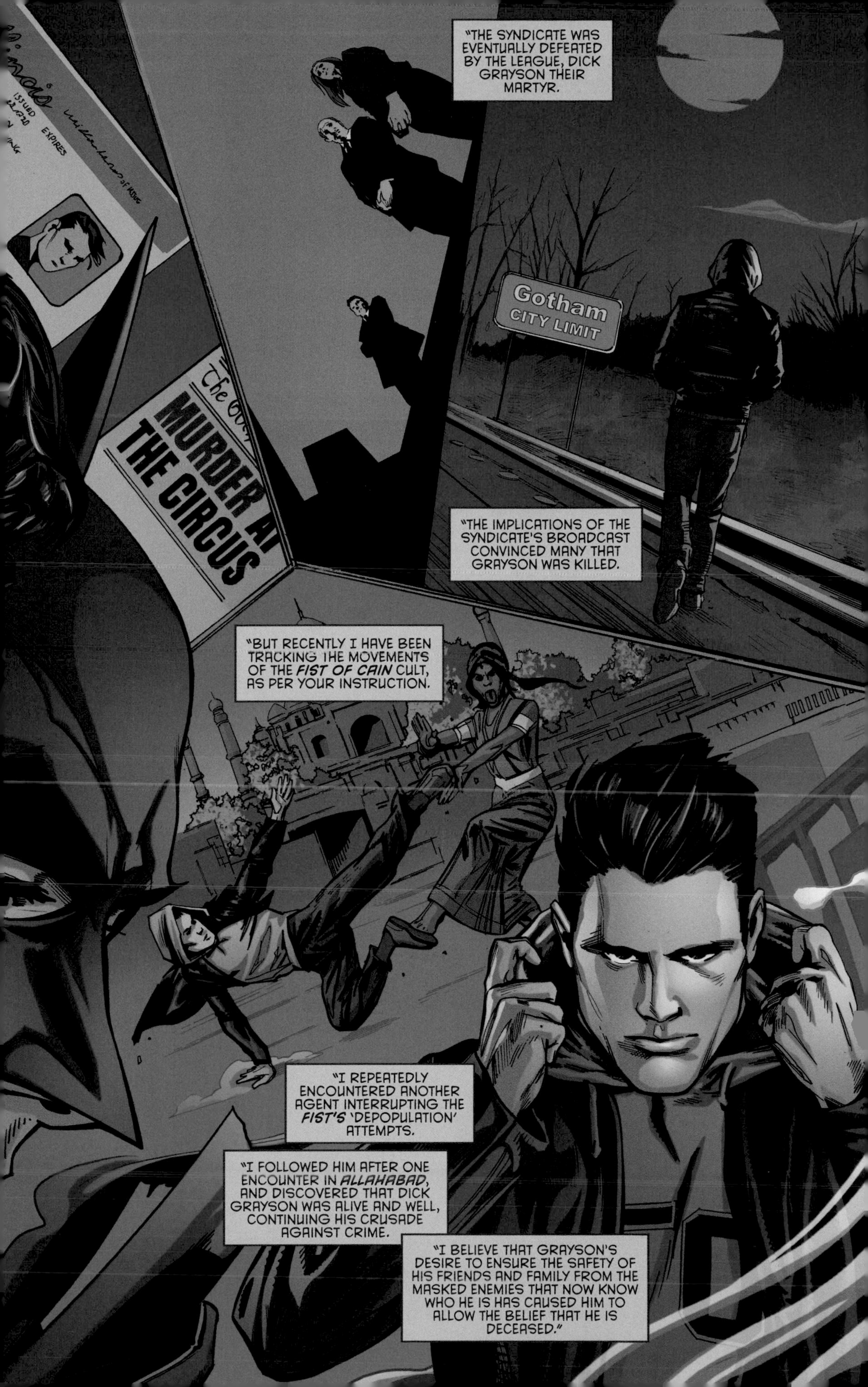
"THE SYNDICATE WAS EVENTUALLY DEFEATED BY THE LEAGUE, DICK GRAYSON THEIR MARTYR.
Gotham CITY LIMIT
MURDER AT THE CIRCUS
"THE IMPLICATIONS OF THE SYNDICATE'S BROADCAST CONVINCED MANY THAT GRAYSON WAS KILLED.
"BUT RECENTLY I HAVE BEEN TRACKING THE MOVEMENTS OF THE FIST OF CAIN CULT, AS PER YOUR INSTRUCTION.
"I REPEATEDLY ENCOUNTERED ANOTHER AGENT INTERRUPTING THE FIST'S 'DEPOPULATION' ATTEMPTS.
"I FOLLOWED HIM AFTER ONE ENCOUNTER IN ALLAHABAD, AND DISCOVERED THAT DICK GRAYSON WAS ALIVE AND WELL, CONTINUING HIS CRUSADE AGAINST CRIME.
"I BELIEVE THAT GRAYSON'S DESIRE TO ENSURE THE SAFETY OF HIS FRIENDS AND FAMILY FROM THE MASKED ENEMIES THAT NOW KNOW WHO HE IS HAS CAUSED HIM TO ALLOW THE BELIEF THAT HE IS DECEASED."

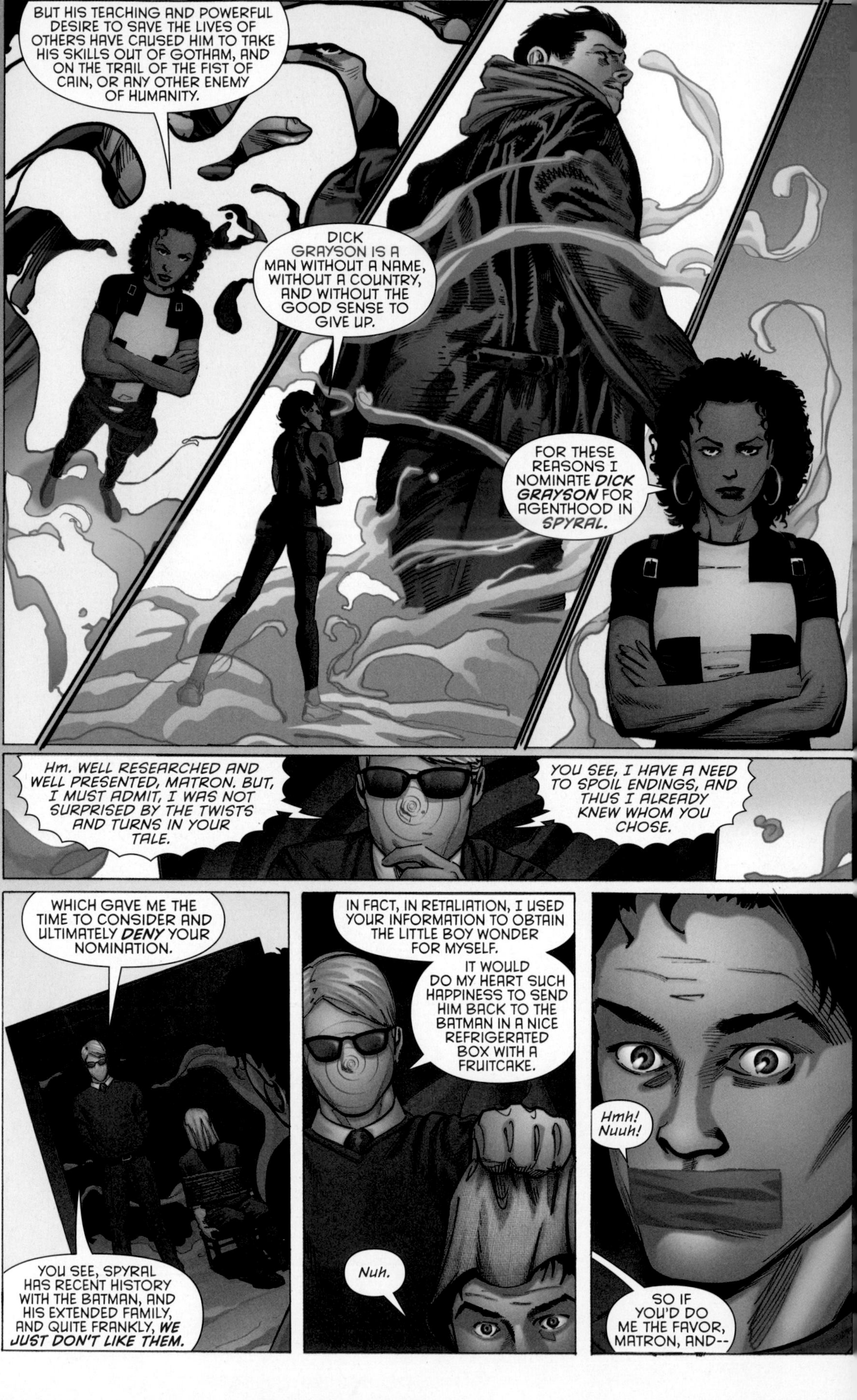
BUT HIS TEACHING AND POWERFUL DESIRE TO SAVE THE LIVES OF OTHERS HAVE CAUSED HIM TO TAKE HIS SKILLS OUT OF GOTHAM, AND ON THE TRAIL OF THE FIST OF CAIN, OR ANY OTHER ENEMY OF HUMANITY.
DICK GRAYSON IS A MAN WITHOUT A NAME, WITHOUT A COUNTRY, AND WITHOUT THE GOOD SENSE TO GIVE UP.
FOR THESE REASONS I NOMINATE DICK GRAYSON FOR AGENTHOOD IN SPYRAL.
Hm. WELL RESEARCHED AND WELL PRESENTED, MATRON. BUT, I MUST ADMIT, I WAS NOT SURPRISED BY THE TWISTS AND TURNS IN YOUR TALE.
YOU SEE, I HAVE A NEED TO SPOIL ENDINGS, AND THUS I ALREADY KNEW WHOM YOU CHOSE.
WHICH GAVE ME THE TIME TO CONSIDER AND ULTIMATELY DENY YOUR NOMINATION.
YOU SEE, SPYRAL HAS RECENT HISTORY WITH THE BATMAN, AND HIS EXTENDED FAMILY, AND QUITE FRANKLY, WE JUST DON'T LIKE THEM.
IN FACT, IN RETALIATION, I USED YOUR INFORMATION TO OBTAIN THE LITTLE BOY WONDER FOR MYSELF.
IT WOULD DO MY HEART SUCH HAPPINESS TO SEND HIM BACK TO THE BATMAN IN A NICE REFRIGERATED BOX WITH A FRUITCAKE.
Nuh.
Hmh! Nuuh!
SO IF YOU'D DO ME THE FAVOR, MATRON, AND--

"YOU MAY BRING HIM IN, MATRON. AND IF HE ACCEPTS...

NOW.

"...I TRUST YOUR JUDGMENT THAT GRAYSON WILL MAKE A FINE *AGENT 37*."

...SO, THE WHEELS ARE COMING OFF OF THE PENGUIN'S ZAMBONI OF DOOM, RIGHT? AND HE'S FREAKING OUT, SQUAWKING, "*WAK!* WHY WON'T MY MACHINE WORK? *WAK!*"

AND, RIGHT BEFORE I KICKED HIM IN HIS STUPID FACE, I SAID "HEY PENGUIN! LOOK! *HAPPY FEET!*"

WAIT...LOOK'S LIKE *MONSIEUR ALABASTER'S* INFO WAS CORRECT. I'VE GOT TWO *H.I.V.E.* AGENTS CHECKING THE FIST'S DROP SPOT.

EVERY MOMENT WE'VE SPENT WAITING MAKES ME ASK MYSELF WHY YOU INSIST ON SHARING YOUR INANE STORIES WITH ME.

AW, C'MON, HELENA. YOU KNOW WHY--

--BECAUSE TO KNOW ME IS TO *LOVE* ME.

C'MON. THE BORING PART OF THE JOB IS OVER. NOW, THE GOOD PART...

...WE'VE GOT SOME LIVES TO SAVE.

THE CANDIDATE

WRITER / TIM SEELEY   PLOT BY TIM SEELEY & TOM KING   ARTIST / STEPHEN MOONEY
COLORIST / JEROMY COX   LETTERER / CARLOS M. MANGUAL

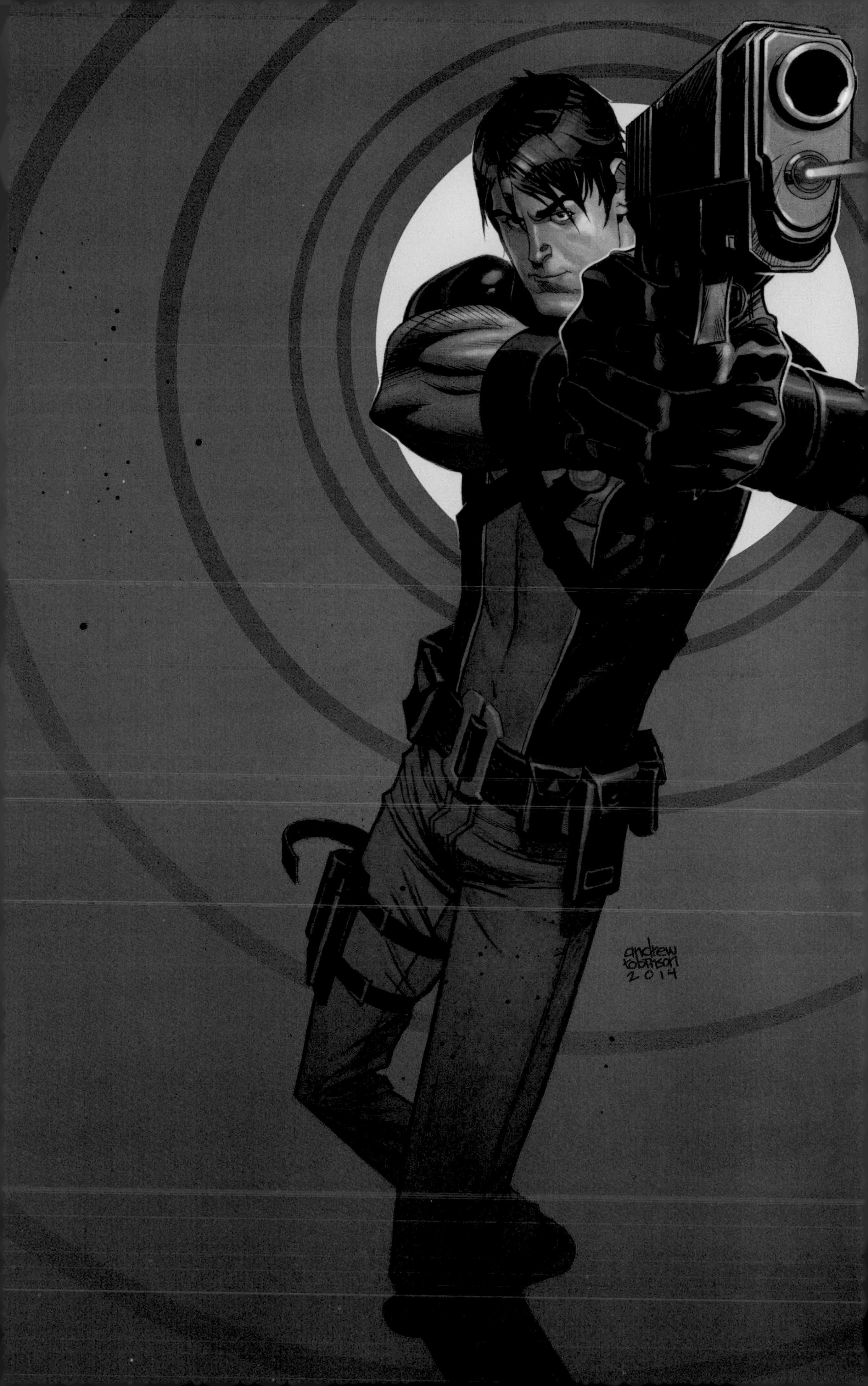
andrew robinson
2014

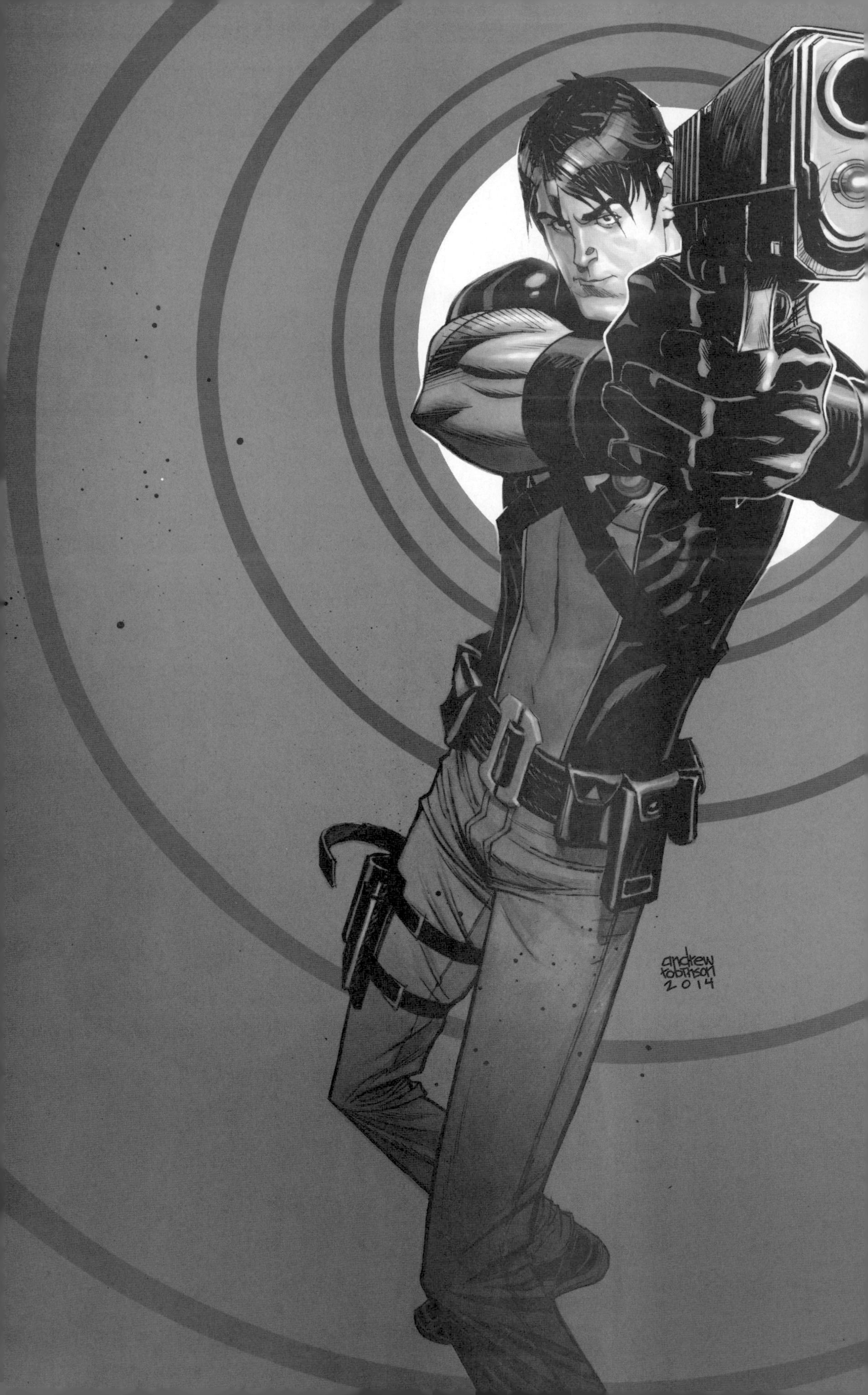
andrew robinson
2014

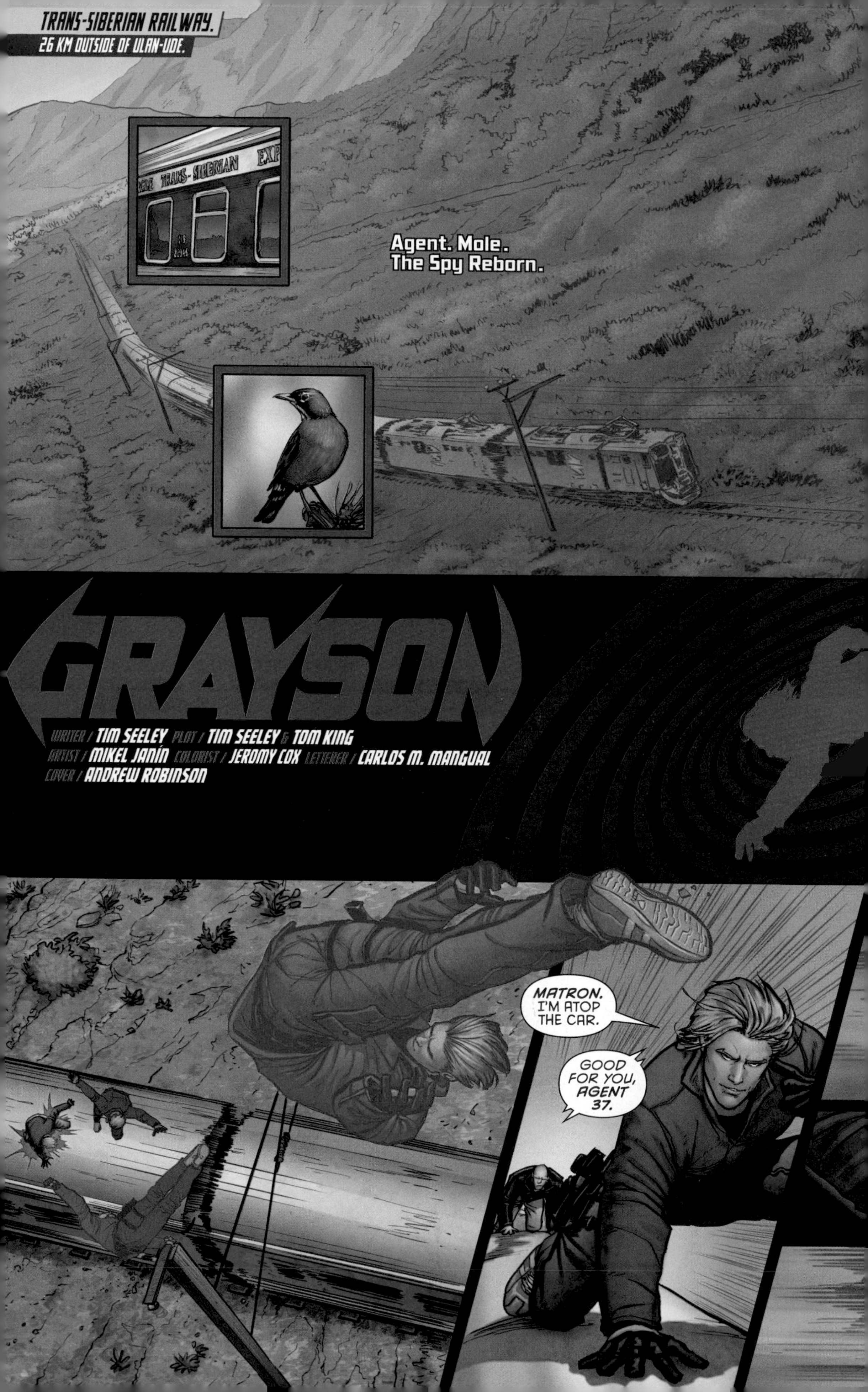
TRANS-SIBERIAN RAILWAY.
26 KM OUTSIDE OF ULAN-UDE.
TRANS-SIBERIAN EXP
Agent. Mole. The Spy Reborn.
GRAYSON
WRITER / TIM SEELEY PLOT / TIM SEELEY & TOM KING
ARTIST / MIKEL JANÍN COLORIST / JEROMY COX LETTERER / CARLOS M. MANGUAL
COVER / ANDREW ROBINSON
MATRON. I'M ATOP THE CAR.
GOOD FOR YOU, AGENT 37.

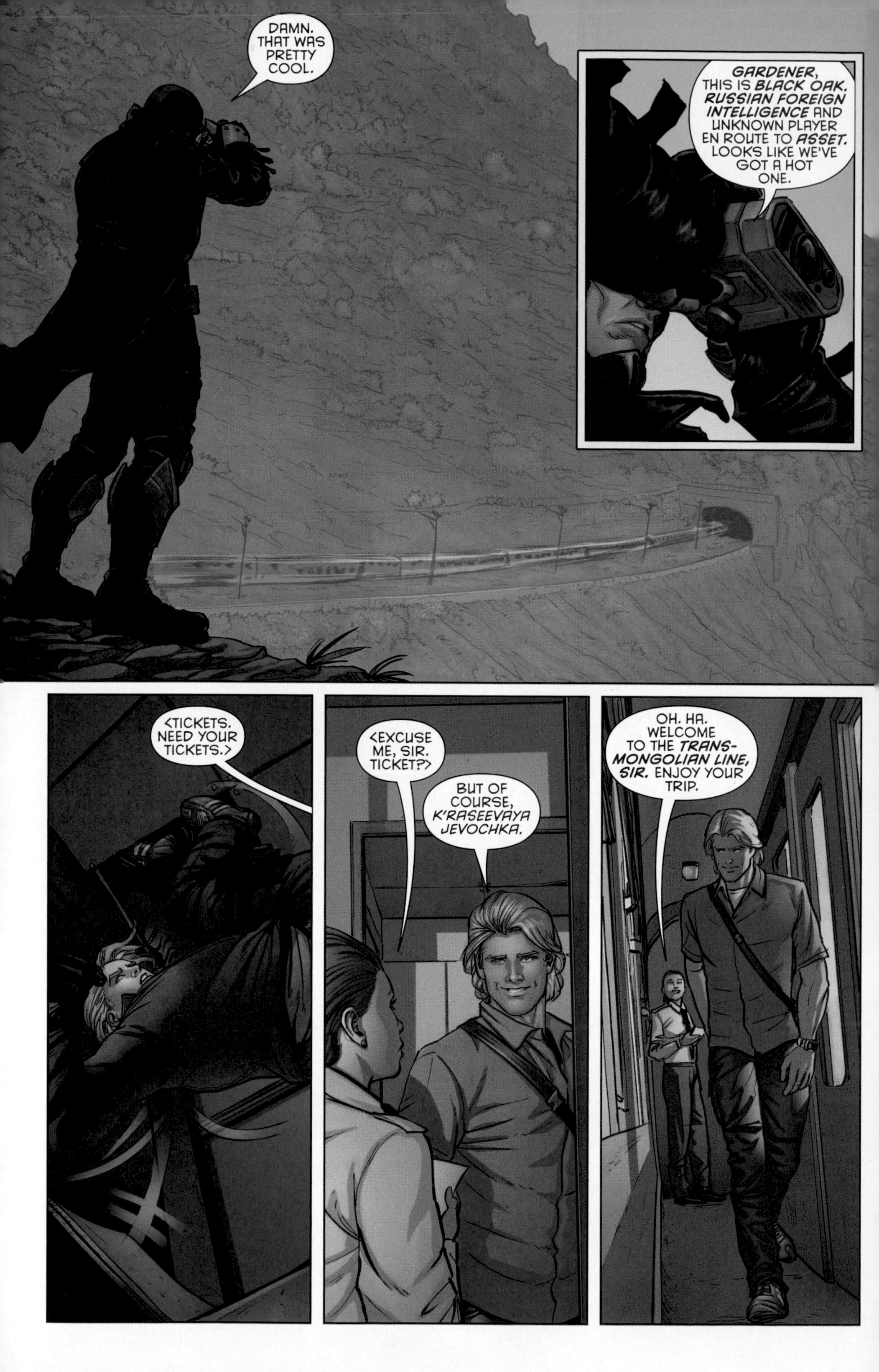
DAMN. THAT WAS PRETTY COOL.
GARDENER, THIS IS BLACK OAK. RUSSIAN FOREIGN INTELLIGENCE AND UNKNOWN PLAYER EN ROUTE TO ASSET. LOOKS LIKE WE'VE GOT A HOT ONE.
<TICKETS. NEED YOUR TICKETS.>
<EXCUSE ME, SIR. TICKET?>
BUT OF COURSE, K'RASEEVAYA JEVOCHKA.
OH. HA. WELCOME TO THE TRANS-MONGOLIAN LINE, SIR. ENJOY YOUR TRIP.

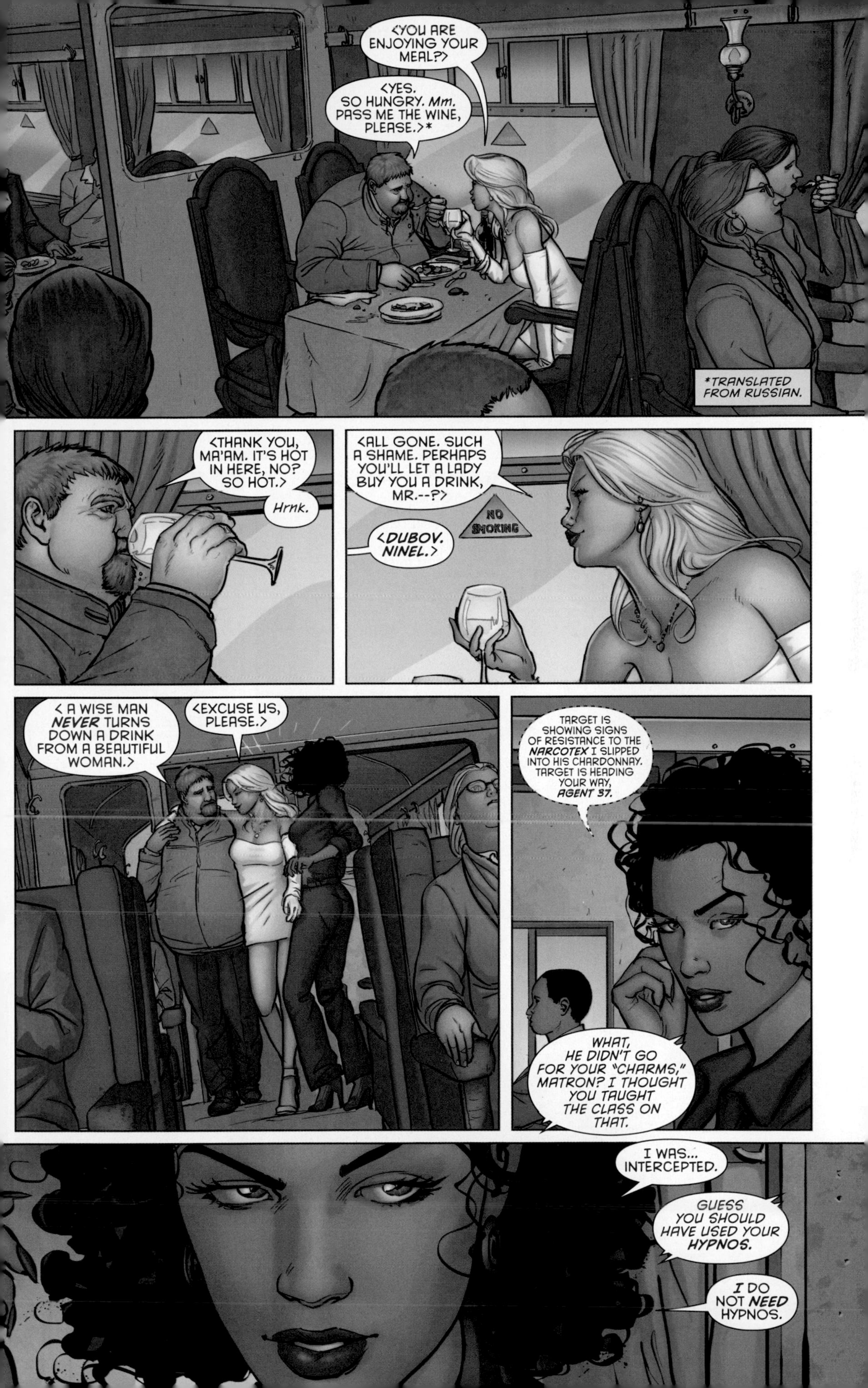
<YOU ARE ENJOYING YOUR MEAL?>
<YES. SO HUNGRY. *Mm.* PASS ME THE WINE, PLEASE.>*
*TRANSLATED FROM RUSSIAN.
<THANK YOU, MA'AM. IT'S HOT IN HERE, NO? SO HOT.>
Hrnk.
<ALL GONE. SUCH A SHAME. PERHAPS YOU'LL LET A LADY BUY YOU A DRINK, MR.--?>
NO SMOKING
<***DUBOV. NINEL.***>
< A WISE MAN ***NEVER*** TURNS DOWN A DRINK FROM A BEAUTIFUL WOMAN.>
<EXCUSE US, PLEASE.>
TARGET IS SHOWING SIGNS OF RESISTANCE TO THE ***NARCOTEX*** I SLIPPED INTO HIS CHARDONNAY. TARGET IS HEADING YOUR WAY, ***AGENT 37.***
WHAT, HE DIDN'T GO FOR YOUR "CHARMS," MATRON? I THOUGHT YOU TAUGHT THE CLASS ON THAT.
I WAS... INTERCEPTED.
GUESS YOU SHOULD HAVE USED YOUR ***HYPNOS.***
I DO NOT ***NEED*** HYPNOS.

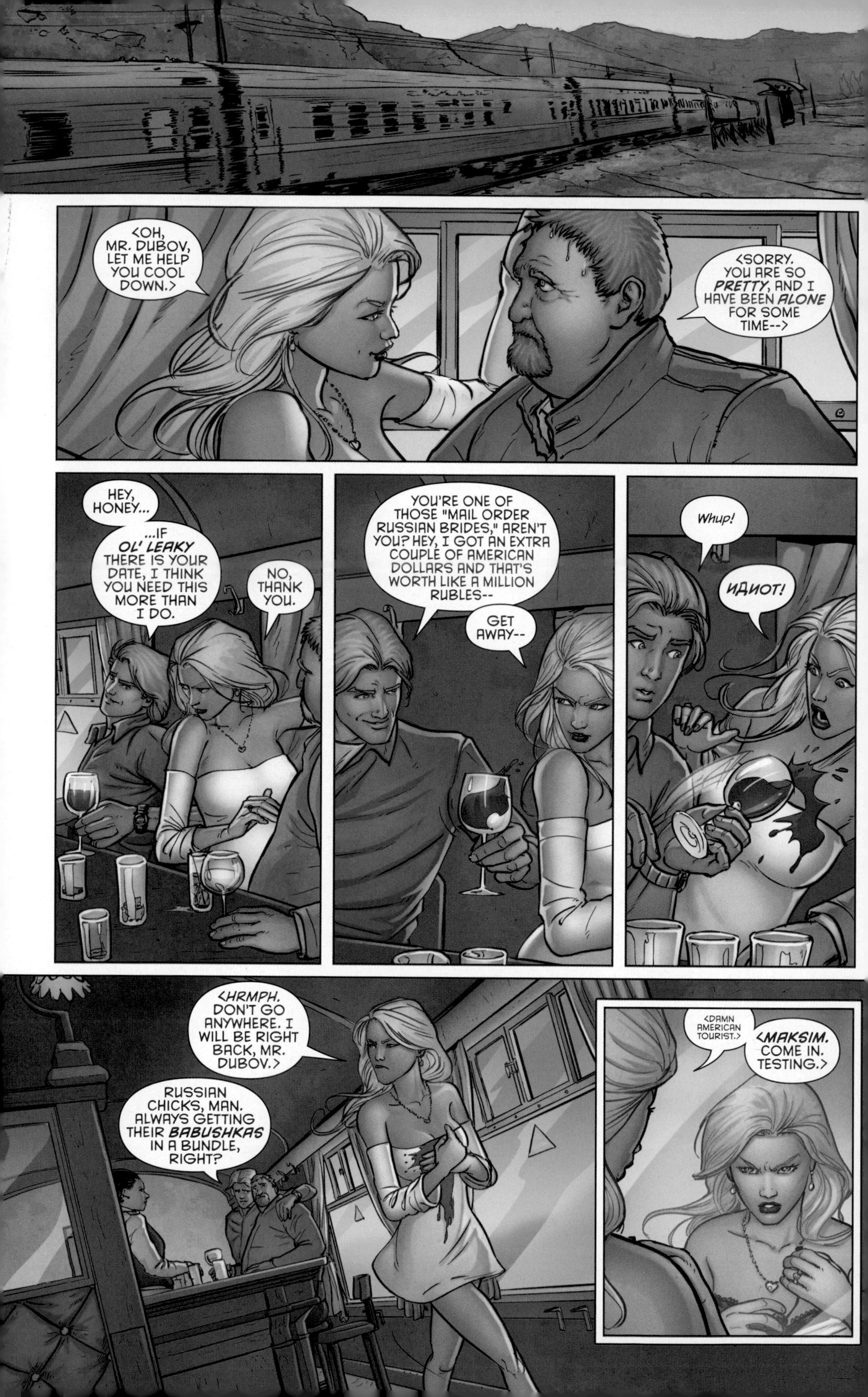
<OH, MR. DUBOV, LET ME HELP YOU COOL DOWN.>
<SORRY. YOU ARE SO PRETTY, AND I HAVE BEEN ALONE FOR SOME TIME-->
HEY, HONEY...
...IF OL' LEAKY THERE IS YOUR DATE, I THINK YOU NEED THIS MORE THAN I DO.
NO, THANK YOU.
YOU'RE ONE OF THOSE "MAIL ORDER RUSSIAN BRIDES," AREN'T YOU? HEY, I GOT AN EXTRA COUPLE OF AMERICAN DOLLARS AND THAT'S WORTH LIKE A MILLION RUBLES--
GET AWAY--
Whup!
ИДИОТ!
<HRMPH. DON'T GO ANYWHERE. I WILL BE RIGHT BACK, MR. DUBOV.>
RUSSIAN CHICKS, MAN. ALWAYS GETTING THEIR BABUSHKAS IN A BUNDLE, RIGHT?
<DAMN AMERICAN TOURIST.>
<MAKSIM. COME IN. TESTING.>

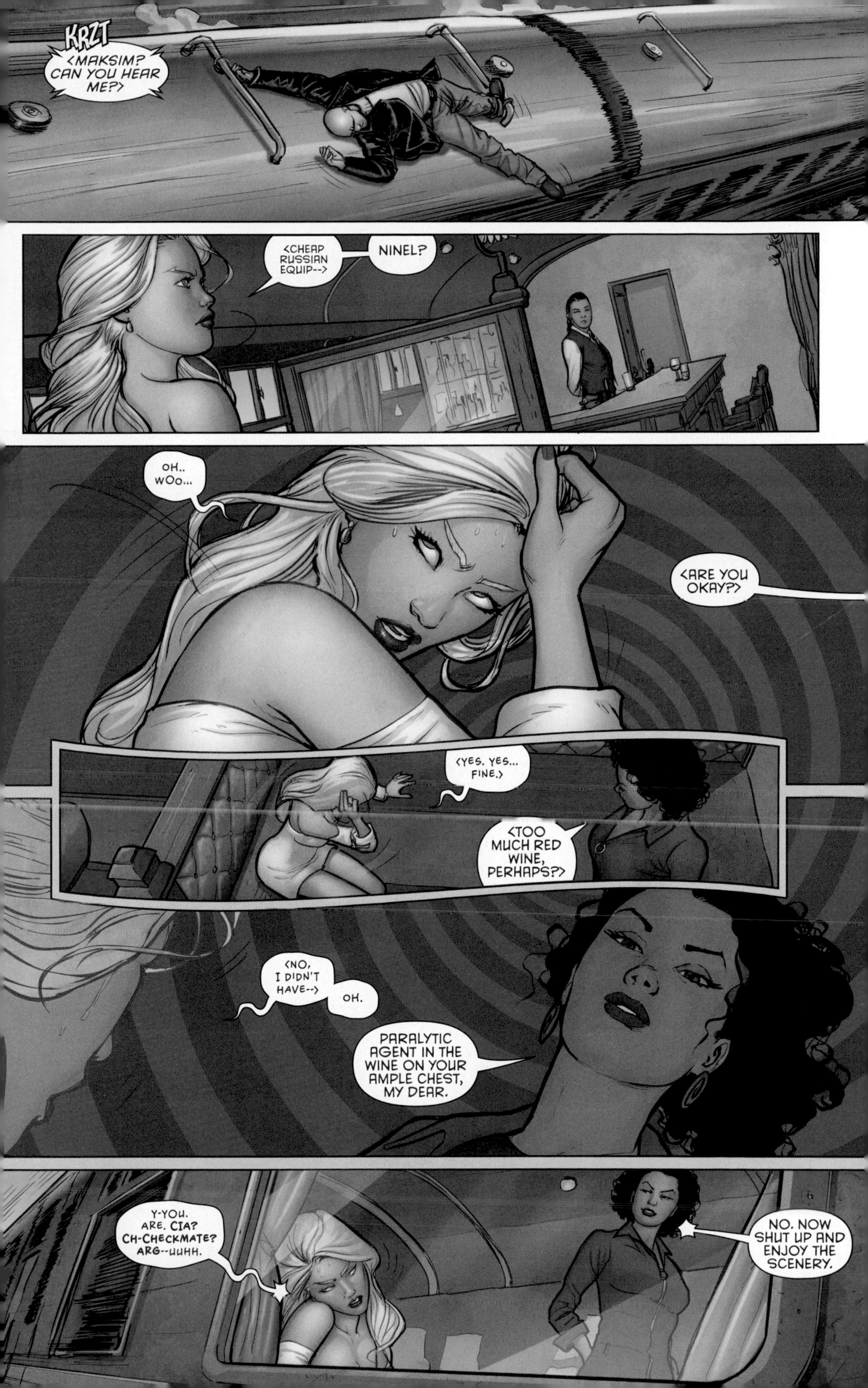
KRZT
<MAKSIM? CAN YOU HEAR ME?>
<CHEAP RUSSIAN EQUIP-->
NINEL?
OH.. WOO...
<ARE YOU OKAY?>
<YES. YES... FINE.>
<TOO MUCH RED WINE, PERHAPS?>
<NO, I DIDN'T HAVE-->
OH.
PARALYTIC AGENT IN THE WINE ON YOUR AMPLE CHEST, MY DEAR.
Y-YOU. ARE. CIA? CH-CHECKMATE? ARG--UUHH.
NO. NOW SHUT UP AND ENJOY THE SCENERY.

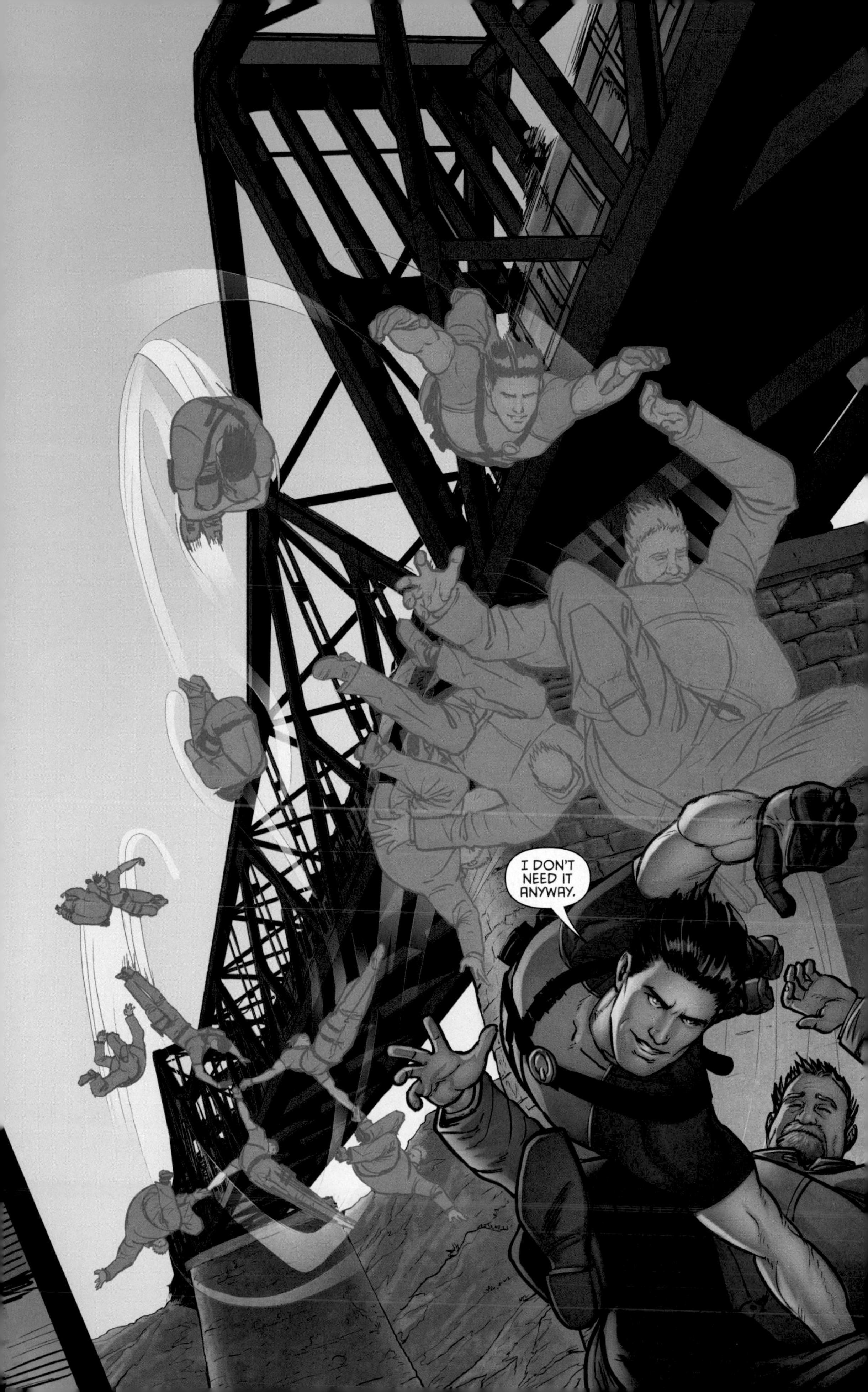
I DON'T NEED IT ANYWAY.

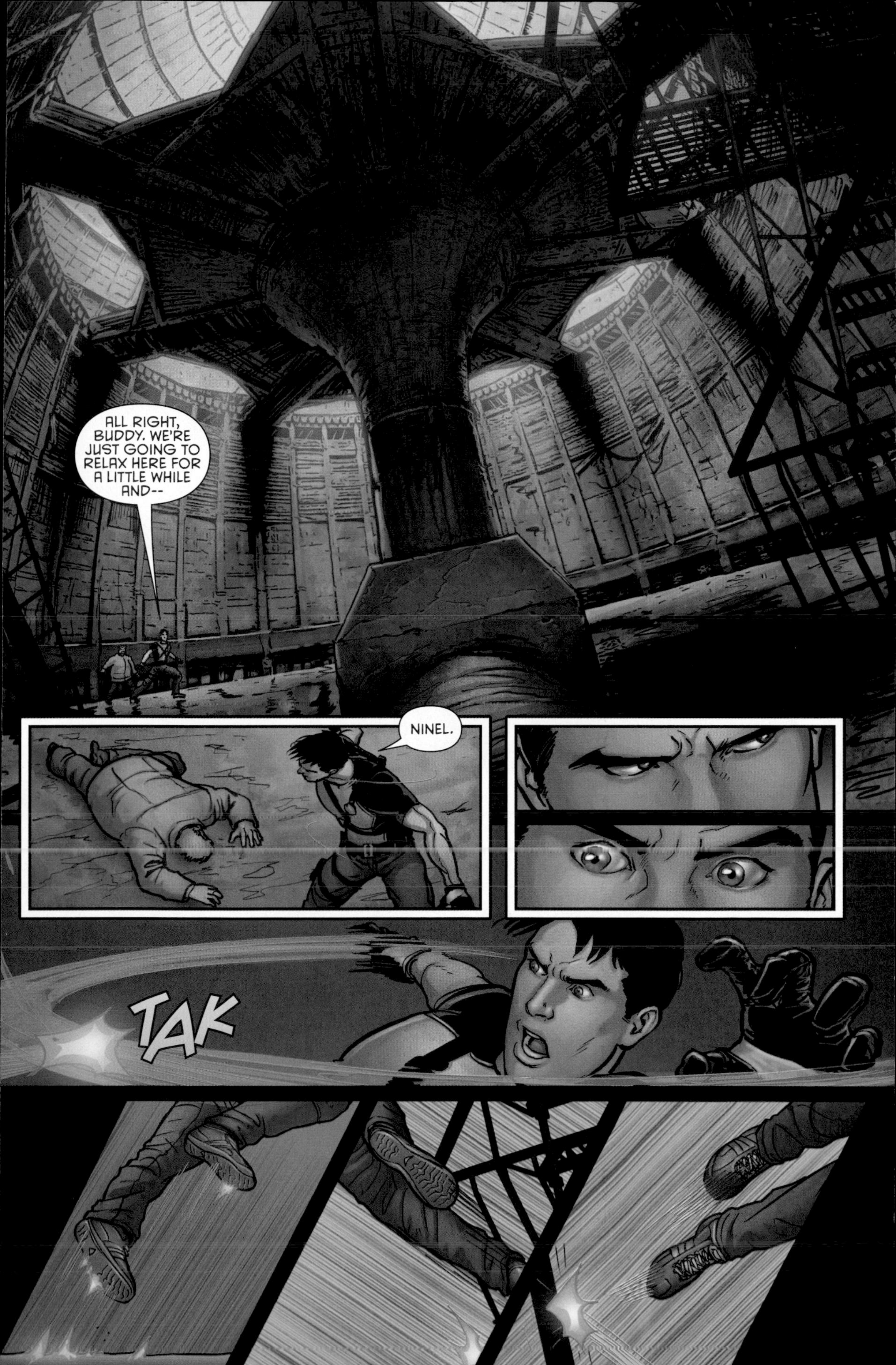
ALL RIGHT, BUDDY. WE'RE JUST GOING TO RELAX HERE FOR A LITTLE WHILE AND--
NINEL.
TAK

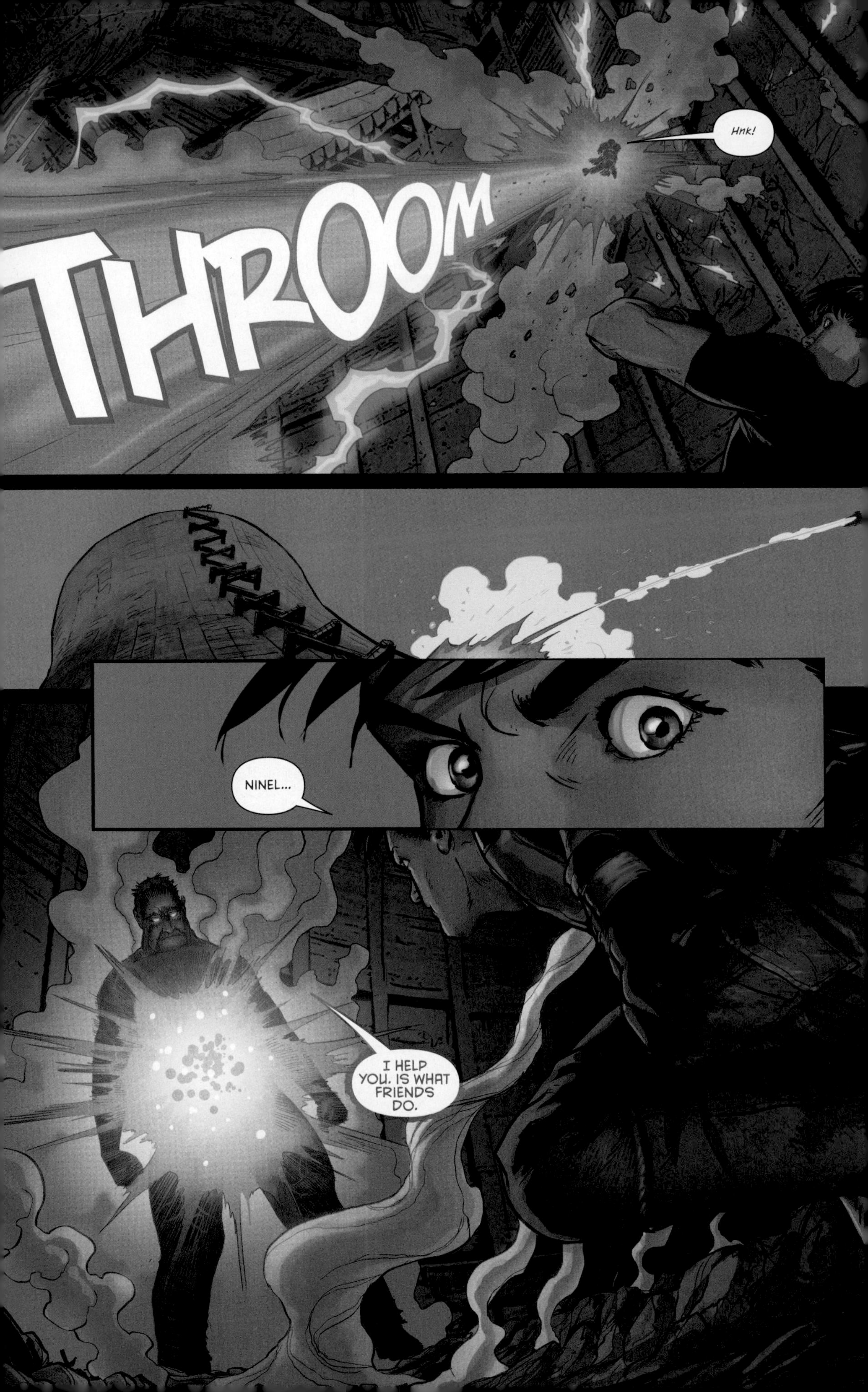
Hnk!
THROOM
NINEL...
I HELP YOU. IS WHAT FRIENDS DO.

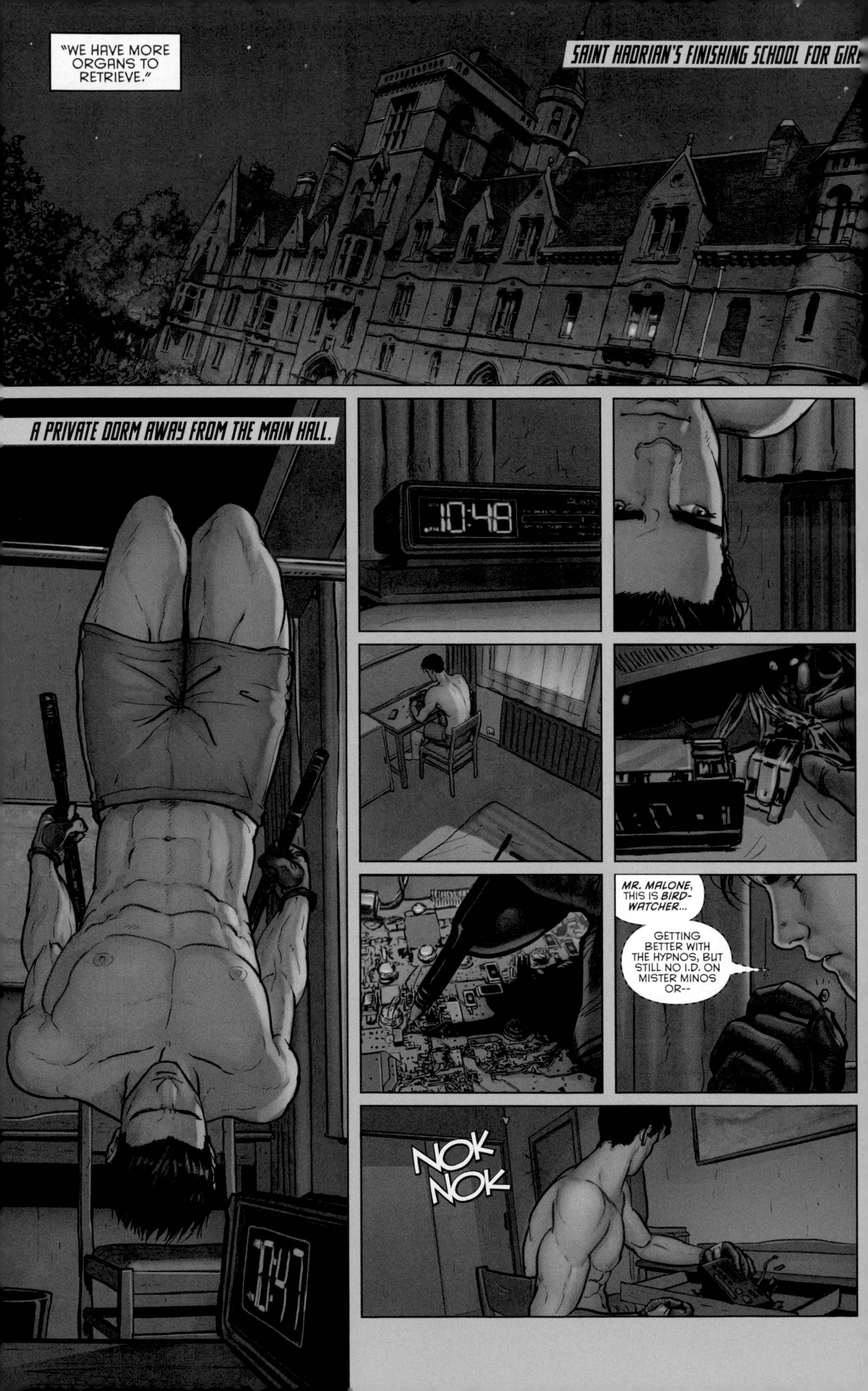
"WE HAVE MORE ORGANS TO RETRIEVE."
SAINT HADRIAN'S FINISHING SCHOOL FOR GIR
A PRIVATE DORM AWAY FROM THE MAIN HALL.
MR. MALONE, THIS IS BIRD-WATCHER...
GETTING BETTER WITH THE HYPNOS, BUT STILL NO I.D. ON MISTER MINOS OR--
NOK NOK

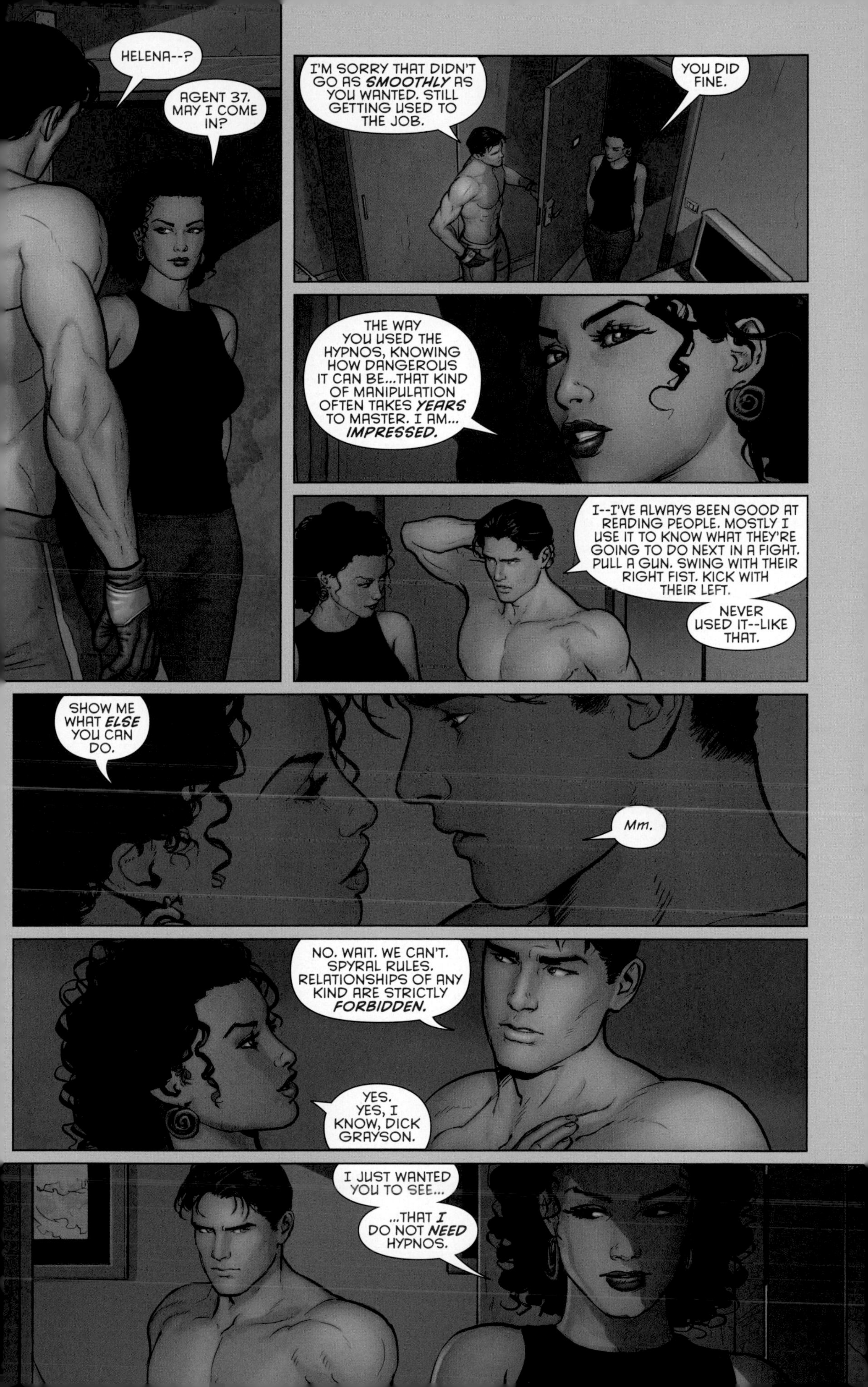

HELENA--?
AGENT 37. MAY I COME IN?
I'M SORRY THAT DIDN'T GO AS SMOOTHLY AS YOU WANTED. STILL GETTING USED TO THE JOB.
YOU DID FINE.
THE WAY YOU USED THE HYPNOS, KNOWING HOW DANGEROUS IT CAN BE...THAT KIND OF MANIPULATION OFTEN TAKES YEARS TO MASTER. I AM... IMPRESSED.
I--I'VE ALWAYS BEEN GOOD AT READING PEOPLE. MOSTLY I USE IT TO KNOW WHAT THEY'RE GOING TO DO NEXT IN A FIGHT. PULL A GUN. SWING WITH THEIR RIGHT FIST. KICK WITH THEIR LEFT.
NEVER USED IT--LIKE THAT.
SHOW ME WHAT ELSE YOU CAN DO.
Mm.
NO. WAIT. WE CAN'T. SPYRAL RULES. RELATIONSHIPS OF ANY KIND ARE STRICTLY FORBIDDEN.
YES. YES, I KNOW, DICK GRAYSON.
I JUST WANTED YOU TO SEE...
...THAT I DO NOT NEED HYPNOS.

AH, HOW LIKE A WEB IT ALL IS... EVERYTHING CONNECTED. AN EVER-WEAVING LOOP, TYING US ALL TOGETHER.

MISTER MINOS. RESULTS CONFIRMED. THE ORGAN IS INDEED PART OF THE *PARAGON PROTOCOL.* ORIGIN *TEMPLATE* CONFIRMED AND UPLOADED.

THANK YOU, *FRAU NETZ.* YOU ARE EVERY BIT THE GENIUS YOUR *FATHER* WAS.

AND WHERE HE ONCE USED SPYRAL TO *KILL* SUPER-HUMANS, WE WILL USE IT TO FIND THE IDENTITIES OF THESE MEN AND WOMEN WHO CROWD OUR SKIES.

WITH GOD-HOOD MUST COME *TRANSPARENCY.*

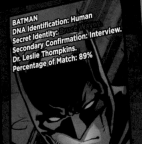

POWER CANNOT BE MASKED.

BATMAN
DNA Identification: Human
Secret Identity: Bruce Wayne
Secondary Confirmation: Interview.
Dr. Leslie Thompkins.
Percentage of Match: 89%

CYBORG
DNA Identification: Human: Unknown
Possibly of "Apokolips" origin.
Secret Identity: Victor Stone
Secondary Confirmation: Blood records
Percentage of Match: 90%

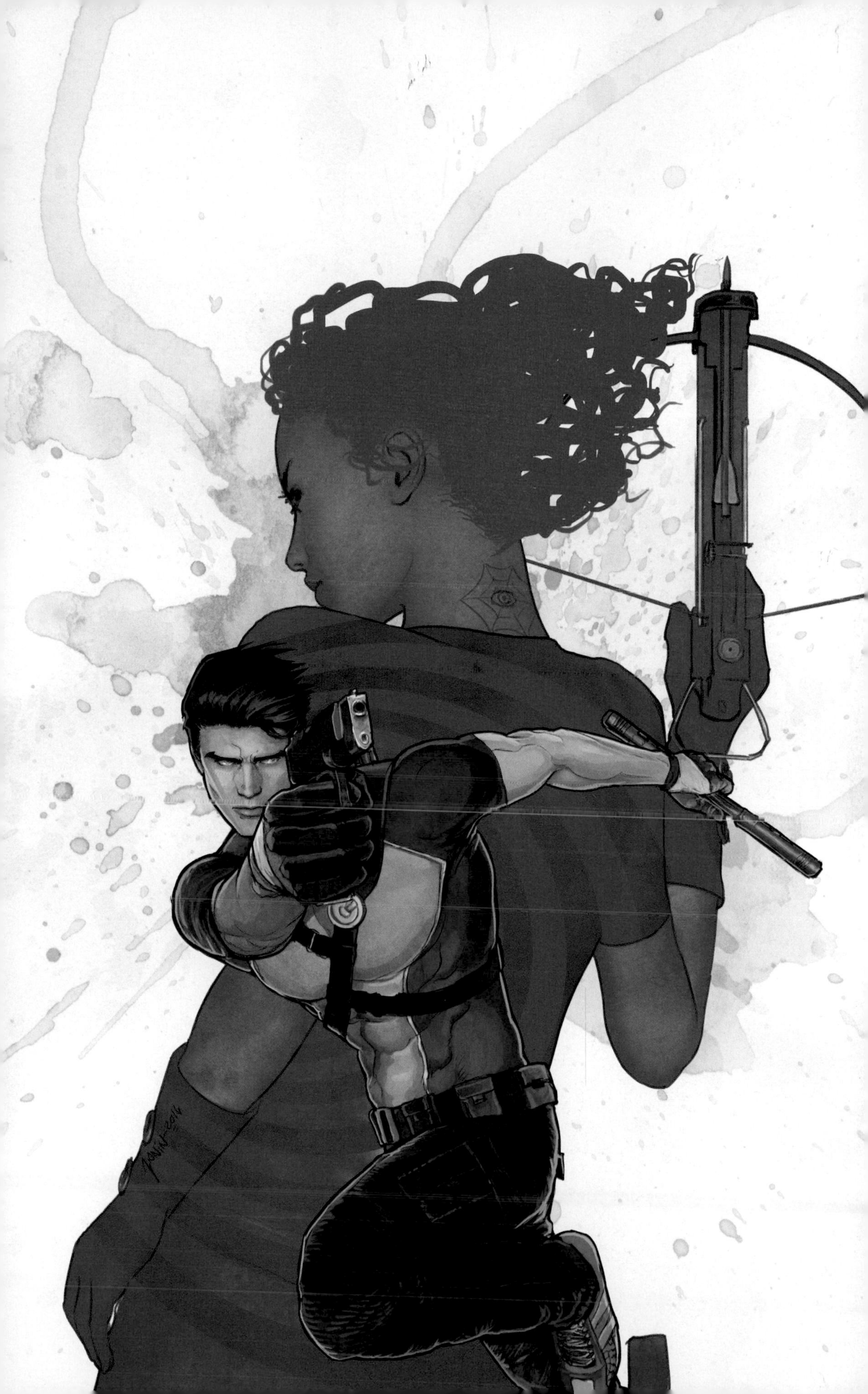

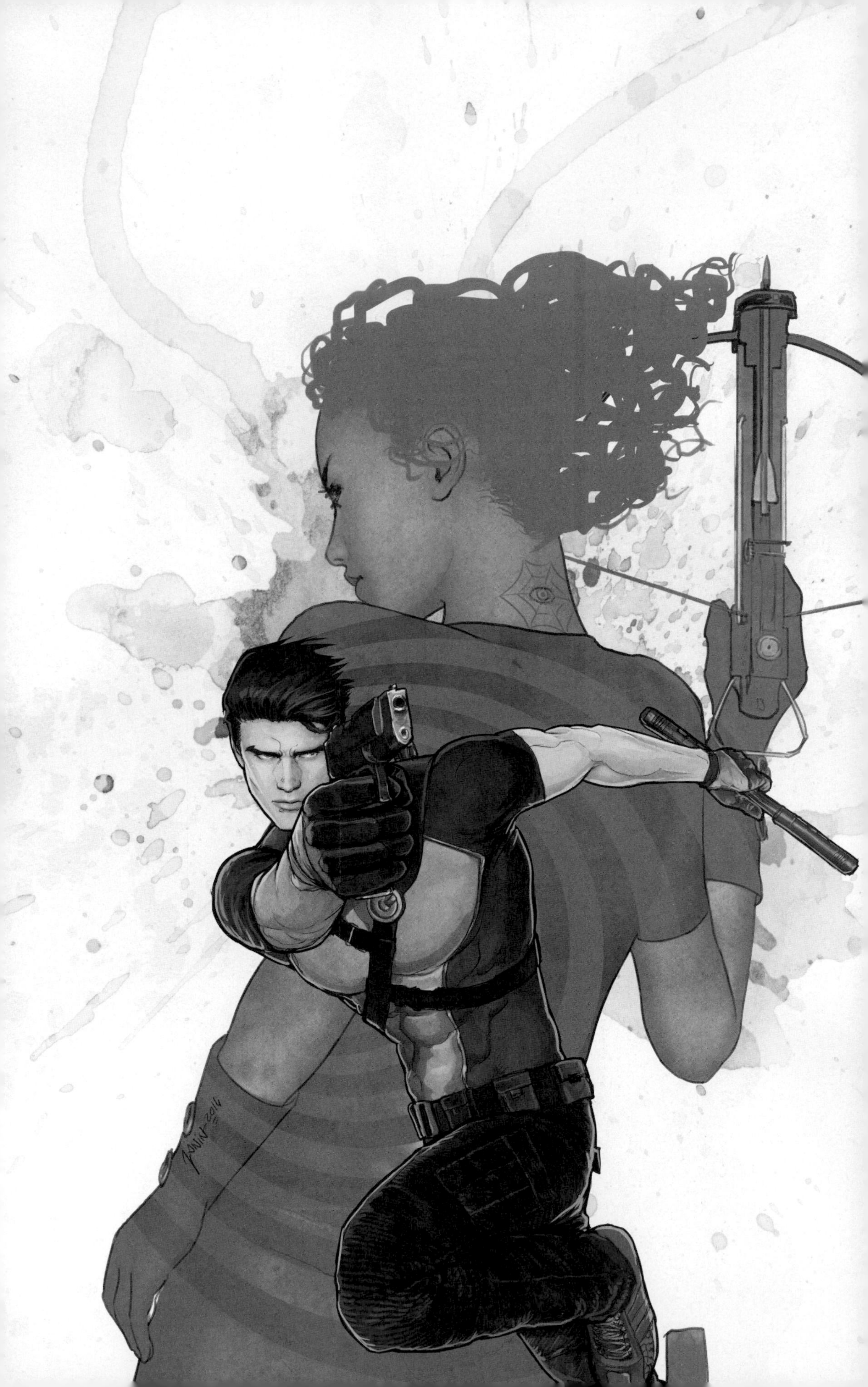

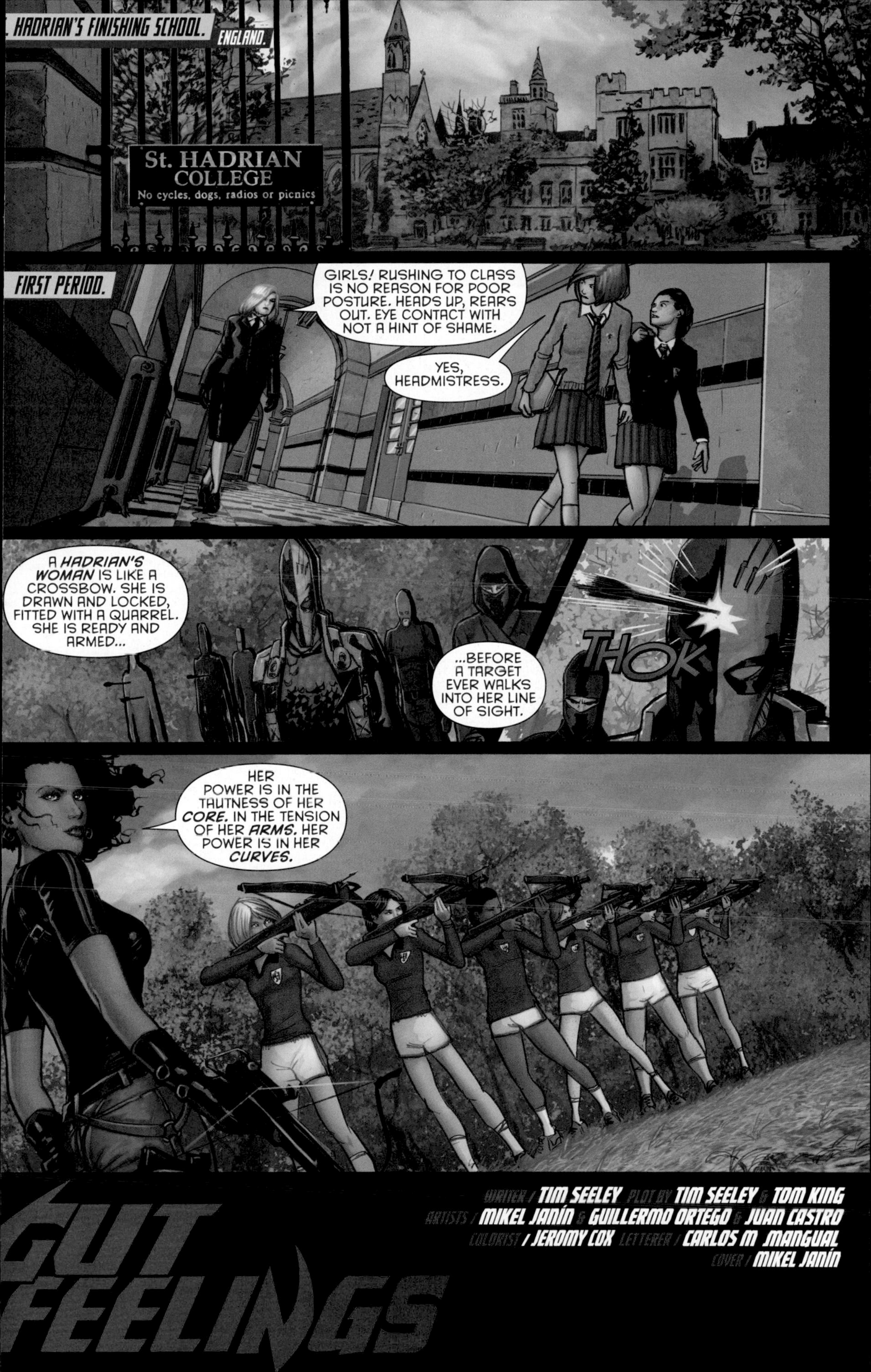
HADRIAN'S FINISHING SCHOOL.
ENGLAND.
St. HADRIAN COLLEGE
No cycles, dogs, radios or picnics
FIRST PERIOD.
GIRLS! RUSHING TO CLASS IS NO REASON FOR POOR POSTURE. HEADS UP, REARS OUT. EYE CONTACT WITH NOT A HINT OF SHAME.
YES, HEADMISTRESS.
A HADRIAN'S WOMAN IS LIKE A CROSSBOW. SHE IS DRAWN AND LOCKED, FITTED WITH A QUARREL. SHE IS READY AND ARMED...
...BEFORE A TARGET EVER WALKS INTO HER LINE OF SIGHT.
THOK
HER POWER IS IN THE TAUTNESS OF HER CORE. IN THE TENSION OF HER ARMS. HER POWER IS IN HER CURVES.
GUT FEELINGS
WRITER / TIM SEELEY PLOT BY TIM SEELEY & TOM KING
ARTISTS / MIKEL JANÍN & GUILLERMO ORTEGO & JUAN CASTRO
COLORIST / JEROMY COX LETTERER / CARLOS M. MANGUAL
COVER / MIKEL JANÍN

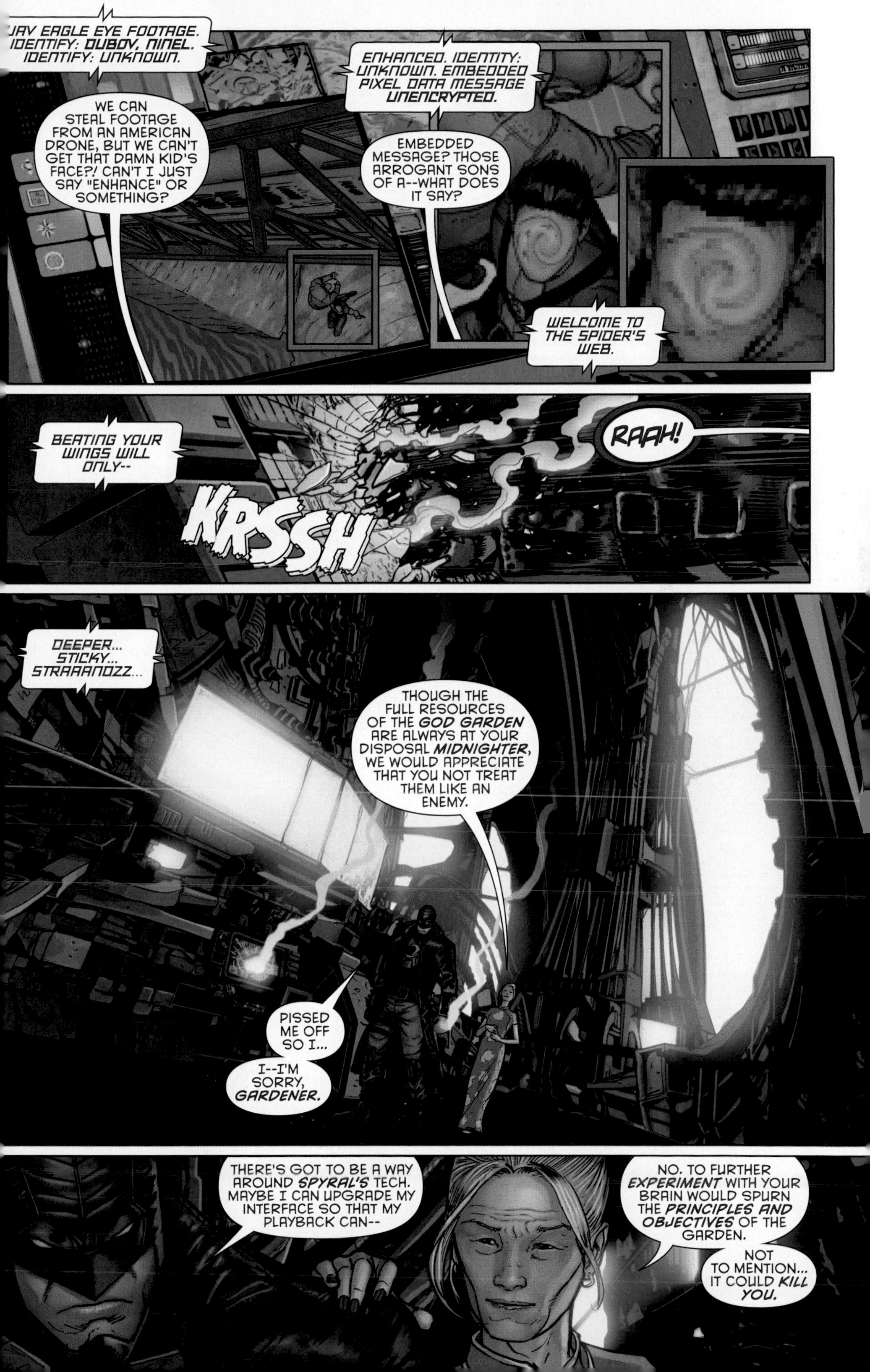
UAV EAGLE EYE FOOTAGE. IDENTIFY: DUBOV, NINEL. IDENTIFY: UNKNOWN.
WE CAN STEAL FOOTAGE FROM AN AMERICAN DRONE, BUT WE CAN'T GET THAT DAMN KID'S FACE?! CAN'T I JUST SAY "ENHANCE" OR SOMETHING?
ENHANCED. IDENTITY: UNKNOWN. EMBEDDED PIXEL DATA MESSAGE UNENCRYPTED.
EMBEDDED MESSAGE? THOSE ARROGANT SONS OF A--WHAT DOES IT SAY?
WELCOME TO THE SPIDER'S WEB.
BEATING YOUR WINGS WILL ONLY--
RAAH!
KRSSH
DEEPER... STICKY... STRAAANOZZ...
THOUGH THE FULL RESOURCES OF THE GOD GARDEN ARE ALWAYS AT YOUR DISPOSAL MIDNIGHTER, WE WOULD APPRECIATE THAT YOU NOT TREAT THEM LIKE AN ENEMY.
PISSED ME OFF SO I...
I--I'M SORRY, GARDENER.
THERE'S GOT TO BE A WAY AROUND SPYRAL'S TECH. MAYBE I CAN UPGRADE MY INTERFACE SO THAT MY PLAYBACK CAN--
NO. TO FURTHER EXPERIMENT WITH YOUR BRAIN WOULD SPURN THE PRINCIPLES AND OBJECTIVES OF THE GARDEN.
NOT TO MENTION... IT COULD KILL YOU.

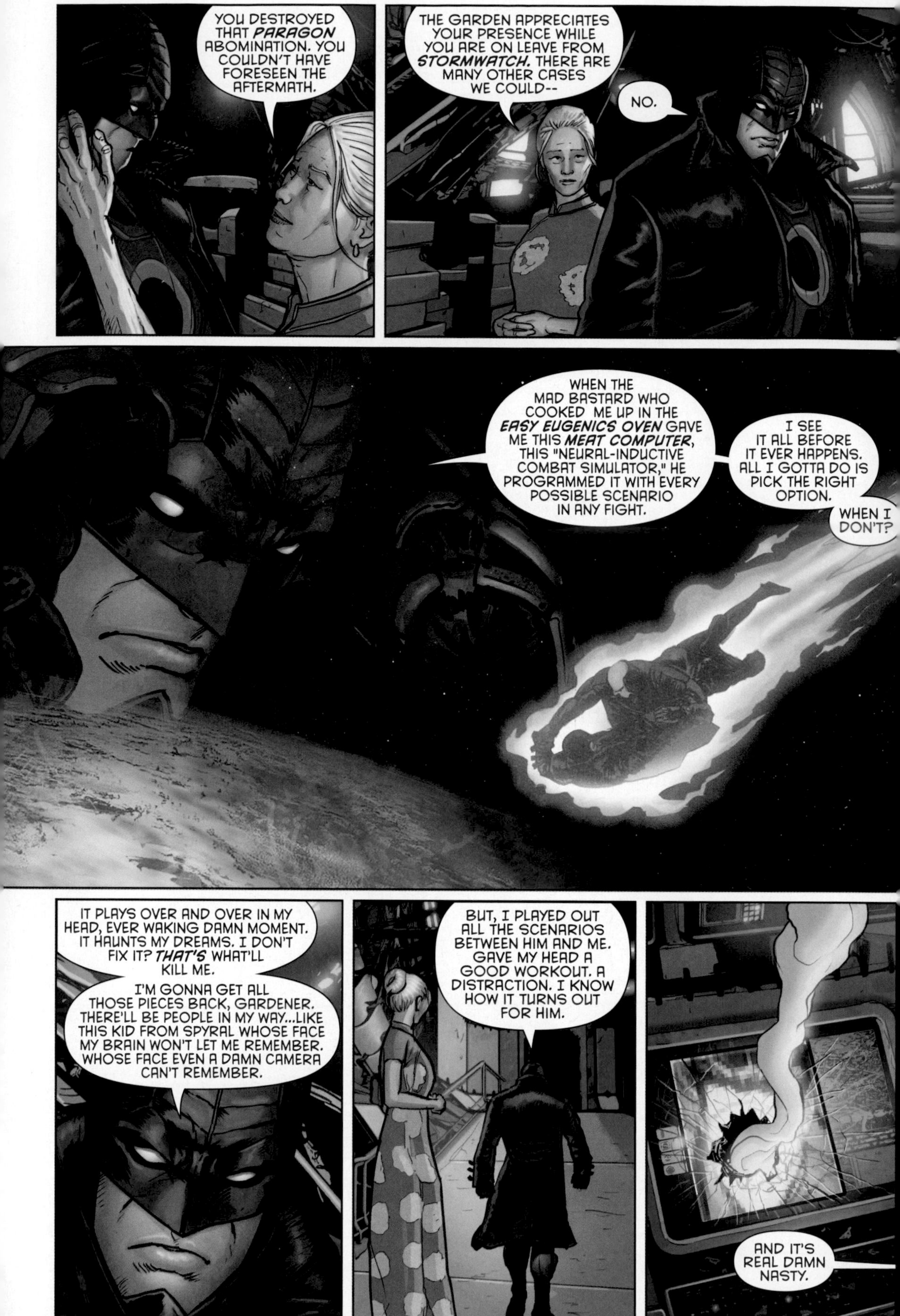
YOU DESTROYED THAT PARAGON ABOMINATION. YOU COULDN'T HAVE FORESEEN THE AFTERMATH.
THE GARDEN APPRECIATES YOUR PRESENCE WHILE YOU ARE ON LEAVE FROM STORMWATCH. THERE ARE MANY OTHER CASES WE COULD--
NO.
WHEN THE MAD BASTARD WHO COOKED ME UP IN THE EASY EUGENICS OVEN GAVE ME THIS MEAT COMPUTER, THIS "NEURAL-INDUCTIVE COMBAT SIMULATOR," HE PROGRAMMED IT WITH EVERY POSSIBLE SCENARIO IN ANY FIGHT.
I SEE IT ALL BEFORE IT EVER HAPPENS. ALL I GOTTA DO IS PICK THE RIGHT OPTION.
WHEN I DON'T?
IT PLAYS OVER AND OVER IN MY HEAD, EVER WAKING DAMN MOMENT. IT HAUNTS MY DREAMS. I DON'T FIX IT? THAT'S WHAT'LL KILL ME.
I'M GONNA GET ALL THOSE PIECES BACK, GARDENER. THERE'LL BE PEOPLE IN MY WAY...LIKE THIS KID FROM SPYRAL WHOSE FACE MY BRAIN WON'T LET ME REMEMBER. WHOSE FACE EVEN A DAMN CAMERA CAN'T REMEMBER.
BUT, I PLAYED OUT ALL THE SCENARIOS BETWEEN HIM AND ME. GAVE MY HEAD A GOOD WORKOUT. A DISTRACTION. I KNOW HOW IT TURNS OUT FOR HIM.
AND IT'S REAL DAMN NASTY.

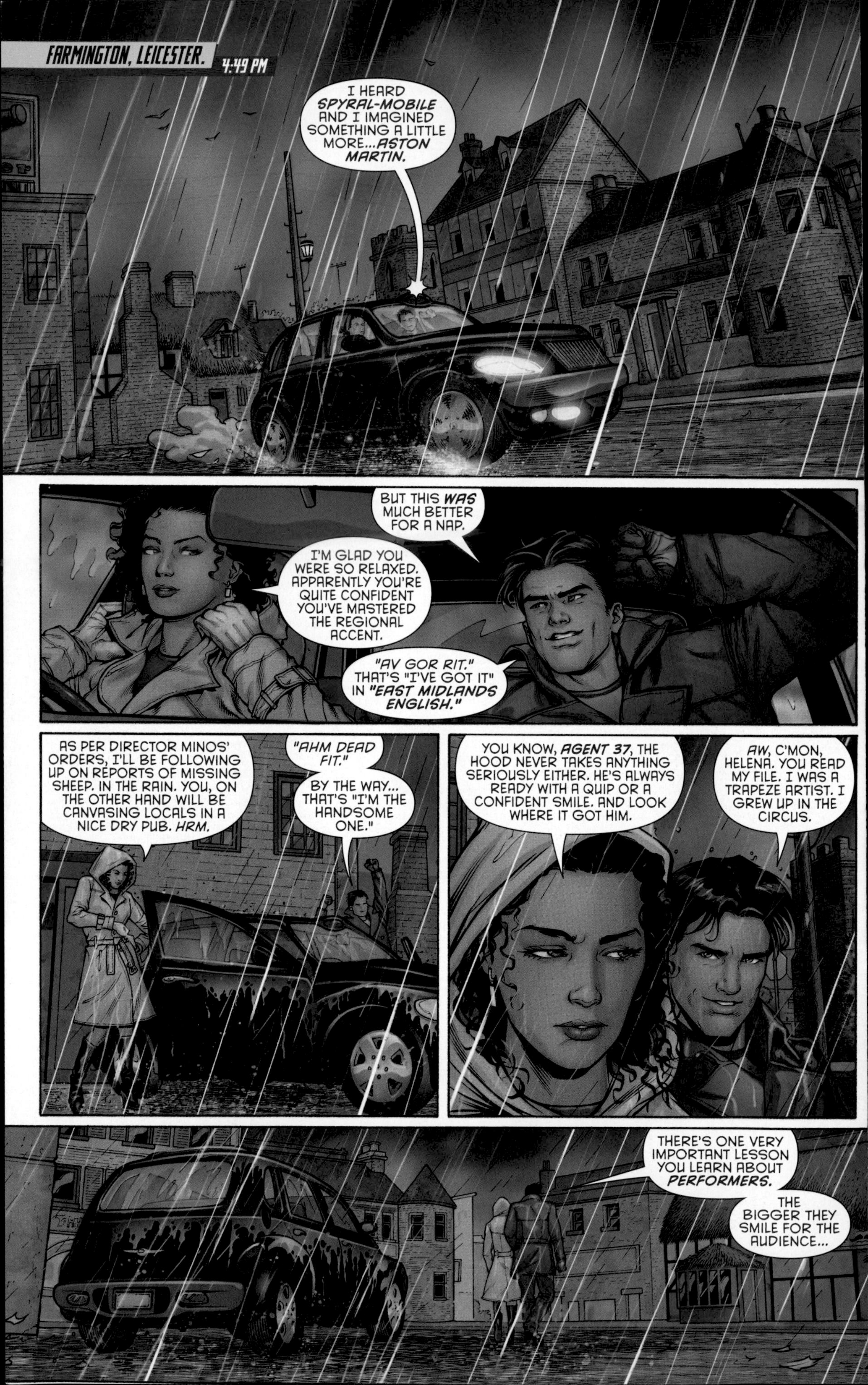
FARMINGTON, LEICESTER.
4:49 PM
I HEARD SPYRAL-MOBILE AND I IMAGINED SOMETHING A LITTLE MORE...ASTON MARTIN.
BUT THIS WAS MUCH BETTER FOR A NAP.
I'M GLAD YOU WERE SO RELAXED. APPARENTLY YOU'RE QUITE CONFIDENT YOU'VE MASTERED THE REGIONAL ACCENT.
"AV GOR RIT." THAT'S "I'VE GOT IT" IN "EAST MIDLANDS ENGLISH."
AS PER DIRECTOR MINOS' ORDERS, I'LL BE FOLLOWING UP ON REPORTS OF MISSING SHEEP. IN THE RAIN. YOU, ON THE OTHER HAND WILL BE CANVASING LOCALS IN A NICE DRY PUB. HRM.
"AHM DEAD FIT."
BY THE WAY... THAT'S "I'M THE HANDSOME ONE."
YOU KNOW, AGENT 37, THE HOOD NEVER TAKES ANYTHING SERIOUSLY EITHER. HE'S ALWAYS READY WITH A QUIP OR A CONFIDENT SMILE. AND LOOK WHERE IT GOT HIM.
AW, C'MON, HELENA. YOU READ MY FILE. I WAS A TRAPEZE ARTIST. I GREW UP IN THE CIRCUS.
THERE'S ONE VERY IMPORTANT LESSON YOU LEARN ABOUT PERFORMERS.
THE BIGGER THEY SMILE FOR THE AUDIENCE...

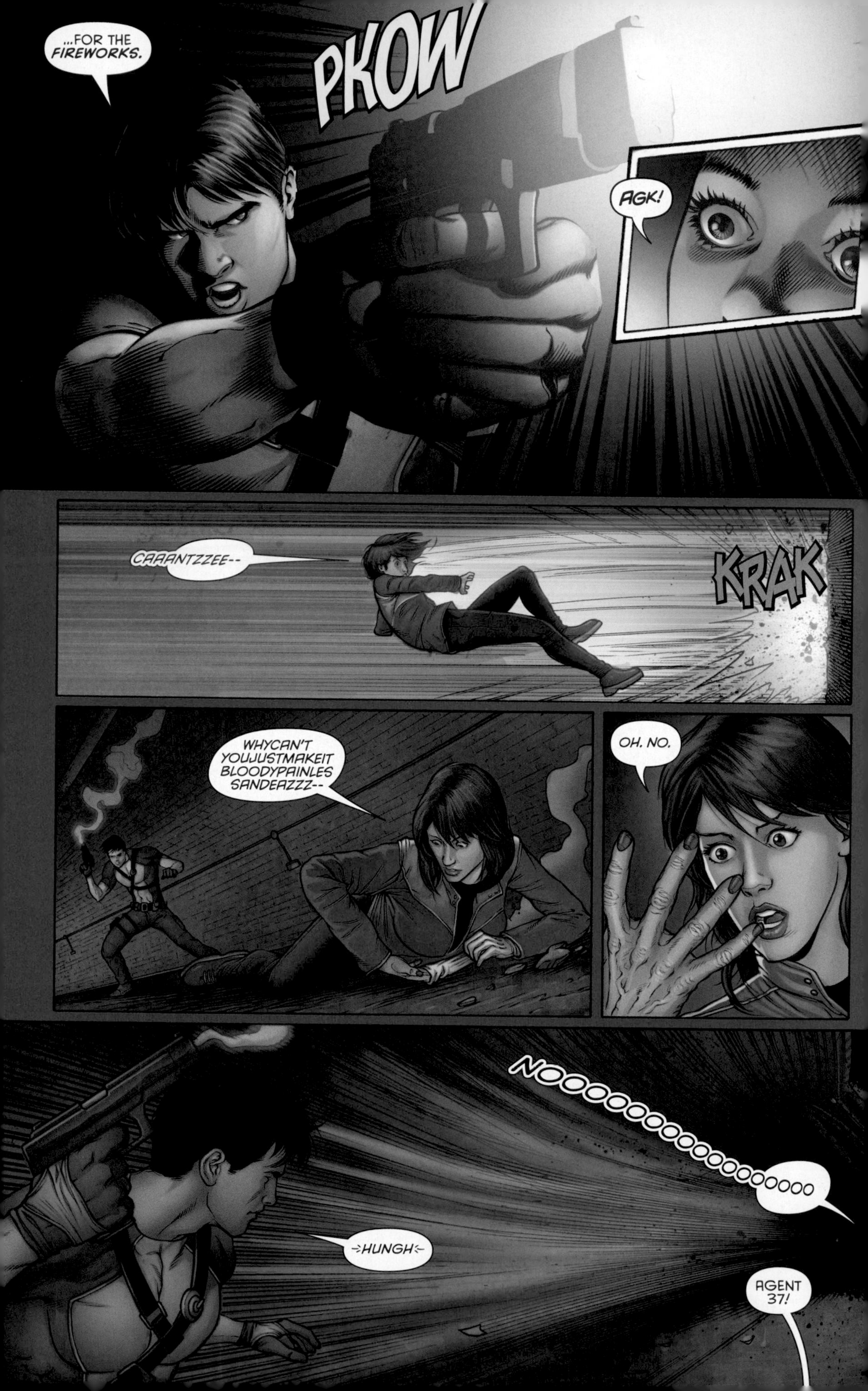

...FOR THE FIREWORKS.
PKOW
AGK!
CAAANTZZEE--
KRAK
WHYCAN'T YOUJUSTMAKEIT BLOODYPAINLES SANDEAZZZ--
OH. NO.
NOOOOOOOOOOOOOOOOOOO
HUNGH
AGENT 37!

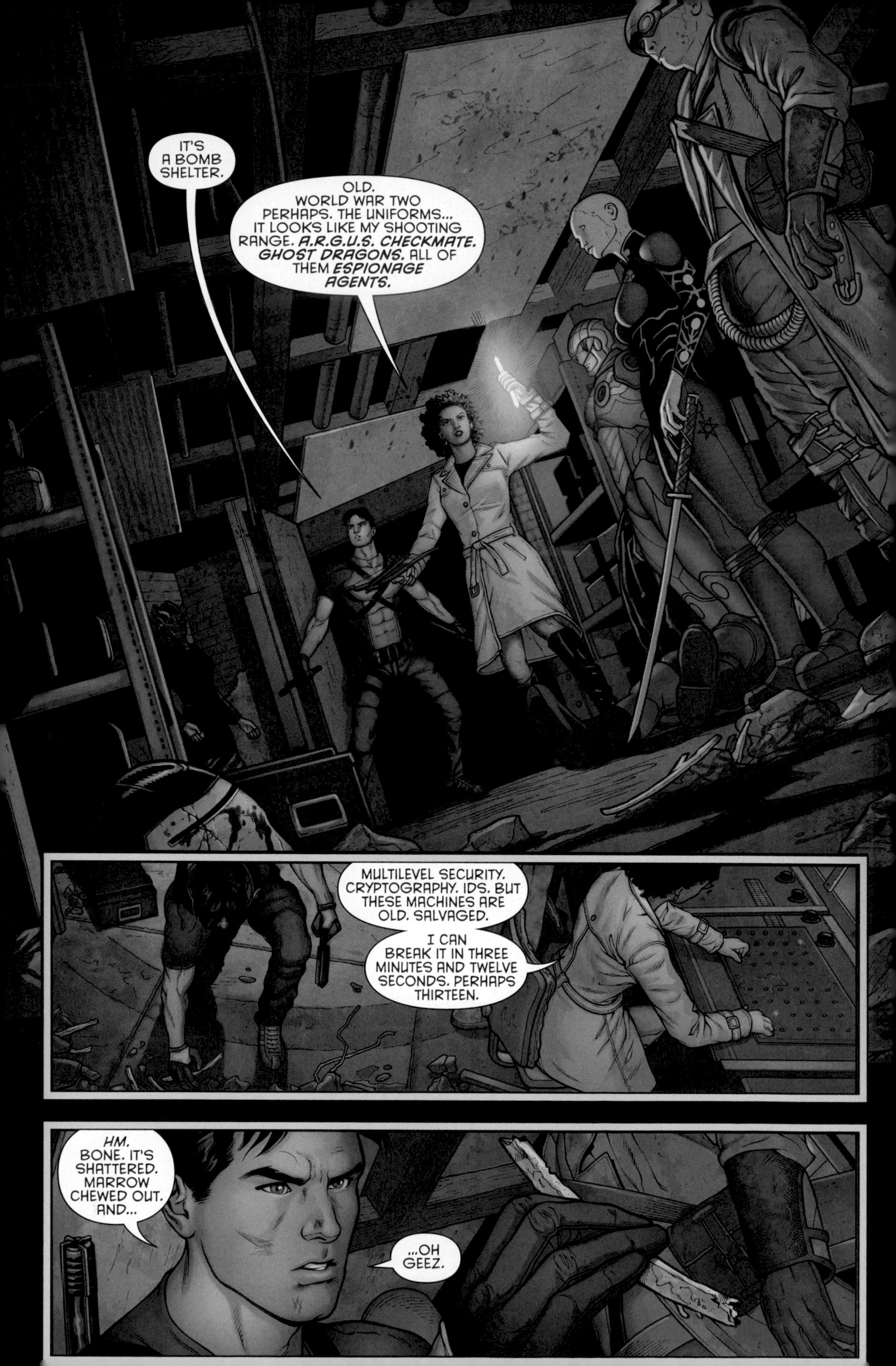
IT'S A BOMB SHELTER.
OLD. WORLD WAR TWO PERHAPS. THE UNIFORMS... IT LOOKS LIKE MY SHOOTING RANGE. *A.R.G.U.S. CHECKMATE. GHOST DRAGONS.* ALL OF THEM *ESPIONAGE AGENTS.*
MULTILEVEL SECURITY. CRYPTOGRAPHY. IDS. BUT THESE MACHINES ARE OLD. SALVAGED.
I CAN BREAK IT IN THREE MINUTES AND TWELVE SECONDS. PERHAPS THIRTEEN.
HM. BONE. IT'S SHATTERED. MARROW CHEWED OUT. AND...
...OH GEEZ.

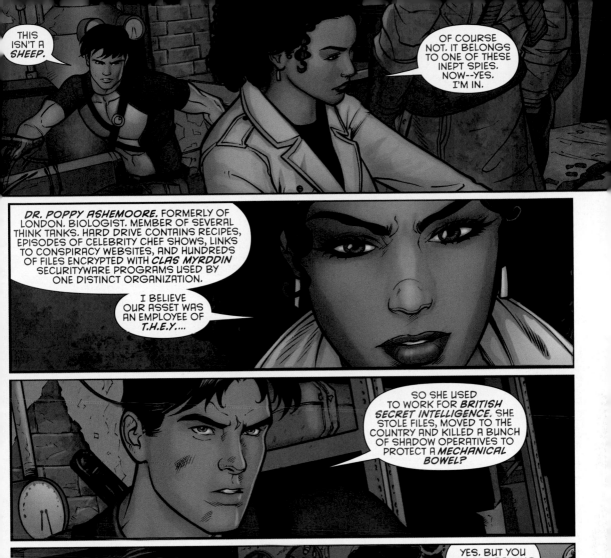

THIS ISN'T A *SHEEP*.

OF COURSE NOT. IT BELONGS TO ONE OF THESE INEPT SPIES. NOW--YES. I'M IN.

DR. POPPY ASHEMOORE. FORMERLY OF LONDON. BIOLOGIST. MEMBER OF SEVERAL THINK TANKS. HARD DRIVE CONTAINS RECIPES, EPISODES OF CELEBRITY CHEF SHOWS, LINKS TO CONSPIRACY WEBSITES, AND HUNDREDS OF FILES ENCRYPTED WITH *CLAS MYRDDIN* SECURITYWARE PROGRAMS USED BY ONE DISTINCT ORGANIZATION.

I BELIEVE OUR ASSET WAS AN EMPLOYEE OF *T.H.E.Y.*...

SO SHE USED TO WORK FOR *BRITISH SECRET INTELLIGENCE.* SHE STOLE FILES, MOVED TO THE COUNTRY AND KILLED A BUNCH OF SHADOW OPERATIVES TO PROTECT A *MECHANICAL BOWEL?*

YES. BUT YOU ARE FORGETTING ONE THING, AGENT 37.

SHE DID NOT JUST KILL THOSE WHO CAME FOR HER.

SHE ATE THEM. YOU CAME DANGEROUSLY CLOSE TO BEING *MERENDA.*

I'M DISTURBED BY THE PLEASURE YOU TOOK IN TELLING ME THAT. NOW, I THINK IT'S TIME YOU MAKE LIKE *JAMES BROWN*...

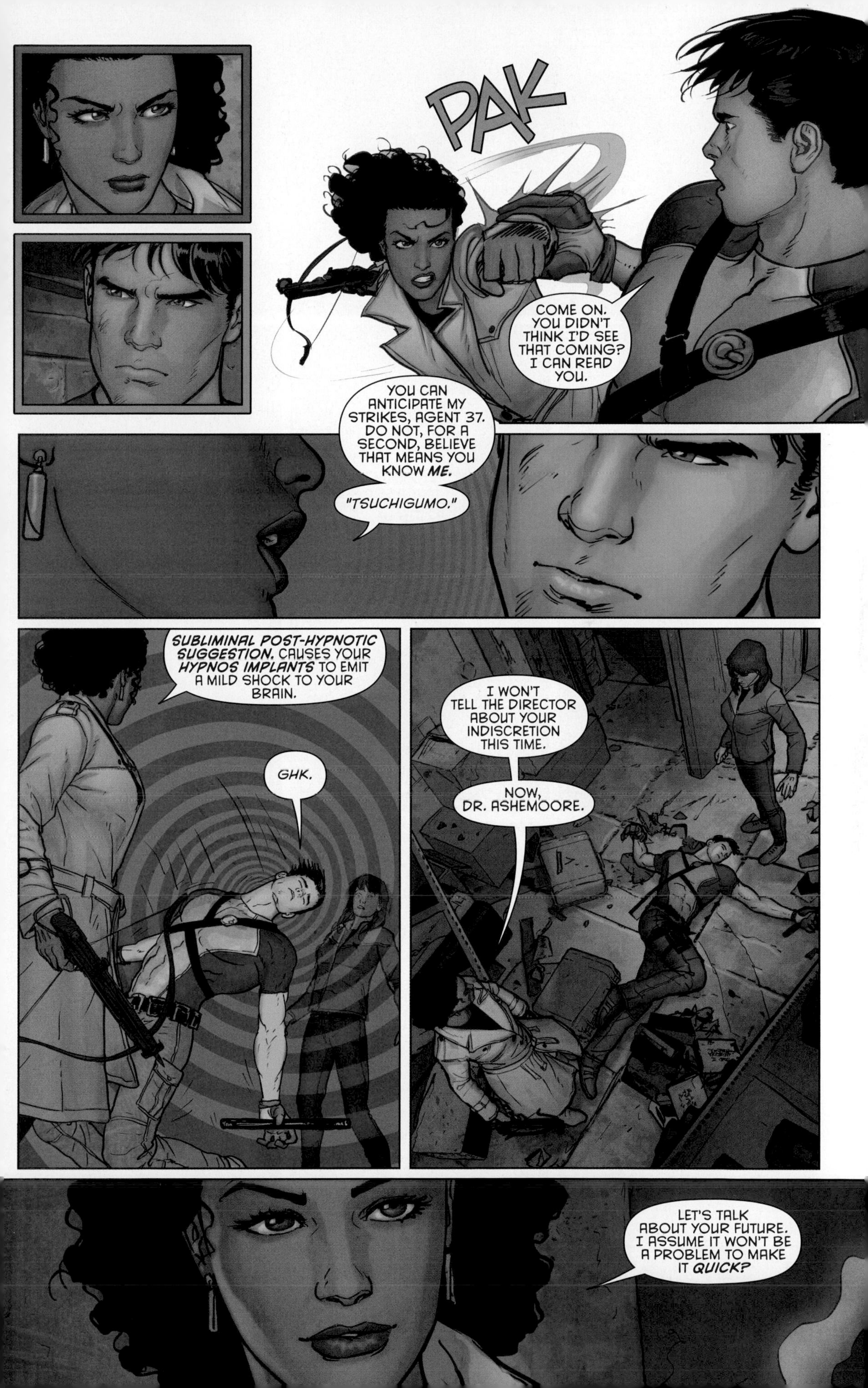
PAK
COME ON. YOU DIDN'T THINK I'D SEE THAT COMING? I CAN READ YOU.
YOU CAN ANTICIPATE MY STRIKES, AGENT 37. DO NOT, FOR A SECOND, BELIEVE THAT MEANS YOU KNOW ME.
"TSUCHIGUMO."
SUBLIMINAL POST-HYPNOTIC SUGGESTION. CAUSES YOUR HYPNOS IMPLANTS TO EMIT A MILD SHOCK TO YOUR BRAIN.
GHK.
I WON'T TELL THE DIRECTOR ABOUT YOUR INDISCRETION THIS TIME.
NOW, DR. ASHEMOORE.
LET'S TALK ABOUT YOUR FUTURE. I ASSUME IT WON'T BE A PROBLEM TO MAKE IT QUICK?

TODAY, WE'LL BE PICKING UP WHERE WE LAST LEFT OFF, BEFORE WE WERE... INTERRUPTED.

AS I WAS SAYING...

...A HADRIAN'S WOMAN IS LIKE A CROSSBOW.

SHE IS DRAWN AND LOCKED, FITTED WITH A QUARREL. SHE IS READY AND ARMED *BEFORE* A TARGET EVER WALKS INTO HER LINE OF SIGHT.

HER POWER IS IN THE TAUTNESS OF HER *CORE*. IN THE TENSION OF HER *ARMS*. HER POWER IS IN HER *CURVES*.

SHE IS *SILENT*. SHE IS *ELEGANT*. SHE IS UNAWARE OF THE NOISE AND DISTRACTION AROUND HER.

SHE IS UNCONCERNED WITH RIGHTEOUSNESS OR VIRTUE.

SHE EXISTS ONLY FOR THE PROMPT AND UNERRING DELIVERY...

THUNK

...OF HER CHARGE.

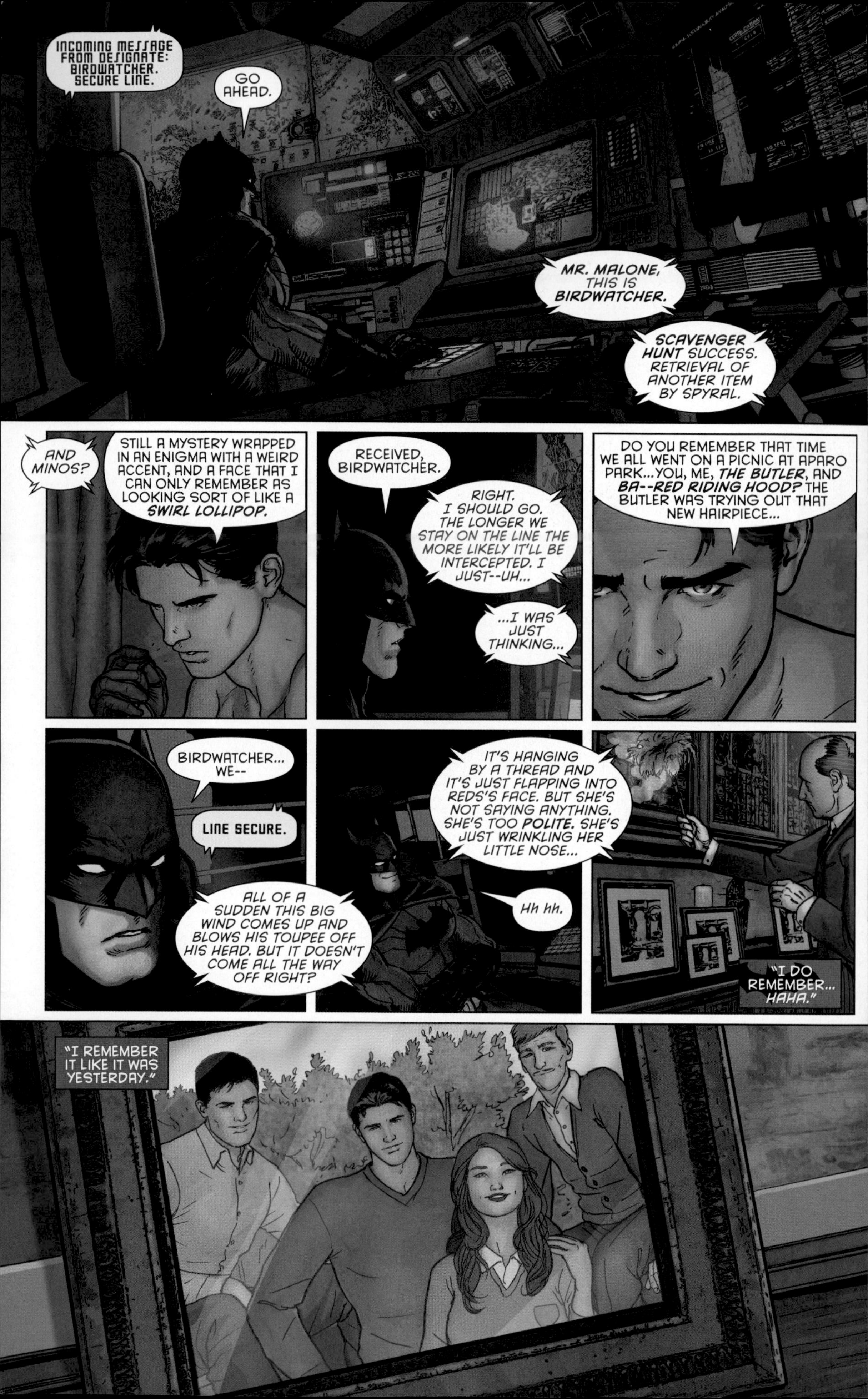
INCOMING MESSAGE FROM DESIGNATE: BIRDWATCHER. SECURE LINE.
GO AHEAD.
MR. MALONE, THIS IS BIRDWATCHER.
SCAVENGER HUNT SUCCESS. RETRIEVAL OF ANOTHER ITEM BY SPYRAL.
AND MINOS?
STILL A MYSTERY WRAPPED IN AN ENIGMA WITH A WEIRD ACCENT, AND A FACE THAT I CAN ONLY REMEMBER AS LOOKING SORT OF LIKE A SWIRL LOLLIPOP.
RECEIVED, BIRDWATCHER.
RIGHT. I SHOULD GO. THE LONGER WE STAY ON THE LINE THE MORE LIKELY IT'LL BE INTERCEPTED. I JUST--UH...
...I WAS JUST THINKING...
DO YOU REMEMBER THAT TIME WE ALL WENT ON A PICNIC AT APARO PARK...YOU, ME, THE BUTLER, AND BA--RED RIDING HOOD? THE BUTLER WAS TRYING OUT THAT NEW HAIRPIECE...
BIRDWATCHER... WE--
LINE SECURE.
ALL OF A SUDDEN THIS BIG WIND COMES UP AND BLOWS HIS TOUPEE OFF HIS HEAD. BUT IT DOESN'T COME ALL THE WAY OFF RIGHT?
IT'S HANGING BY A THREAD AND IT'S JUST FLAPPING INTO REDS'S FACE. BUT SHE'S NOT SAYING ANYTHING. SHE'S TOO POLITE. SHE'S JUST WRINKLING HER LITTLE NOSE...
Hh hh.
"I DO REMEMBER... HAHA."
"I REMEMBER IT LIKE IT WAS YESTERDAY."

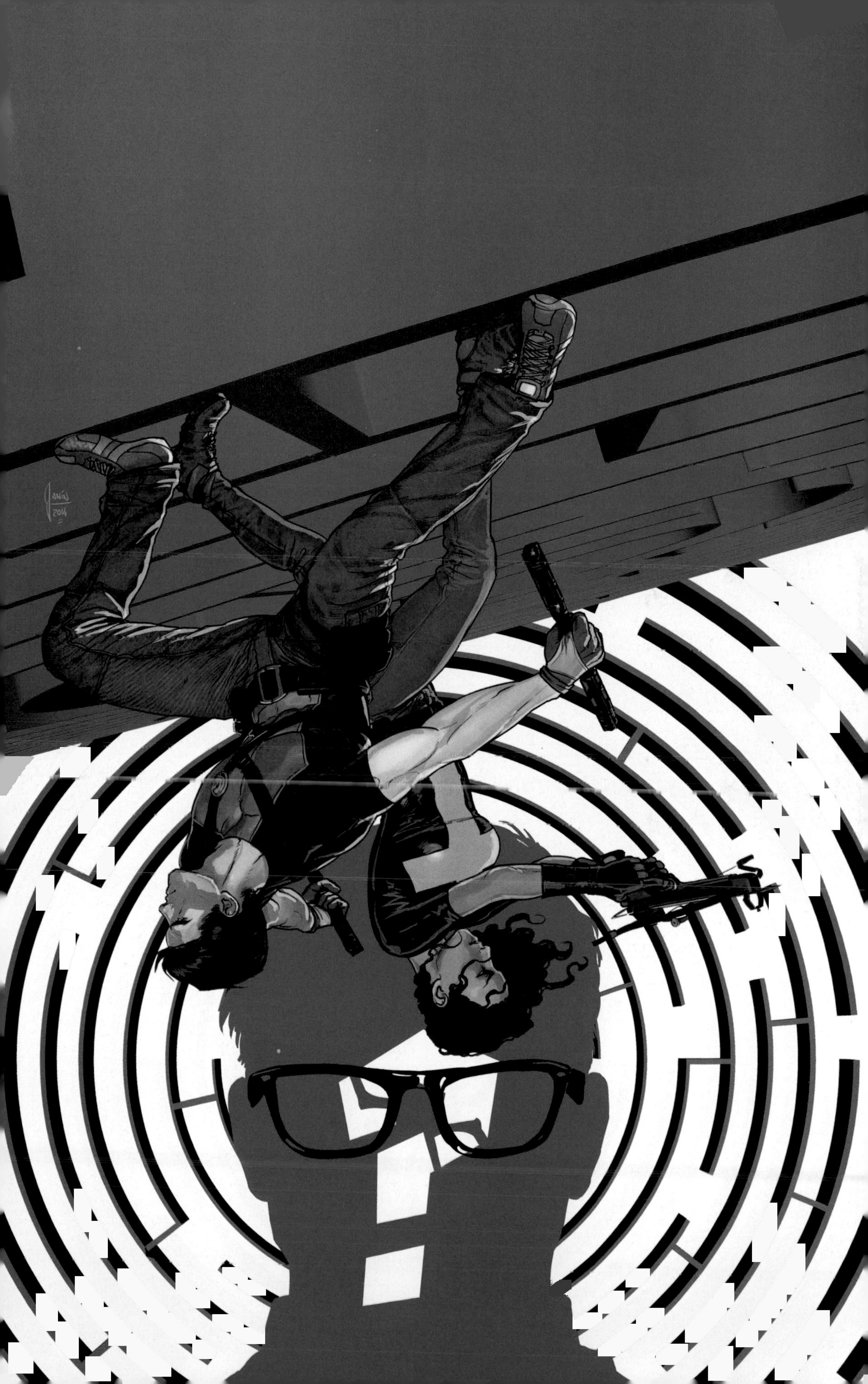

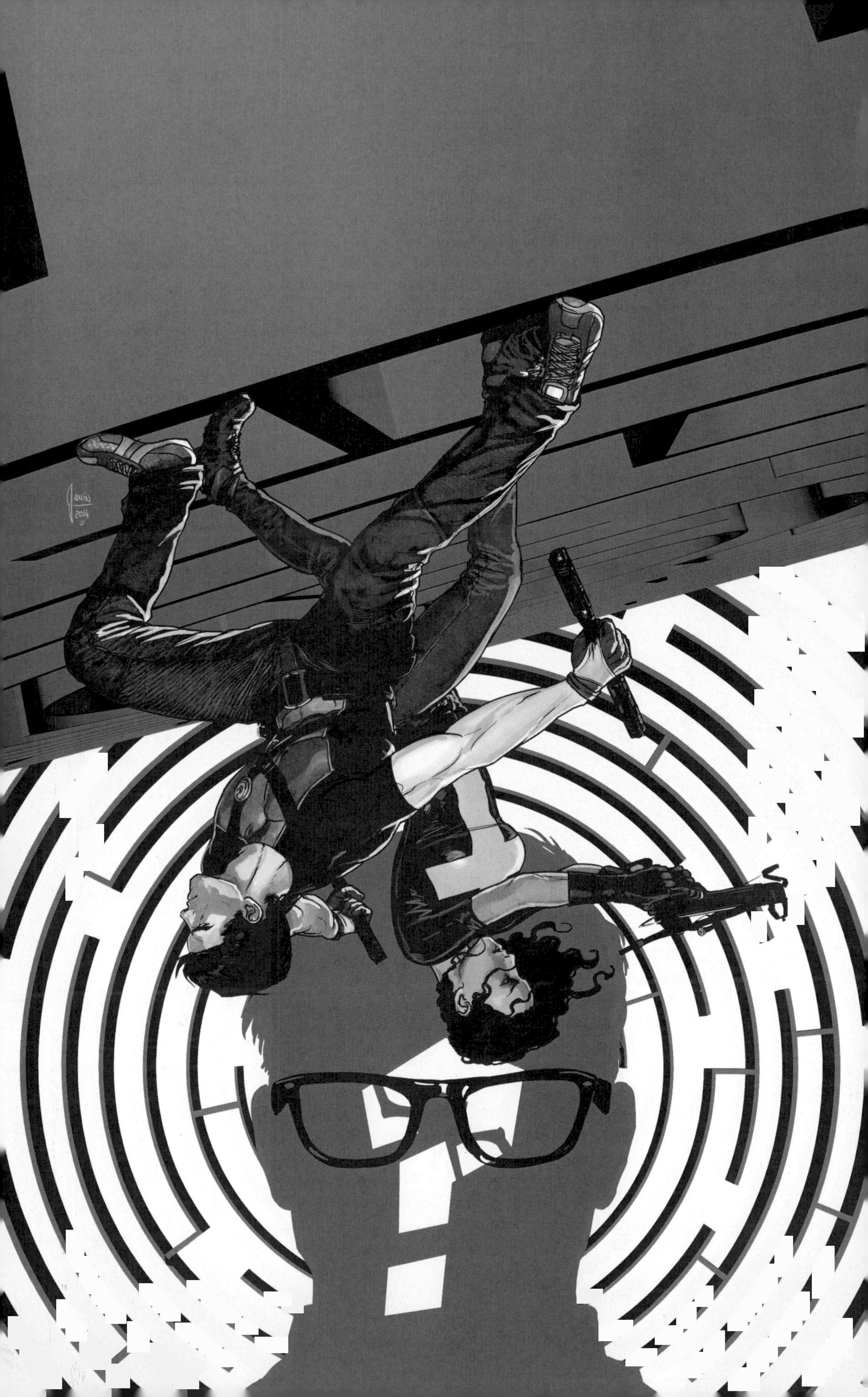

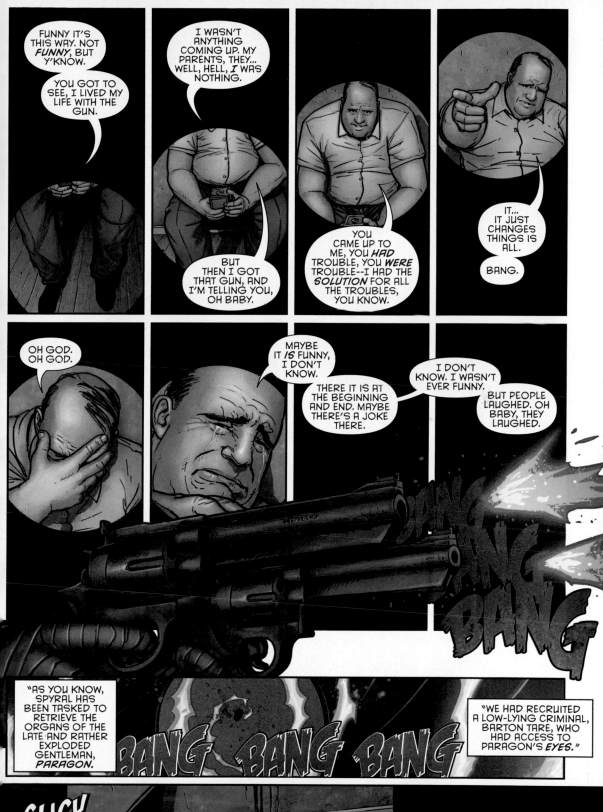

REALLY? THIS IS HOW THE GREAT WING-KNIGHT SHOOTS?

I SEE WHY MR. MINOS HAS *AGENT 1* AND ME BAILING YOU OUT ON THIS MISSION.

NIGHTWING.

AND YOU SHOULD SEE ME WITH A *SLINGSHOT,* AGENT 8.

BANG

BANG BANG

DAMN--

YOU'RE PULLING YOUR SHOTS DOWN AND LEFT.

YOU'RE *ANTICIPATING* THE SHOT, WHIPPING YOUR HAND RIGHT BEFORE IT GOES OFF.

KS 02

K4 03

KS 03

KS 02

5X

KS 02

K4 03

YOU JUST NEED SOME FINGER DISCIPLINE.

STOP THINKING ABOUT THE *GUN.*

START THINKING ABOUT THE *TARGET.*

FOCUS ON THE BACK SITES. THEN PUT YOUR FRONT SITE BETWEEN THEM.

GO SLOW. LINE IT UP. GLIDE IT IN.

NOW, YOU'RE READY. BUT REMEMBER, DON'T ANTICIPATE THE EXPLOSION. *CAUSE* THE EXPLOSION.

CAN YOU DO THAT, WING-KNIGHT? CAN YOU DO THAT FOR ME?

THAT'S NOT MY NAME.

MY NAME IS...

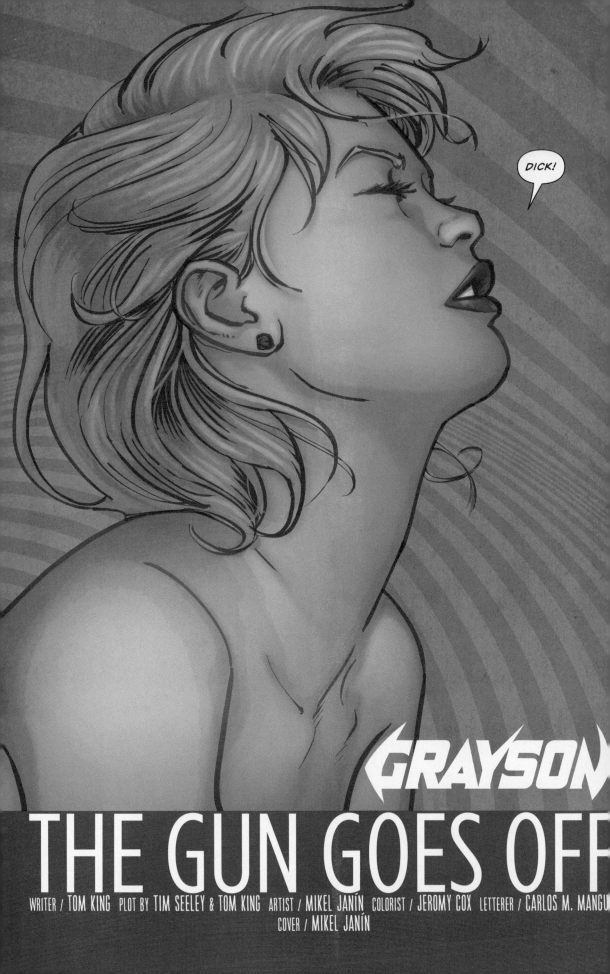

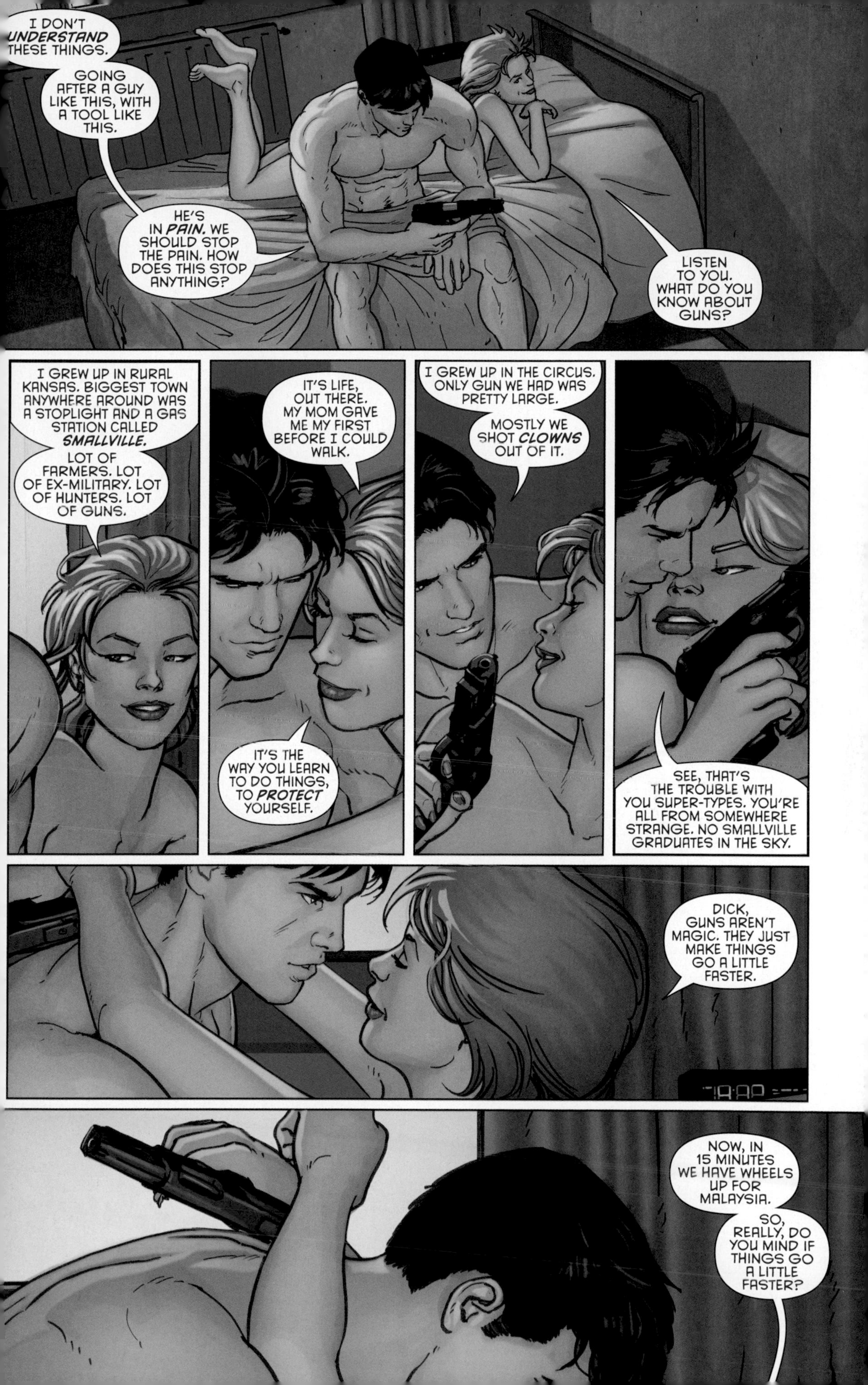
I DON'T *UNDERSTAND* THESE THINGS.
GOING AFTER A GUY LIKE THIS, WITH A TOOL LIKE THIS.
HE'S IN *PAIN.* WE SHOULD STOP THE PAIN. HOW DOES THIS STOP ANYTHING?
LISTEN TO YOU. WHAT DO YOU KNOW ABOUT GUNS?
I GREW UP IN RURAL KANSAS. BIGGEST TOWN ANYWHERE AROUND WAS A STOPLIGHT AND A GAS STATION CALLED *SMALLVILLE.*
LOT OF FARMERS. LOT OF EX-MILITARY. LOT OF HUNTERS. LOT OF GUNS.
IT'S LIFE, OUT THERE. MY MOM GAVE ME MY FIRST BEFORE I COULD WALK.
IT'S THE WAY YOU LEARN TO DO THINGS, TO *PROTECT* YOURSELF.
I GREW UP IN THE CIRCUS. ONLY GUN WE HAD WAS PRETTY LARGE.
MOSTLY WE SHOT *CLOWNS* OUT OF IT.
SEE, THAT'S THE TROUBLE WITH YOU SUPER-TYPES. YOU'RE ALL FROM SOMEWHERE STRANGE. NO SMALLVILLE GRADUATES IN THE SKY.
DICK, GUNS AREN'T MAGIC. THEY JUST MAKE THINGS GO A LITTLE FASTER.
NOW, IN 15 MINUTES WE HAVE WHEELS UP FOR MALAYSIA.
SO, REALLY, DO YOU MIND IF THINGS GO A LITTLE FASTER?

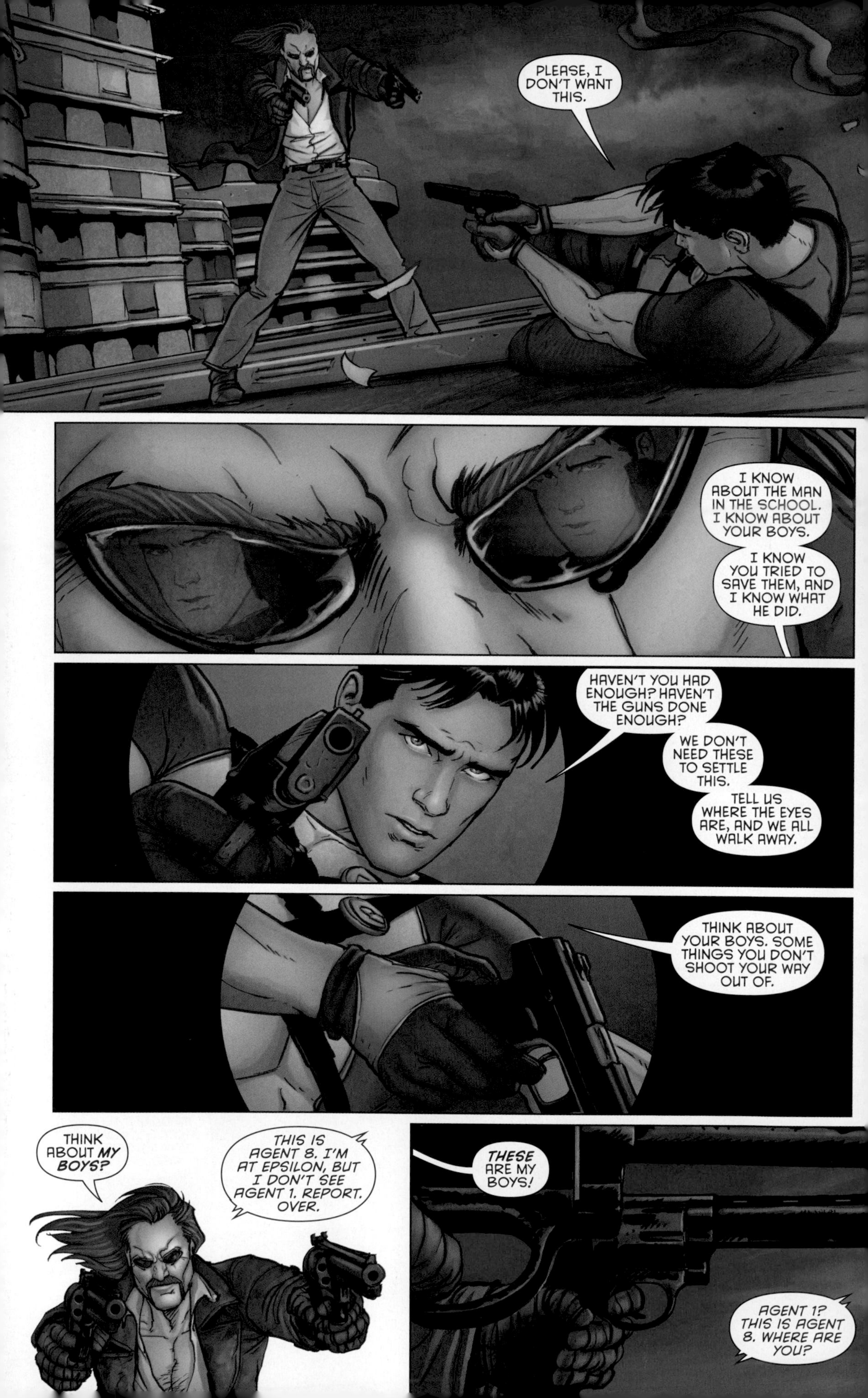
PLEASE, I DON'T WANT THIS.
I KNOW ABOUT THE MAN IN THE SCHOOL. I KNOW ABOUT YOUR BOYS.
I KNOW YOU TRIED TO SAVE THEM, AND I KNOW WHAT HE DID.
HAVEN'T YOU HAD ENOUGH? HAVEN'T THE GUNS DONE ENOUGH?
WE DON'T NEED THESE TO SETTLE THIS.
TELL US WHERE THE EYES ARE, AND WE ALL WALK AWAY.
THINK ABOUT YOUR BOYS. SOME THINGS YOU DON'T SHOOT YOUR WAY OUT OF.
THINK ABOUT *MY* *BOYS?*
THIS IS AGENT 8. I'M AT EPSILON, BUT I DON'T SEE AGENT 1. REPORT. OVER.
THESE ARE MY BOYS!
AGENT 1? THIS IS AGENT 8. WHERE ARE YOU?

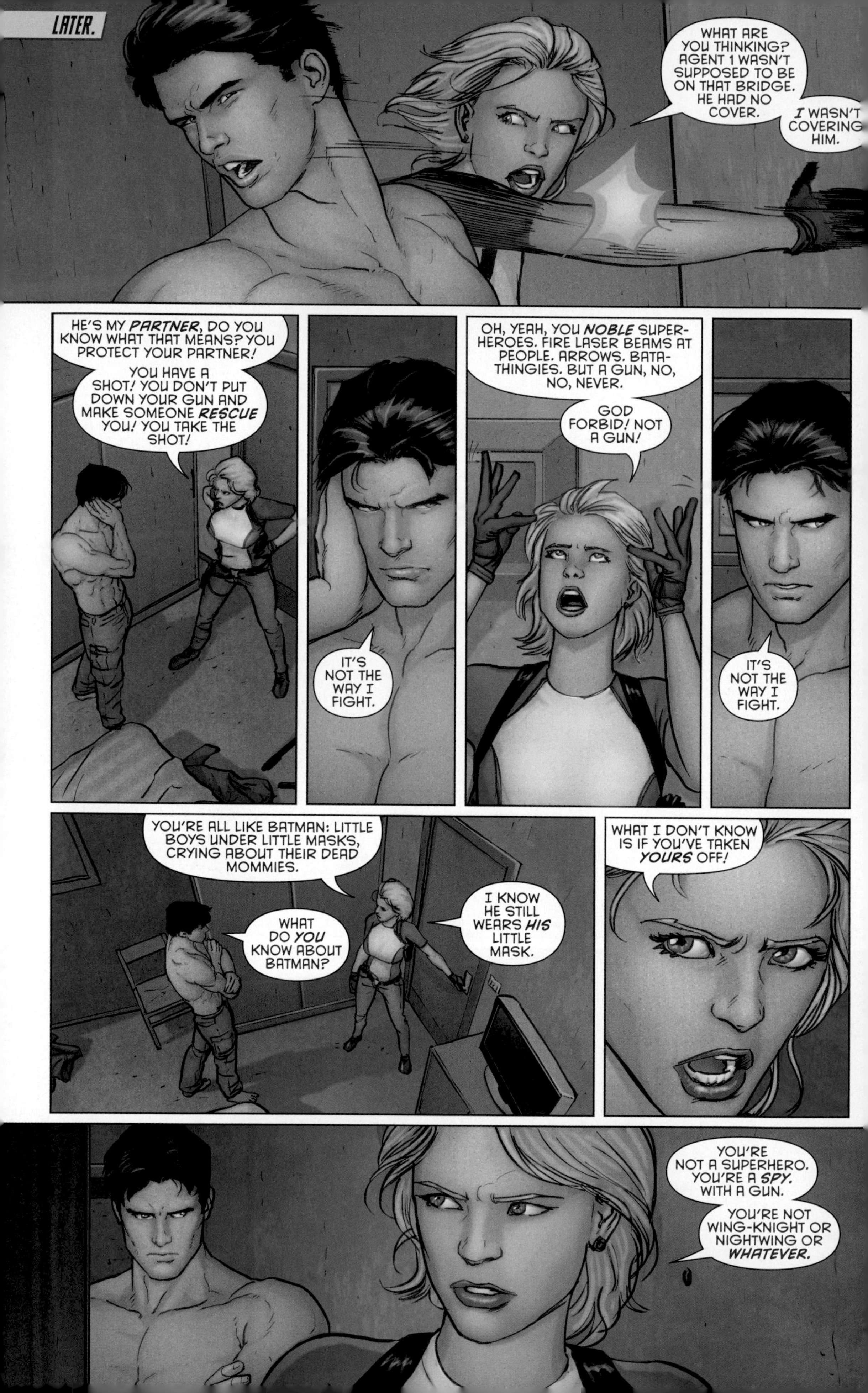
LATER.
WHAT ARE YOU THINKING? AGENT 1 WASN'T SUPPOSED TO BE ON THAT BRIDGE. HE HAD NO COVER.
I WASN'T COVERING HIM.
HE'S MY PARTNER, DO YOU KNOW WHAT THAT MEANS? YOU PROTECT YOUR PARTNER!
YOU HAVE A SHOT! YOU DON'T PUT DOWN YOUR GUN AND MAKE SOMEONE RESCUE YOU! YOU TAKE THE SHOT!
IT'S NOT THE WAY I FIGHT.
OH, YEAH, YOU NOBLE SUPER-HEROES. FIRE LASER BEAMS AT PEOPLE. ARROWS. BATA-THINGIES. BUT A GUN, NO, NO, NEVER.
GOD FORBID! NOT A GUN!
IT'S NOT THE WAY I FIGHT.
YOU'RE ALL LIKE BATMAN: LITTLE BOYS UNDER LITTLE MASKS, CRYING ABOUT THEIR DEAD MOMMIES.
WHAT DO YOU KNOW ABOUT BATMAN?
I KNOW HE STILL WEARS HIS LITTLE MASK.
WHAT I DON'T KNOW IS IF YOU'VE TAKEN YOURS OFF!
YOU'RE NOT A SUPERHERO. YOU'RE A SPY. WITH A GUN.
YOU'RE NOT WING-KNIGHT OR NIGHTWING OR WHATEVER.

"YOU'RE **AGENT 37.**"

...WE CAN CONFIRM FROM THIS AGENT 8 THAT SPYRAL HAS THE BATMAN INFORMATION?

YEAH, SURE.

THAT'S GOOD WORK, BIRDWATCHER. YOU'RE DOING WELL.

YAY. GREAT FOR ME.

...

LOOK, I NEED A FAVOR.

ANYTHING.

THERE'S A GUY, CHRISTOPHE TANNER. HE WAS AT THAT SCHOOL SHOOTING IN GENEVA.

YOU HAVE ANYTHING ON HIM IN THE GOOD COMPUTER?

ONE SECOND...

...I SHOW A CHRISTOPHE TANNER ATTENDING THE GENEVA SCHOOL.

NO, THAT'S A MISTAKE. TRUST ME.

SORRY, YOU'RE CONFIRMED ON THAT, BIRDWATCHER. THAT'S A CHRISTOPHE TANNER, JUNIOR I HAD. ENROLLED THERE THIS FALL. STARTS PRE-SCHOOL THIS WEEK.

GETTING RECORDS NOW ON THE FATHER.

WAIT, **WHAT?**

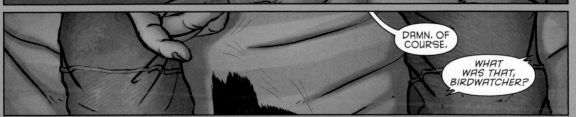

DAMN. OF COURSE.

WHAT WAS THAT, BIRDWATCHER?

A MAN DOESN'T NEED EYES, UNLESS HE'S GOT SOMETHING **WORTH** SEEING.

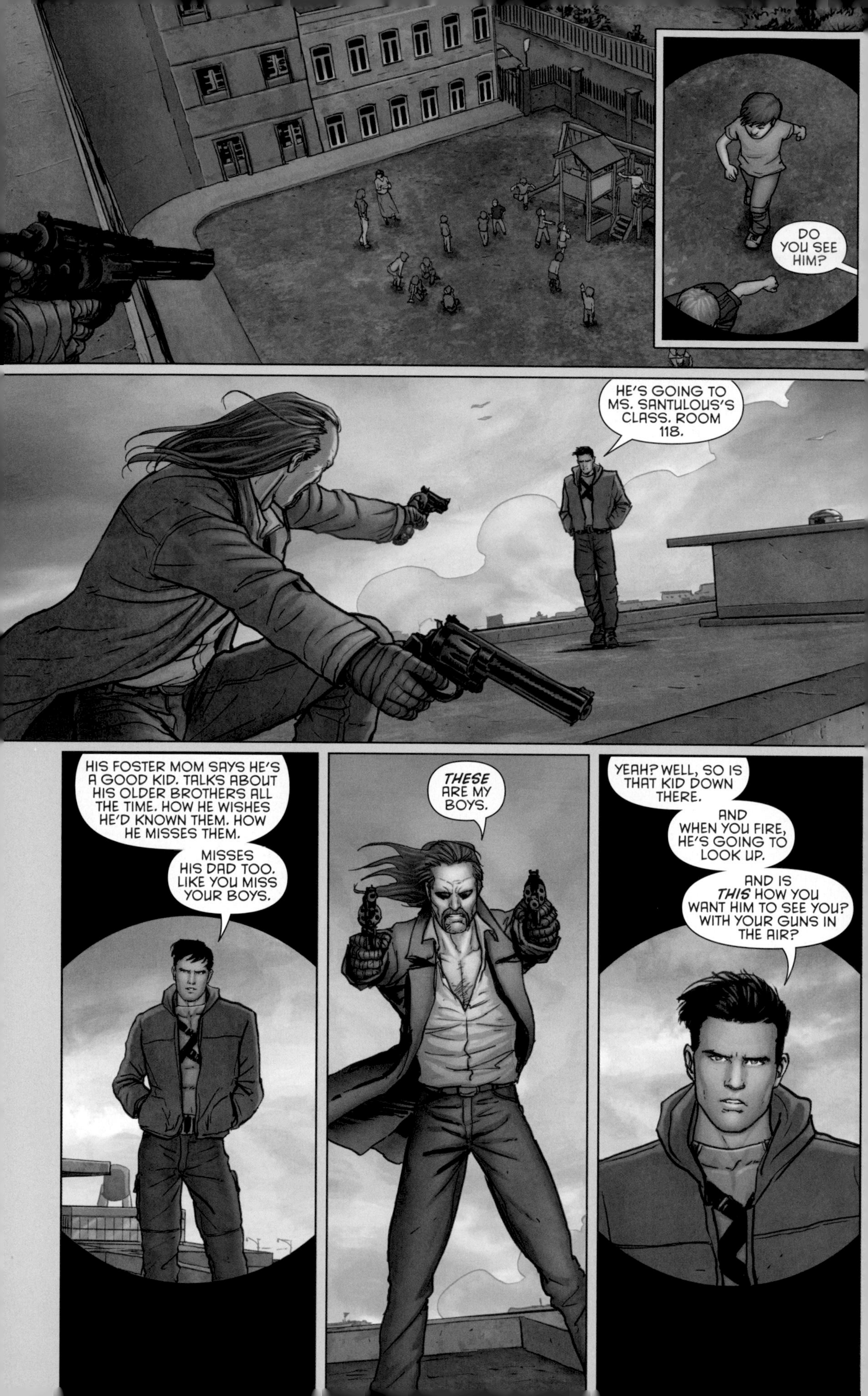
DO YOU SEE HIM?
HE'S GOING TO MS. SANTULOUS'S CLASS. ROOM 118.
HIS FOSTER MOM SAYS HE'S A GOOD KID. TALKS ABOUT HIS OLDER BROTHERS ALL THE TIME. HOW HE WISHES HE'D KNOWN THEM. HOW HE MISSES THEM.
MISSES HIS DAD TOO. LIKE YOU MISS YOUR BOYS.
THESE ARE MY BOYS.
YEAH? WELL, SO IS THAT KID DOWN THERE.
AND WHEN YOU FIRE, HE'S GOING TO LOOK UP.
AND IS THIS HOW YOU WANT HIM TO SEE YOU? WITH YOUR GUNS IN THE AIR?

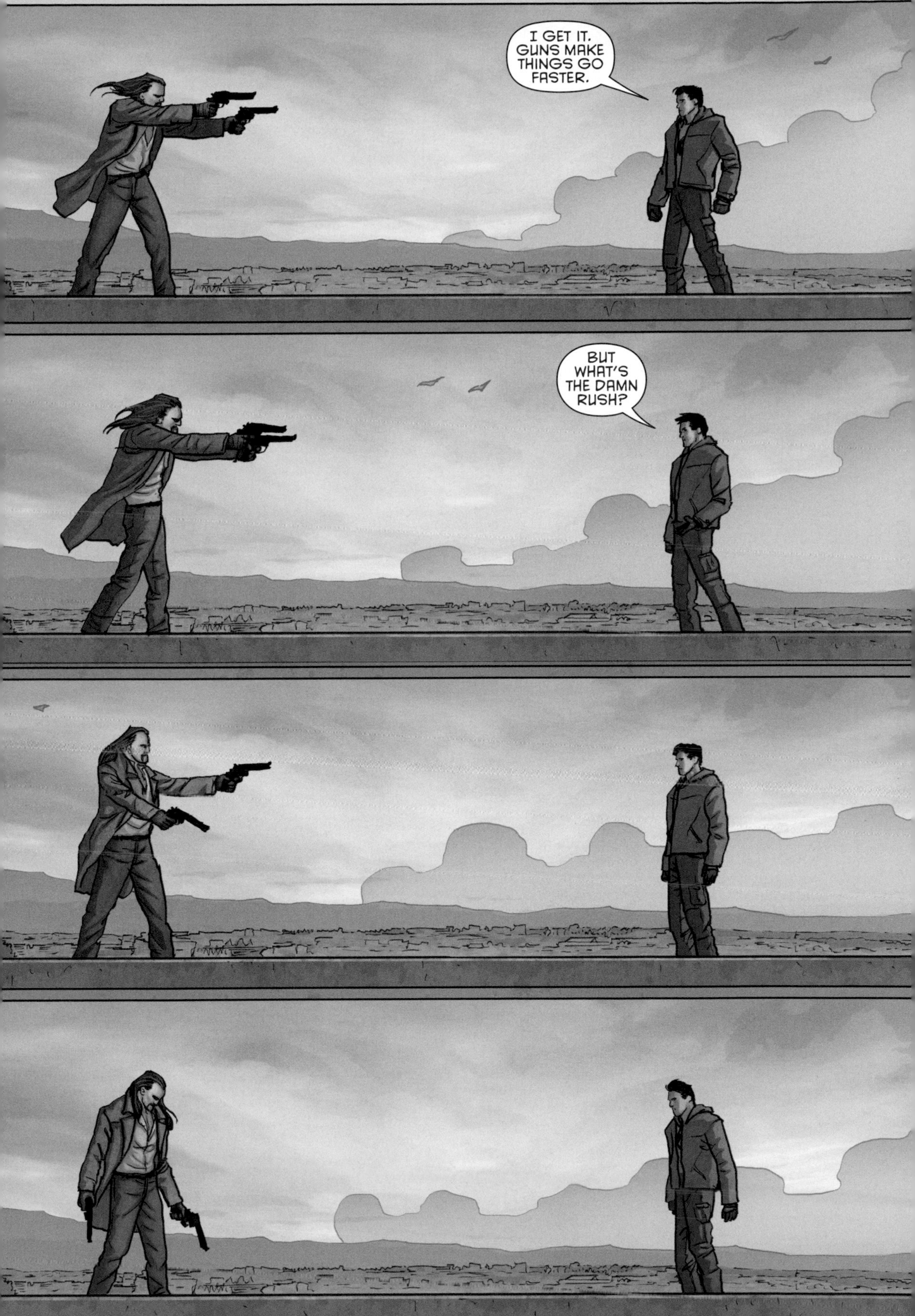
I GET IT. GUNS MAKE THINGS GO FASTER.
BUT WHAT'S THE DAMN RUSH?

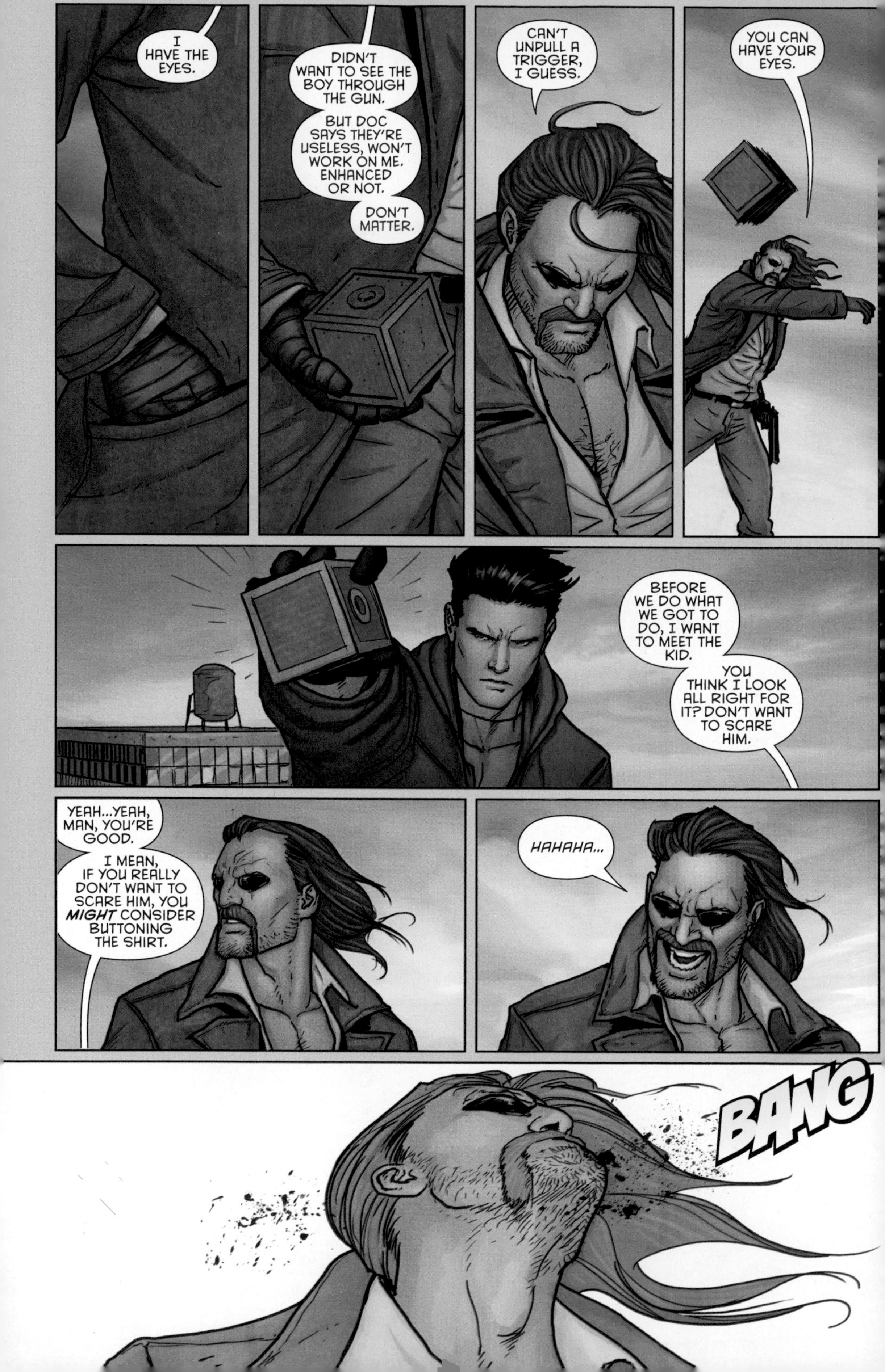
I HAVE THE EYES.
DIDN'T WANT TO SEE THE BOY THROUGH THE GUN.
BUT DOC SAYS THEY'RE USELESS, WON'T WORK ON ME. ENHANCED OR NOT.
DON'T MATTER.
CAN'T UNPULL A TRIGGER, I GUESS.
YOU CAN HAVE YOUR EYES.
BEFORE WE DO WHAT WE GOT TO DO, I WANT TO MEET THE KID.
YOU THINK I LOOK ALL RIGHT FOR IT? DON'T WANT TO SCARE HIM.
YEAH...YEAH, MAN, YOU'RE GOOD.
I MEAN, IF YOU REALLY DON'T WANT TO SCARE HIM, YOU *MIGHT* CONSIDER BUTTONING THE SHIRT.
HAHAHA...
BANG

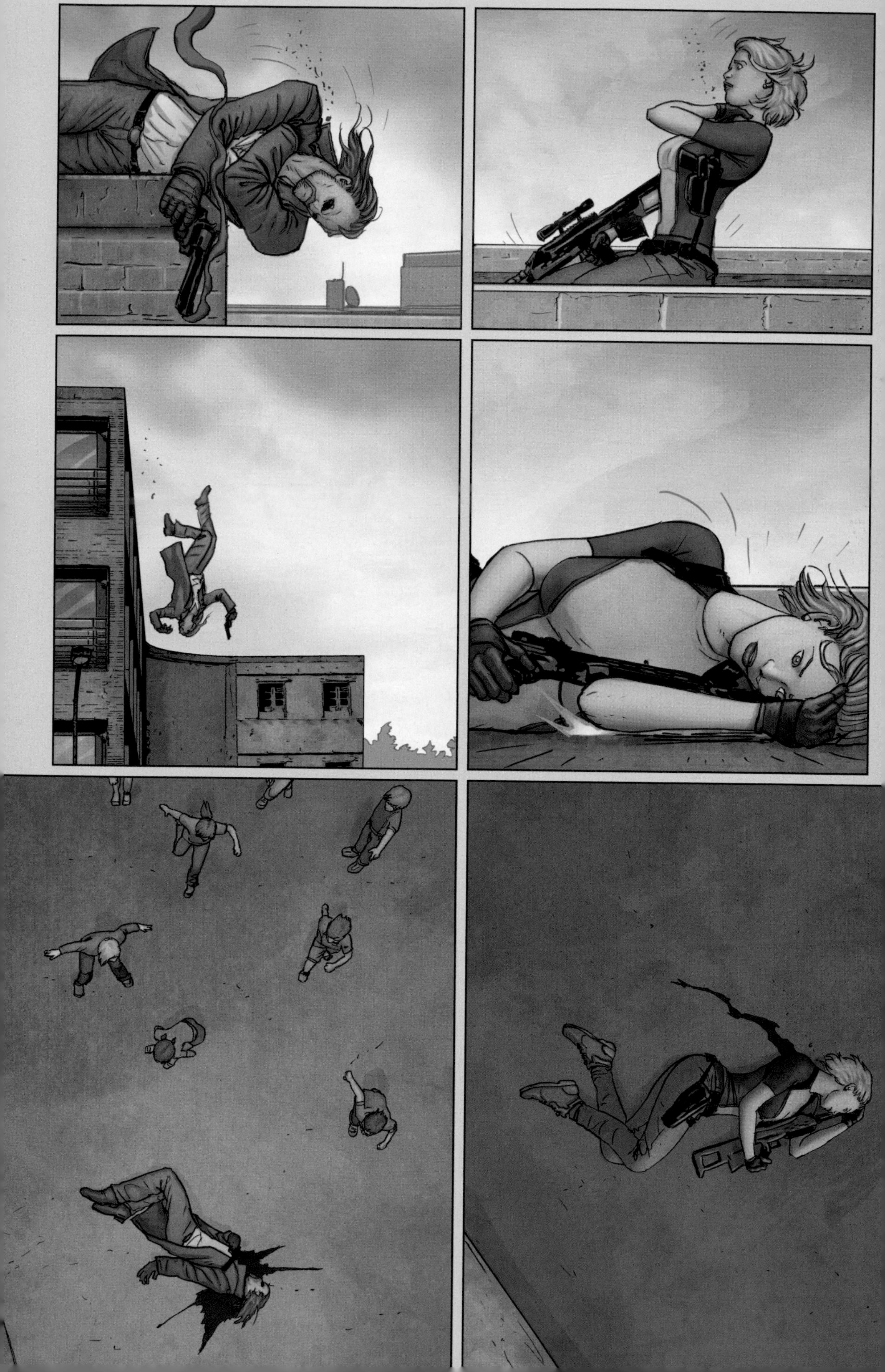

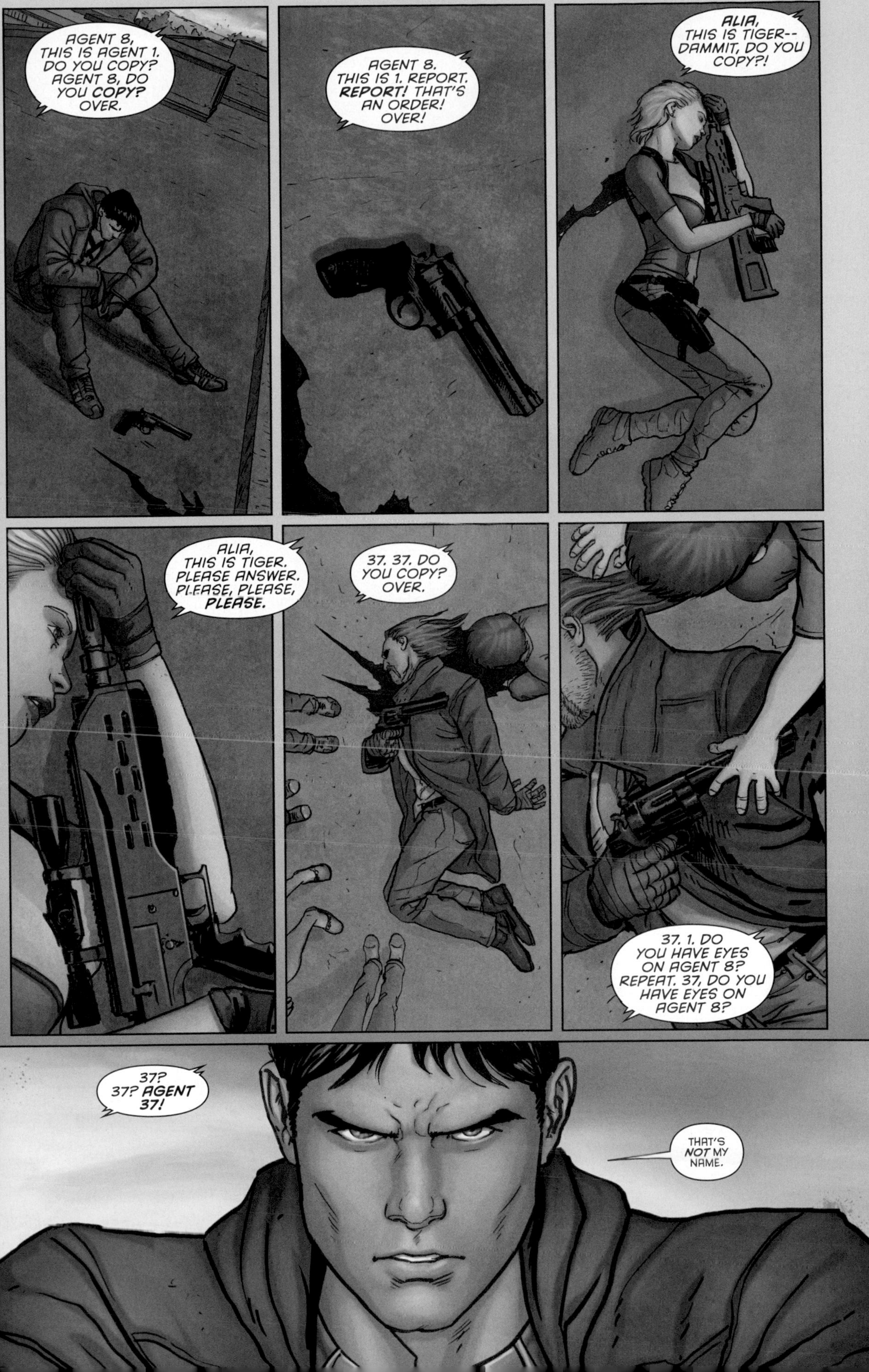
AGENT 8, THIS IS AGENT 1. DO YOU COPY? AGENT 8, DO YOU **COPY?** OVER.
AGENT 8. THIS IS 1. REPORT. **REPORT!** THAT'S AN ORDER! OVER!
ALIA, THIS IS TIGER-- DAMMIT, DO YOU COPY?!
ALIA, THIS IS TIGER. PLEASE ANSWER. PLEASE, PLEASE, ***PLEASE.***
37. 37. DO YOU COPY? OVER.
37. 1. DO YOU HAVE EYES ON AGENT 8? REPEAT. 37, DO YOU HAVE EYES ON AGENT 8?
37? 37? ***AGENT 37!***
THAT'S ***NOT*** MY NAME.

AQUAMAN
Half Human, half Atlantean.
Secret Identity: Arthur Curry
Human Father: Tom Curry (deceased).
Atlantean half-brother: Orm, former ruler of Atlantis.

YOU CAN LEARN SO MUCH FROM A MAN'S EYES.

BUT, THEN AGAIN, WHO NEEDS EYES?

WHEN YOU HAVE *EARS.*

AT 10:48 LAST NIGHT WE DETECTED AN UNAUTHORIZED *SIGNAL* BROADCASTING FROM INSIDE SPYRAL HEADQUARTERS.

SOMEONE SENDING A HIDDEN MESSAGE, USING OUR OWN COMS, THINKING I WOULDN'T BE LISTENING.

I AM *ALWAYS* LISTENING.

I FOUND IT. BUT I CAN'T YET UNDERSTAND IT.

THE ENCRYPTION IS LOVELY AND UNBREAKABLE. SOMEONE HAS WORKED DILIGENTLY, OBSESSIVELY TO KEEP THE CONTENT AND SOURCE OF THIS MESSAGE A SECRET.

MATRON, YOU ARE TO *FIND* THE PERSON RESPONSIBLE FOR THIS TRANSMISSION.

YOU ARE THEN, IN A FORCEFUL MANNER, TO REMIND THAT PERSON THAT WE ARE SPYRAL. AND ALL WILL BE *UNMASKED.*

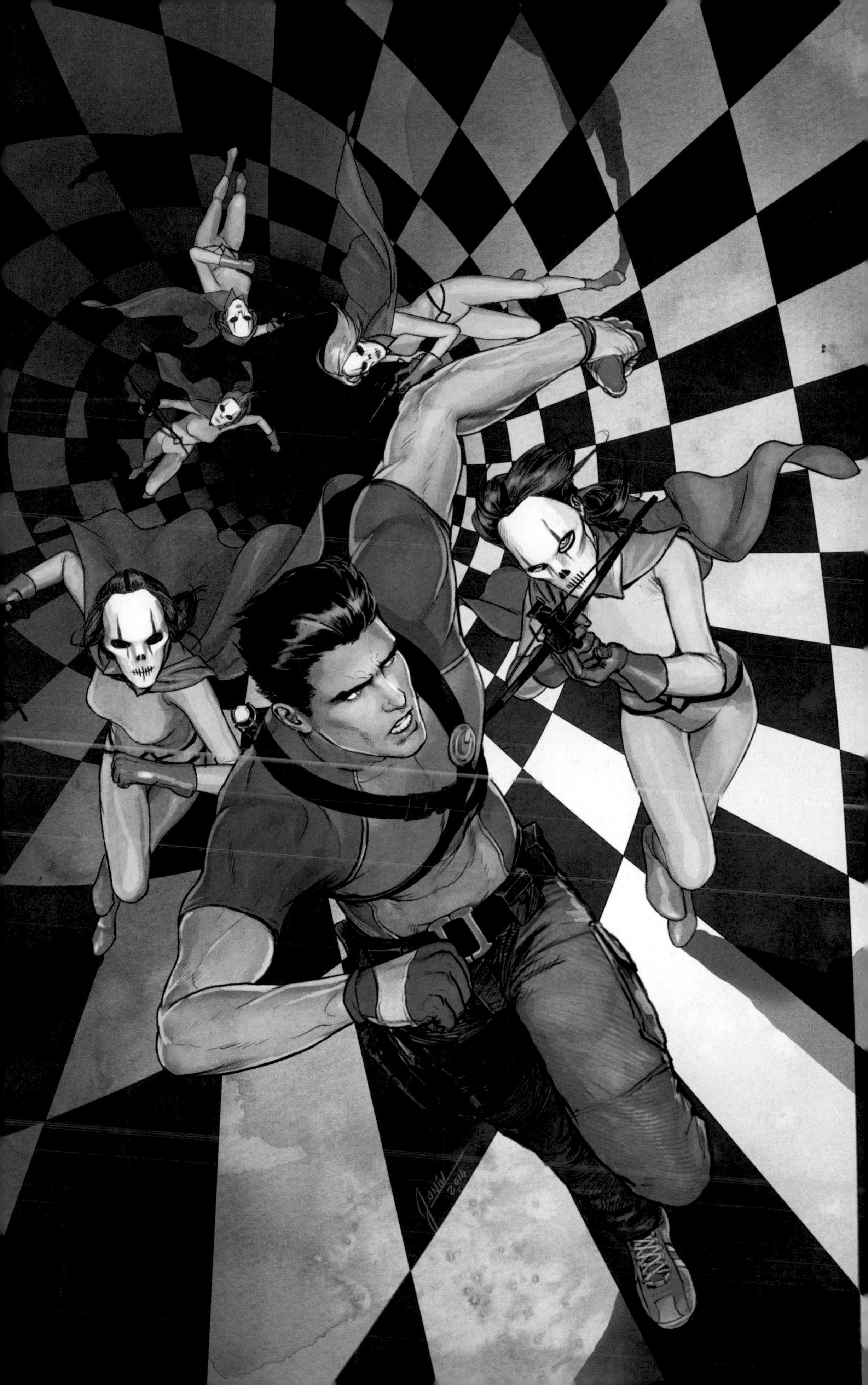

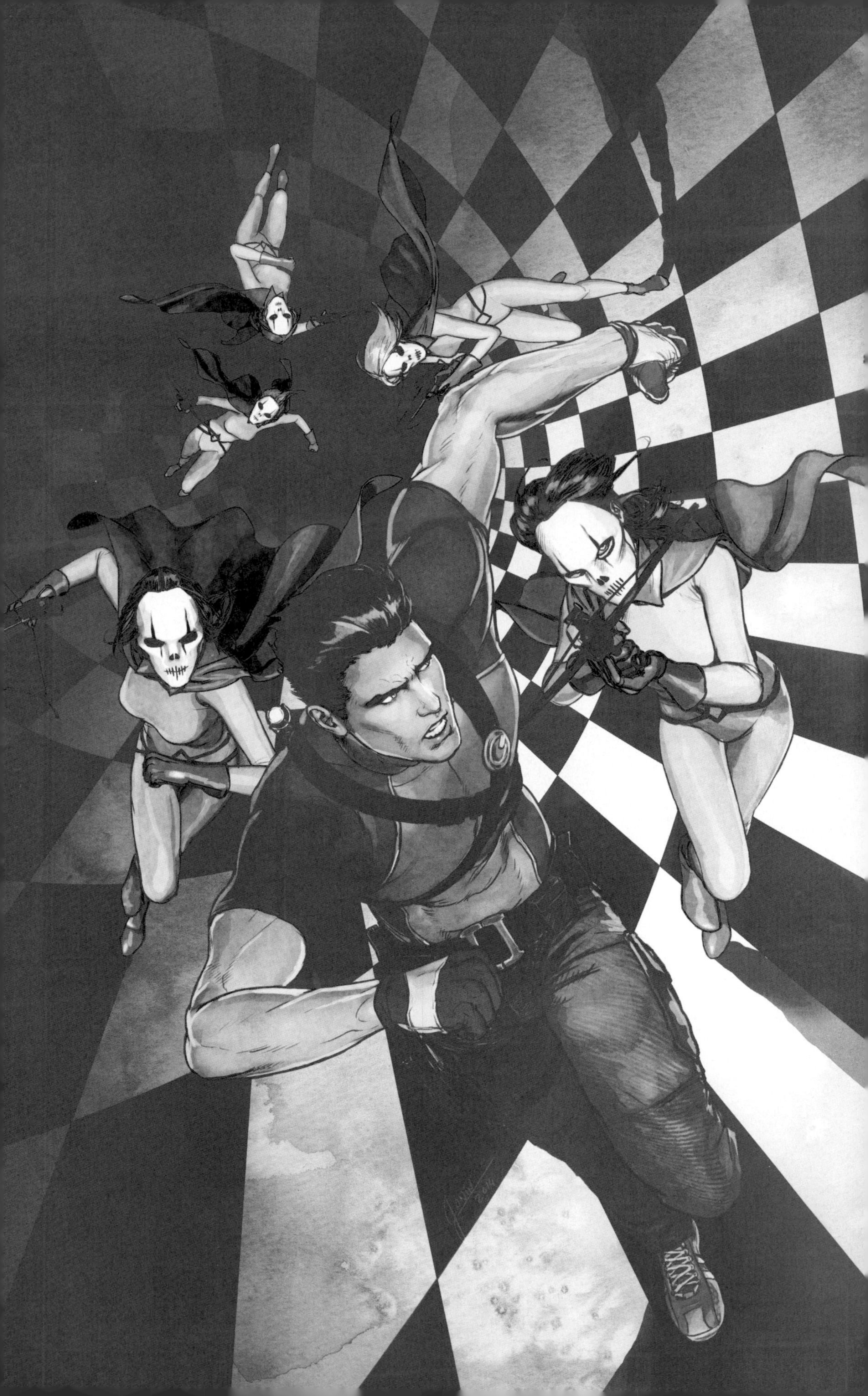

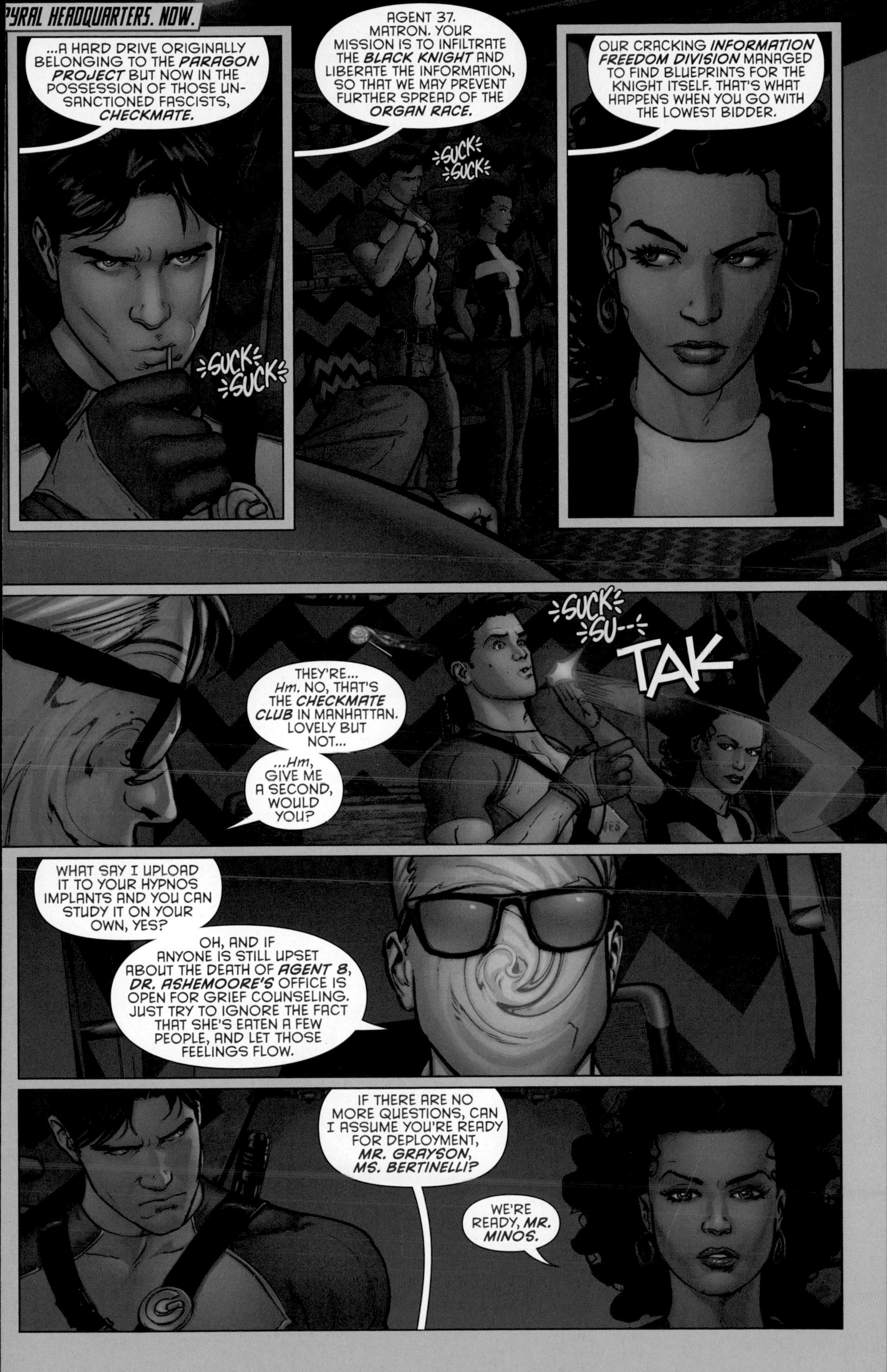
SPYRAL HEADQUARTERS. NOW.
...A HARD DRIVE ORIGINALLY BELONGING TO THE PARAGON PROJECT BUT NOW IN THE POSSESSION OF THOSE UN-SANCTIONED FASCISTS, CHECKMATE.
SUCK SUCK
AGENT 37. MATRON. YOUR MISSION IS TO INFILTRATE THE BLACK KNIGHT AND LIBERATE THE INFORMATION, SO THAT WE MAY PREVENT FURTHER SPREAD OF THE ORGAN RACE.
SUCK SUCK
OUR CRACKING INFORMATION FREEDOM DIVISION MANAGED TO FIND BLUEPRINTS FOR THE KNIGHT ITSELF. THAT'S WHAT HAPPENS WHEN YOU GO WITH THE LOWEST BIDDER.
THEY'RE... Hm. NO, THAT'S THE CHECKMATE CLUB IN MANHATTAN. LOVELY BUT NOT...
...Hm, GIVE ME A SECOND, WOULD YOU?
SUCK SU--
TAK
WHAT SAY I UPLOAD IT TO YOUR HYPNOS IMPLANTS AND YOU CAN STUDY IT ON YOUR OWN, YES?
OH, AND IF ANYONE IS STILL UPSET ABOUT THE DEATH OF AGENT 8, DR. ASHEMOORE'S OFFICE IS OPEN FOR GRIEF COUNSELING. JUST TRY TO IGNORE THE FACT THAT SHE'S EATEN A FEW PEOPLE, AND LET THOSE FEELINGS FLOW.
IF THERE ARE NO MORE QUESTIONS, CAN I ASSUME YOU'RE READY FOR DEPLOYMENT, MR. GRAYSON, MS. BERTINELLI?
WE'RE READY, MR. MINOS.

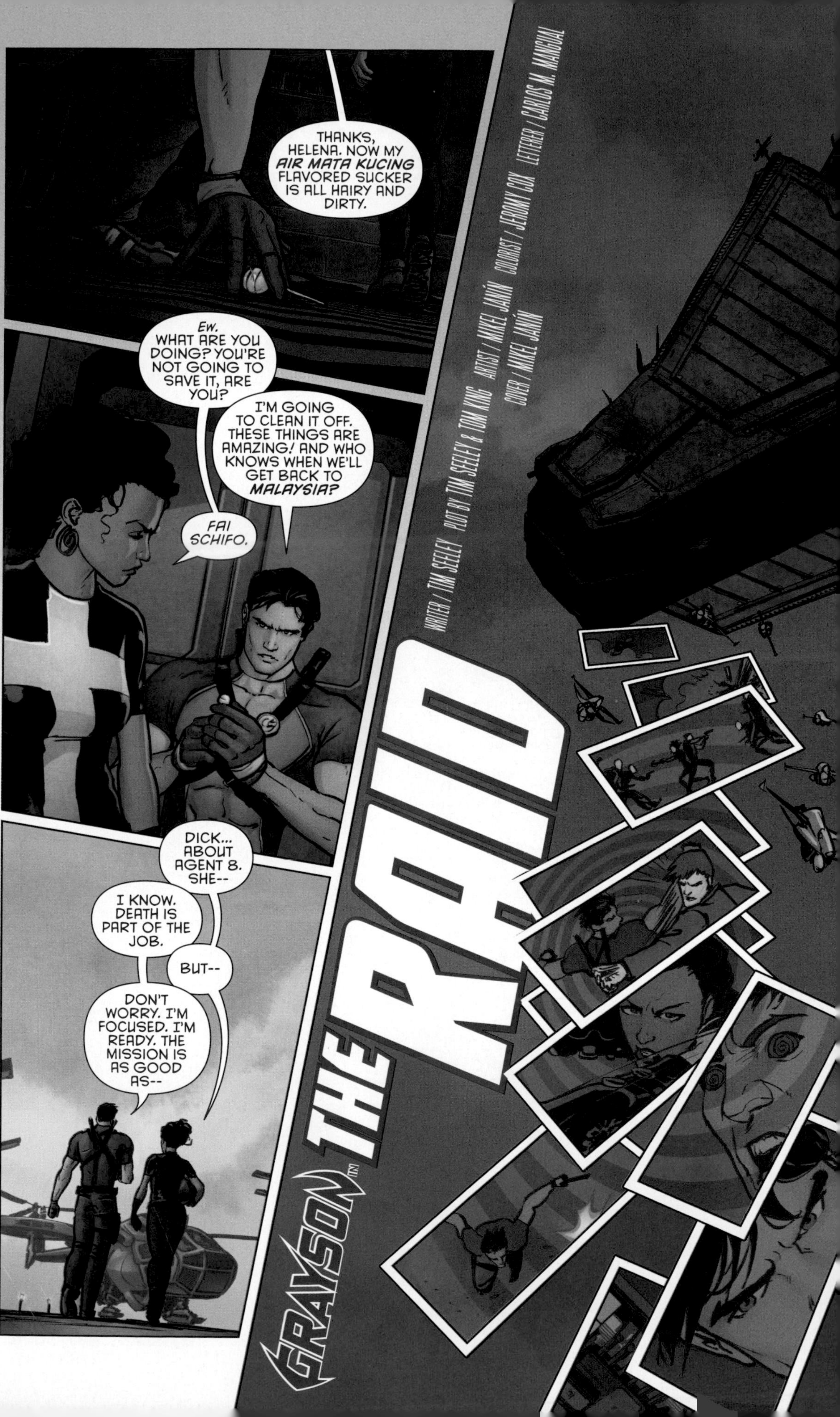
THANKS, HELENA. NOW MY *AIR MATA KUCING* FLAVORED SUCKER IS ALL HAIRY AND DIRTY.
Ew. WHAT ARE YOU DOING? YOU'RE NOT GOING TO SAVE IT, ARE YOU?
I'M GOING TO CLEAN IT OFF. THESE THINGS ARE AMAZING! AND WHO KNOWS WHEN WE'LL GET BACK TO *MALAYSIA?*
FAI SCHIFO.
DICK... ABOUT AGENT 8. SHE--
I KNOW. DEATH IS PART OF THE JOB.
BUT--
DON'T WORRY. I'M FOCUSED. I'M READY. THE MISSION IS AS GOOD AS--
GRAYSON™
THE RAID
WRITER / TIM SEELEY PLOT BY TIM SEELEY & TOM KING ARTIST / MIKEL JANÍN COLORIST / JEROMY COX LETTERER / CARLOS M. MANGUAL
COVER / MIKEL JANÍN

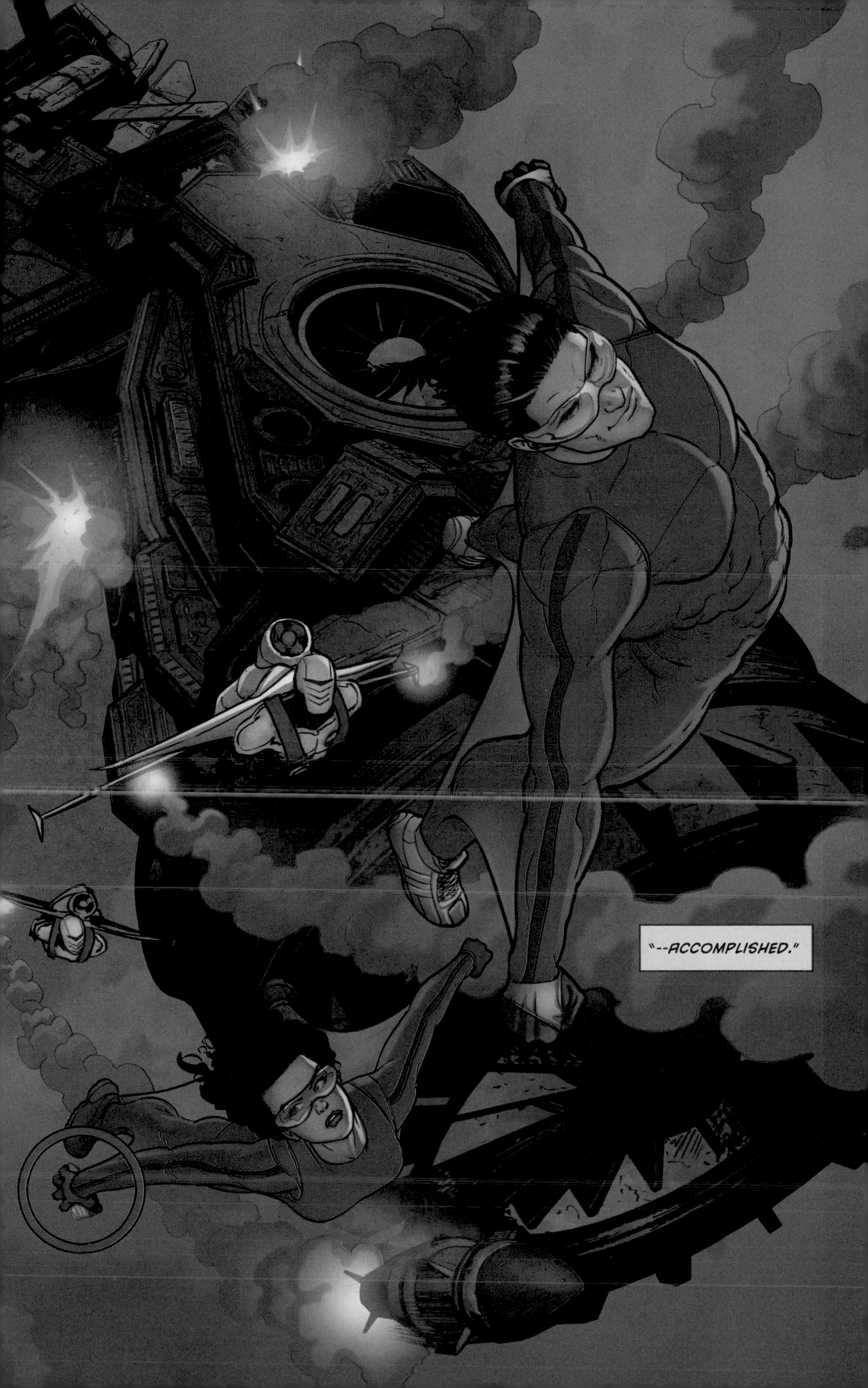
"--ACCOMPLISHED."

LOTTI! YOU BITCH!

HAHA! YOU DAFT LOT! THAT WASN'T EVEN A GOOD IMPRESSION!

NOW, MOVE ON OUT OF THE WAY. WHAT I'VE GOT HERE IS INDISPUTABLE PROOF.

OH, NOW WHAT HAVE YOU MANAGED TO FILM? EVIDENCE THAT WHEN *MS. WEMBERLY* GOES BEHIND THE SHED SHE'S SECRETLY CHANGING INTO *WONDER WOMAN*?

NAW, YE BUNCH OF CHOCOLATE-HOARDIN' HEATHENS. ONE OF MY CAMERAS CAUGHT A RARE AND BEAUTIFUL SIGHT.

A *MAN*. I'LL SHOW YE WHAT I MEAN. BUT MAKE WITH THE SWEETIES, EHM?

YOU'RE NOT TALKING ABOUT THE OLD GUY WHO STEPPED INTO THE CROSSBOW RANGE THE OTHER DAY DRESSED AS A MONK, ARE YOU? YOU CAN *HAVE* HIM.

NO NO. I'M TALKIN' ABOUT SOME PRIME HOLLYWOOD *BEEFCAKE*. NICE BAHOOKIE ON 'IM TOO. COULDN'T GET A GOOD SHOT OF 'IS FACE, BUT WHAT GOOD'S THAT ANYWAY?

SO MANY... ABS...

AY DIOS MIO.

SO WHAT DO YOU SUGGEST WE DO WITH-- THIS?

IT'S SIMPLE, *PARIS*. I SUGGEST WE MOUNT A *"MAN-TY RAID."*

WHY? WHAT GOOD WILL THAT DO?

I DON'T BLOODY KNOW. WHAT DO THE BOYS DO WHEN THEY MOUNT A *PANTY* RAID ON THE GIRLS' CABIN? THEY SCREAM AND PAT THEMSELVES ON THE BACK.

IT'S NOT ABOUT THE *RESULT*...

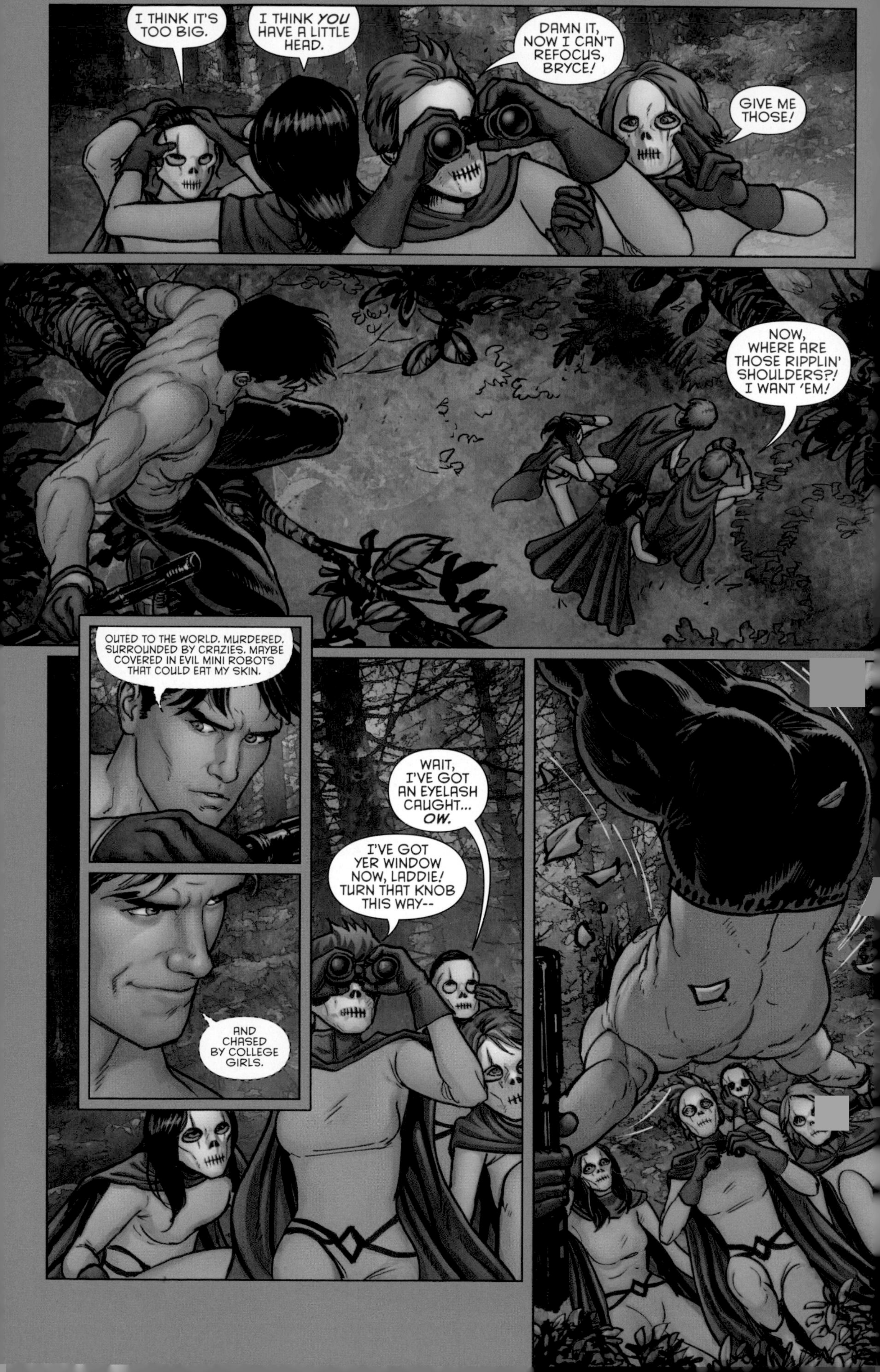
I THINK IT'S TOO BIG.
I THINK *YOU* HAVE A LITTLE HEAD.
DAMN IT, NOW I CAN'T REFOCUS, BRYCE!
GIVE ME THOSE!
NOW, WHERE ARE THOSE RIPPLIN' SHOULDERS?! I WANT 'EM!
OUTED TO THE WORLD. MURDERED. SURROUNDED BY CRAZIES. MAYBE COVERED IN EVIL MINI ROBOTS THAT COULD EAT MY SKIN.
AND CHASED BY COLLEGE GIRLS.
WAIT, I'VE GOT AN EYELASH CAUGHT... **OW.**
I'VE GOT YER WINDOW NOW, LADDIE! TURN THAT KNOB THIS WAY--

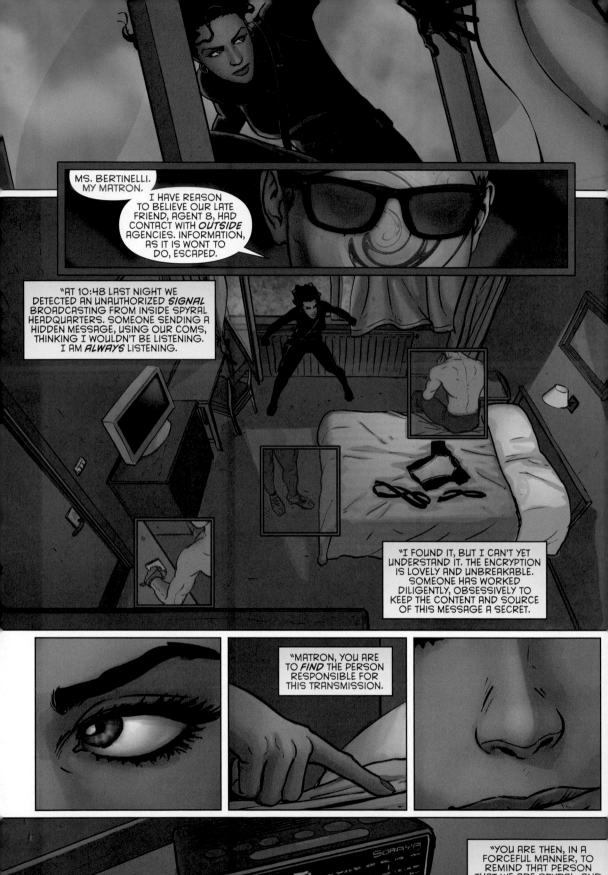

MS. BERTINELLI. MY MATRON. I HAVE REASON TO BELIEVE OUR LATE FRIEND, AGENT 8, HAD CONTACT WITH *OUTSIDE* AGENCIES. INFORMATION, AS IT IS WONT TO DO, ESCAPED.

"AT 10:48 LAST NIGHT WE DETECTED AN UNAUTHORIZED *SIGNAL* BROADCASTING FROM INSIDE SPYRAL HEADQUARTERS. SOMEONE SENDING A HIDDEN MESSAGE, USING OUR COMS, THINKING I WOULDN'T BE LISTENING. I AM *ALWAYS* LISTENING.

"I FOUND IT, BUT I CAN'T YET UNDERSTAND IT. THE ENCRYPTION IS LOVELY AND UNBREAKABLE. SOMEONE HAS WORKED DILIGENTLY, OBSESSIVELY TO KEEP THE CONTENT AND SOURCE OF THIS MESSAGE A SECRET.

"MATRON, YOU ARE TO *FIND* THE PERSON RESPONSIBLE FOR THIS TRANSMISSION.

"YOU ARE THEN, IN A FORCEFUL MANNER, TO REMIND THAT PERSON THAT WE ARE SPYRAL. AND ALL WILL BE *UNMASKED.*"

LEGNER
CLOCK TOWER

GARDEN

ATHLETIC FIELD

DIMAYUGA
HALL

CANTERBURY
HALL

BONNINGTON
HALL

WINDSOR
SPORTS CENTRE

St. Hadrian's
Finishing School.

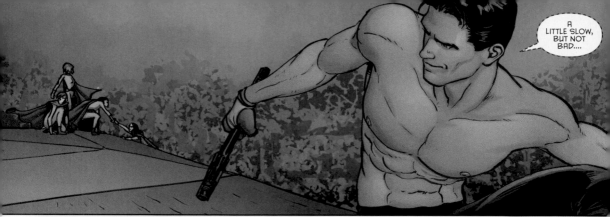

A LITTLE SLOW, BUT NOT BAD....

HE'S UP HERE!

NOWHERE TO GO BUT THE FOOTBALL FIELD NOW, AYE?

AHHH, BAWS.

→SIGH← "BAWS" IS RIGHT.

EVENIN', MATRON.

GIRLS. RETURN TO YOUR DORMS. IMMEDIATELY.

AND YOU, AGENT 37. FOLLOW ME. NOW.

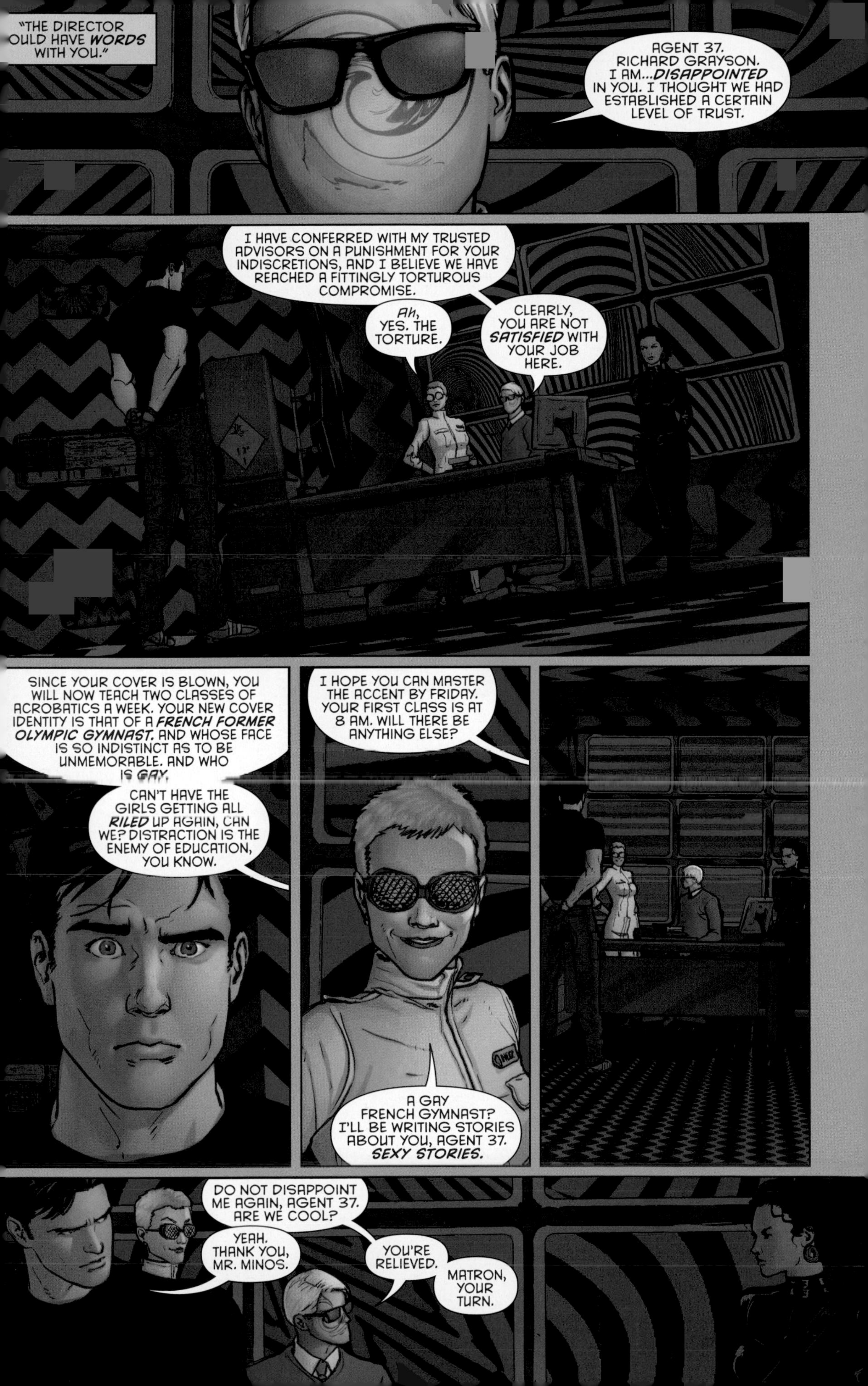
"THE DIRECTOR OULD HAVE WORDS WITH YOU."
AGENT 37. RICHARD GRAYSON. I AM...DISAPPOINTED IN YOU. I THOUGHT WE HAD ESTABLISHED A CERTAIN LEVEL OF TRUST.
I HAVE CONFERRED WITH MY TRUSTED ADVISORS ON A PUNISHMENT FOR YOUR INDISCRETIONS, AND I BELIEVE WE HAVE REACHED A FITTINGLY TORTUROUS COMPROMISE.
AH, YES. THE TORTURE.
CLEARLY, YOU ARE NOT SATISFIED WITH YOUR JOB HERE.
SINCE YOUR COVER IS BLOWN, YOU WILL NOW TEACH TWO CLASSES OF ACROBATICS A WEEK. YOUR NEW COVER IDENTITY IS THAT OF A FRENCH FORMER OLYMPIC GYMNAST. AND WHOSE FACE IS SO INDISTINCT AS TO BE UNMEMORABLE. AND WHO IS GAY.
CAN'T HAVE THE GIRLS GETTING ALL RILED UP AGAIN, CAN WE? DISTRACTION IS THE ENEMY OF EDUCATION, YOU KNOW.
I HOPE YOU CAN MASTER THE ACCENT BY FRIDAY. YOUR FIRST CLASS IS AT 8 AM. WILL THERE BE ANYTHING ELSE?
A GAY FRENCH GYMNAST? I'LL BE WRITING STORIES ABOUT YOU, AGENT 37. SEXY STORIES.
DO NOT DISAPPOINT ME AGAIN, AGENT 37. ARE WE COOL?
YEAH. THANK YOU, MR. MINOS.
YOU'RE RELIEVED.
MATRON, YOUR TURN.

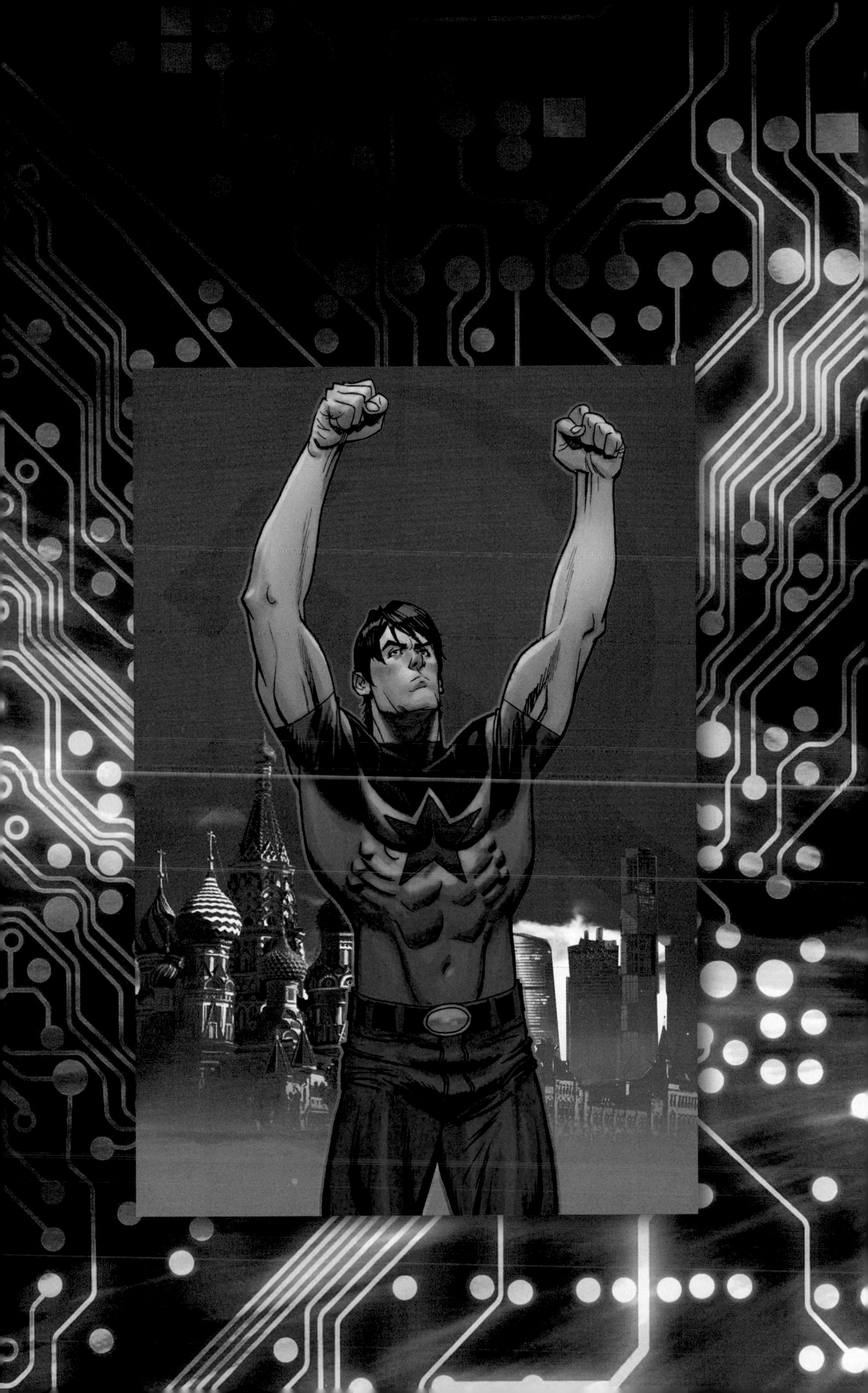

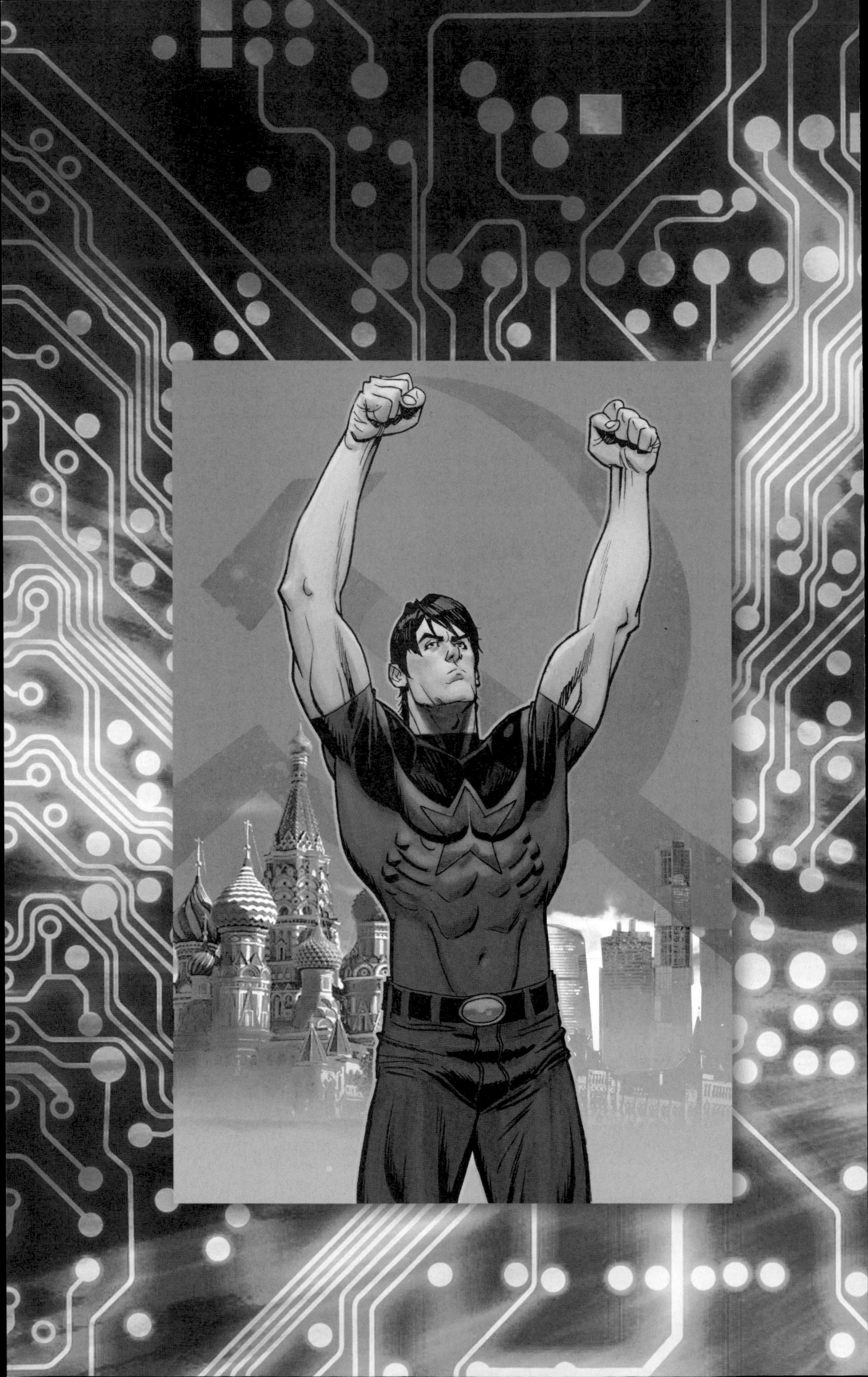

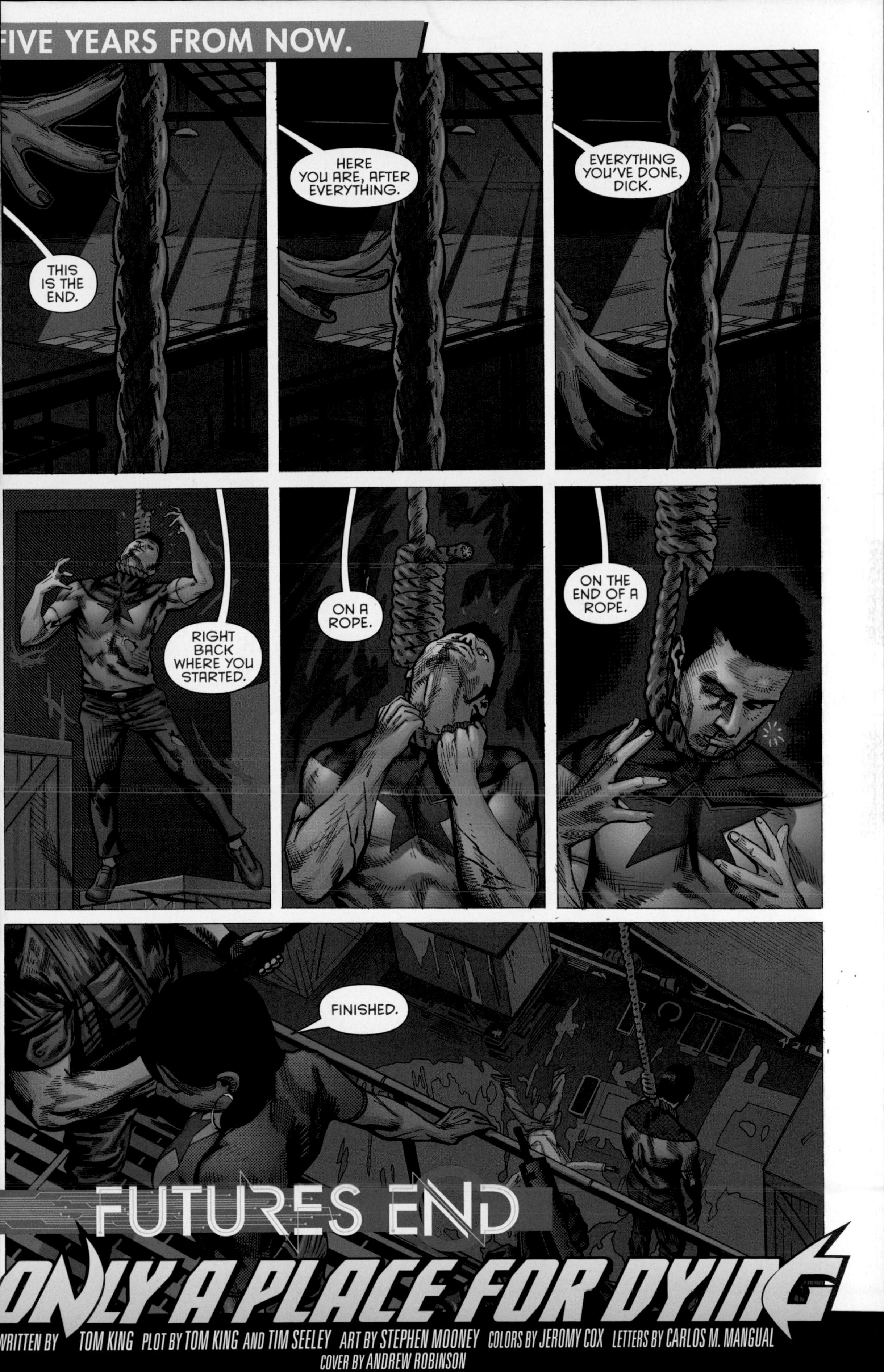

FIVE YEARS FROM NOW.
THIS IS THE END.
HERE YOU ARE, AFTER EVERYTHING.
EVERYTHING YOU'VE DONE, DICK.
RIGHT BACK WHERE YOU STARTED.
ON A ROPE.
ON THE END OF A ROPE.
FINISHED.
FUTURES END
ONLY A PLACE FOR DYING
WRITTEN BY TOM KING PLOT BY TOM KING AND TIM SEELEY ART BY STEPHEN MOONEY COLORS BY JEROMY COX LETTERS BY CARLOS M. MANGUAL
COVER BY ANDREW ROBINSON

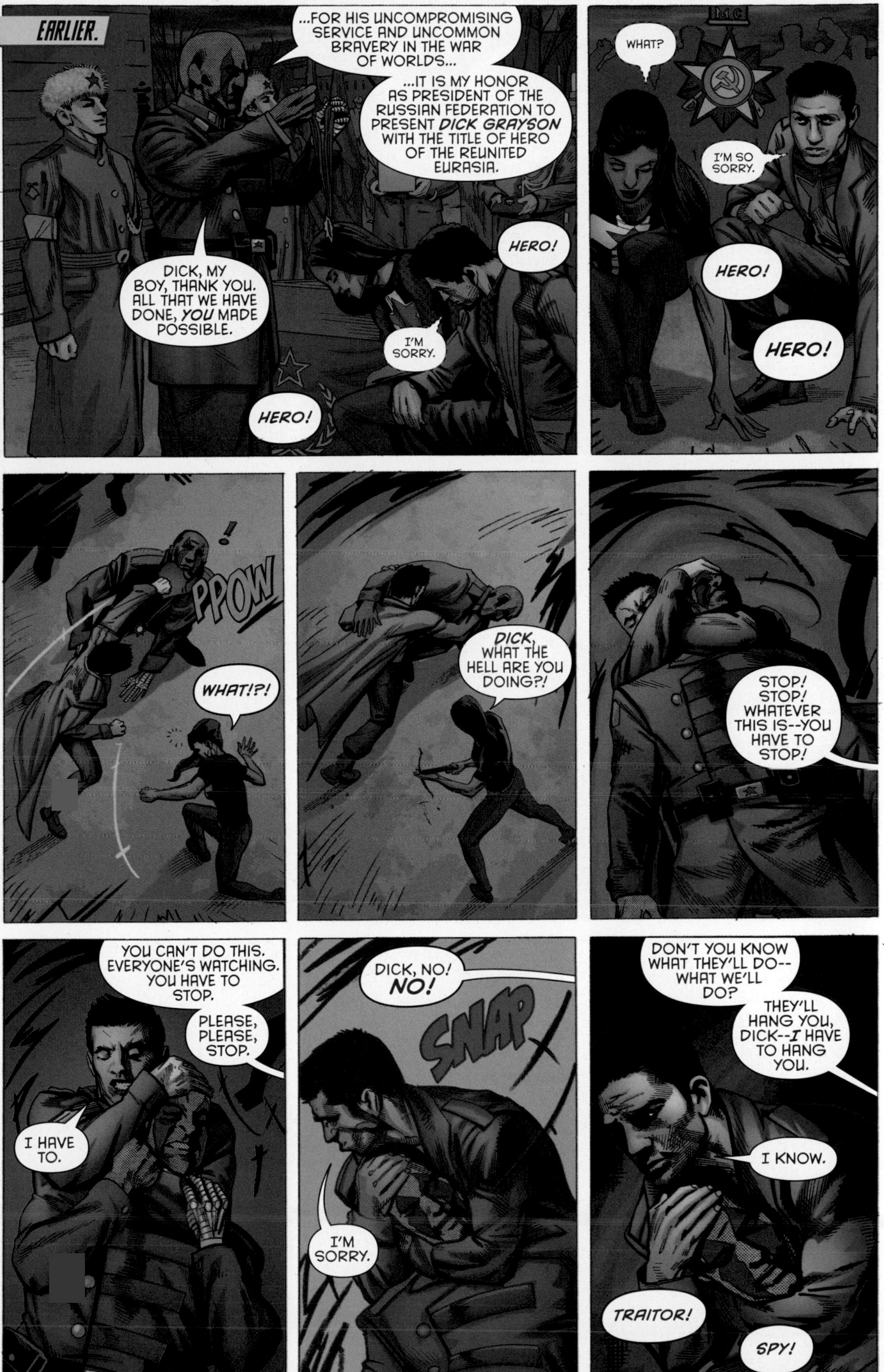
EARLIER.
...FOR HIS UNCOMPROMISING SERVICE AND UNCOMMON BRAVERY IN THE WAR OF WORLDS...
...IT IS MY HONOR AS PRESIDENT OF THE RUSSIAN FEDERATION TO PRESENT DICK GRAYSON WITH THE TITLE OF HERO OF THE REUNITED EURASIA.
DICK, MY BOY, THANK YOU. ALL THAT WE HAVE DONE, YOU MADE POSSIBLE.
HERO!
I'M SORRY.
HERO!
WHAT?
I'M SO SORRY.
HERO!
HERO!
!
PPOW
WHAT!?!
DICK, WHAT THE HELL ARE YOU DOING?!
STOP! STOP! WHATEVER THIS IS--YOU HAVE TO STOP!
YOU CAN'T DO THIS. EVERYONE'S WATCHING. YOU HAVE TO STOP.
PLEASE, PLEASE, STOP.
I HAVE TO.
DICK, NO! NO!
SNAP
I'M SORRY.
DON'T YOU KNOW WHAT THEY'LL DO-- WHAT WE'LL DO?
THEY'LL HANG YOU, DICK--I HAVE TO HANG YOU.
I KNOW.
TRAITOR!
SPY!

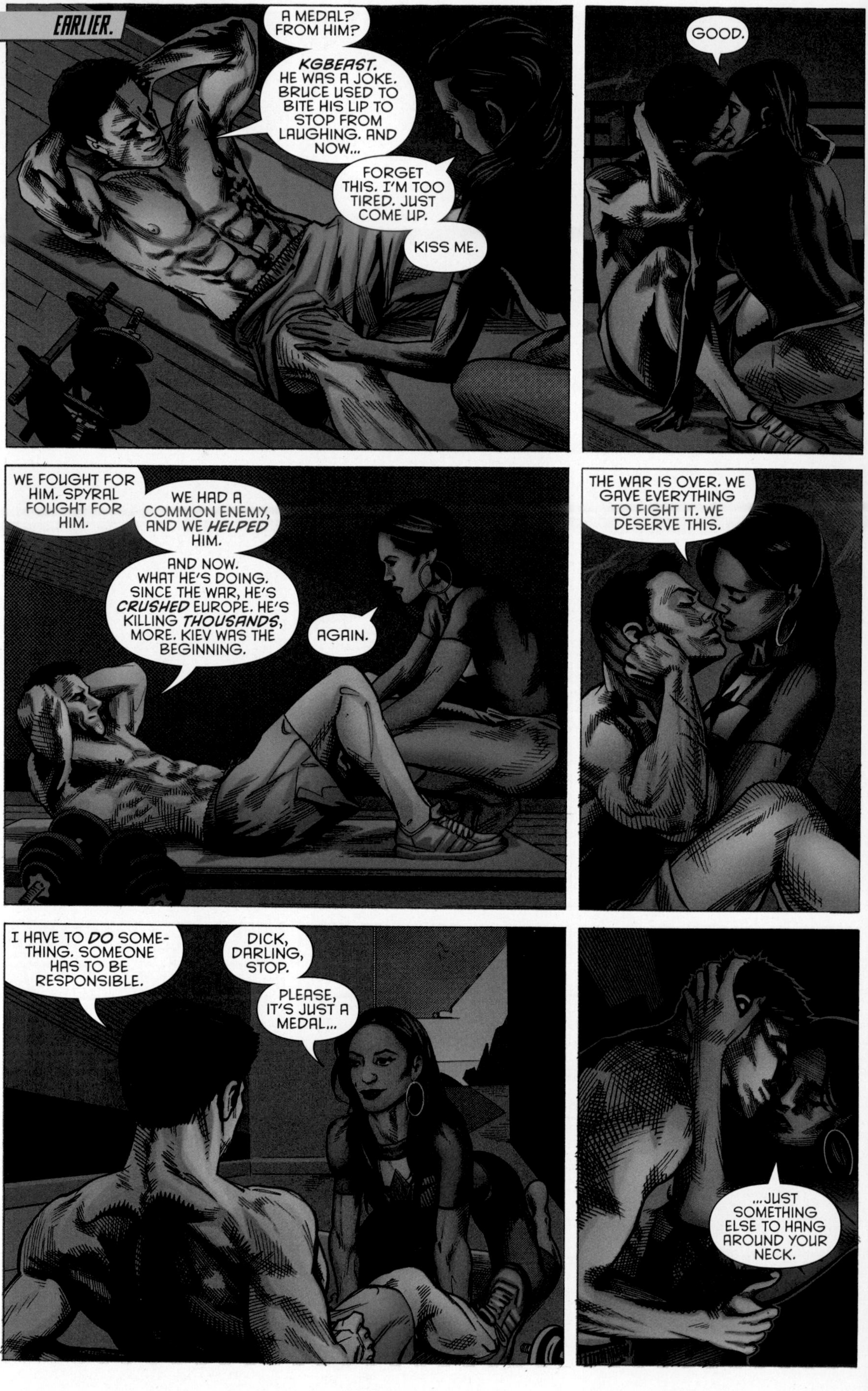
EARLIER.
A MEDAL? FROM HIM?
KGBEAST. HE WAS A JOKE. BRUCE USED TO BITE HIS LIP TO STOP FROM LAUGHING. AND NOW...
FORGET THIS. I'M TOO TIRED. JUST COME UP.
KISS ME.
GOOD.
WE FOUGHT FOR HIM. SPYRAL FOUGHT FOR HIM.
WE HAD A COMMON ENEMY, AND WE HELPED HIM.
AND NOW. WHAT HE'S DOING. SINCE THE WAR, HE'S CRUSHED EUROPE. HE'S KILLING THOUSANDS, MORE. KIEV WAS THE BEGINNING.
AGAIN.
THE WAR IS OVER. WE GAVE EVERYTHING TO FIGHT IT. WE DESERVE THIS.
I HAVE TO DO SOME-THING. SOMEONE HAS TO BE RESPONSIBLE.
DICK, DARLING, STOP.
PLEASE, IT'S JUST A MEDAL...
...JUST SOMETHING ELSE TO HANG AROUND YOUR NECK.

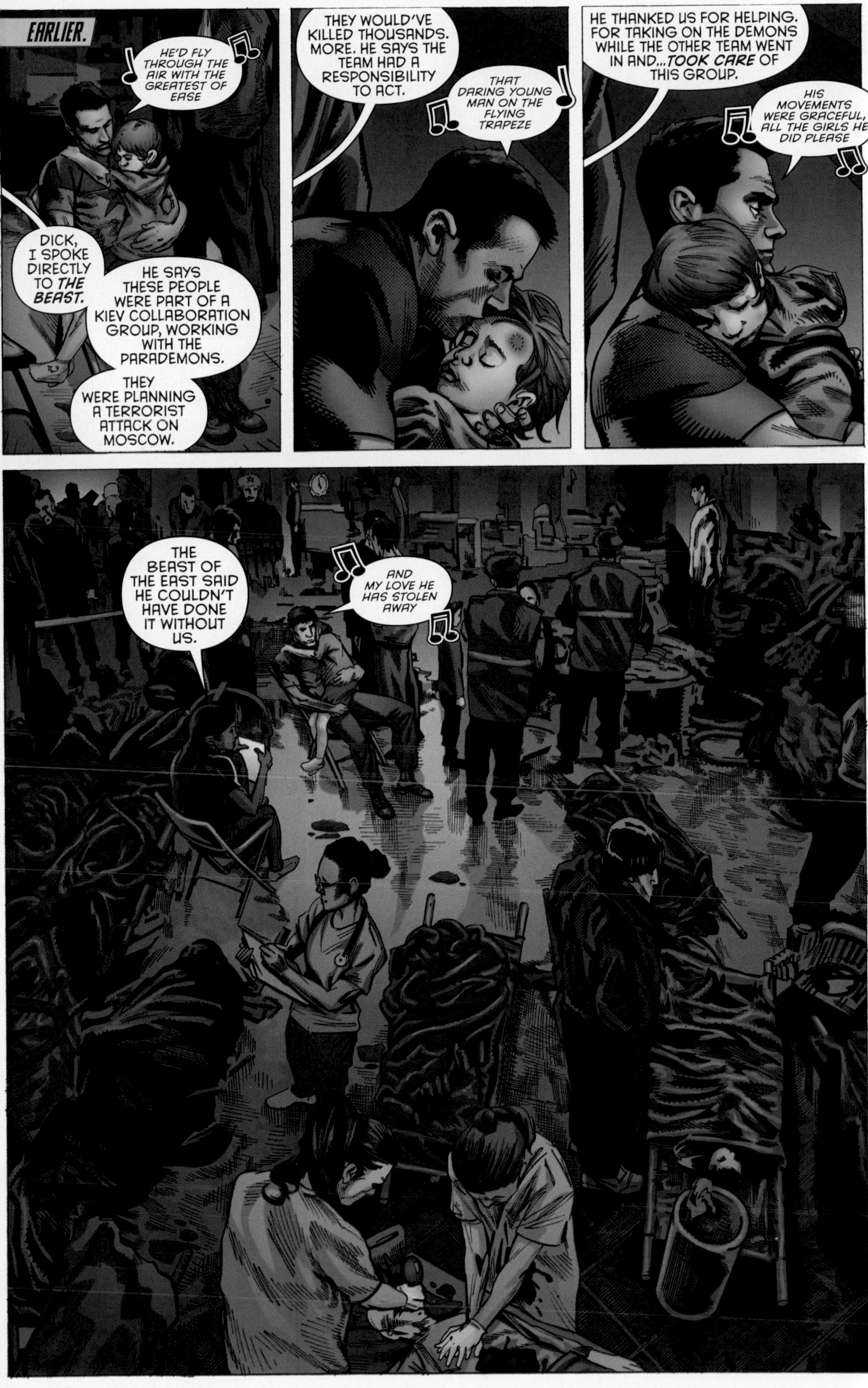
EARLIER.
HE'D FLY THROUGH THE AIR WITH THE GREATEST OF EASE
DICK, I SPOKE DIRECTLY TO THE BEAST.
HE SAYS THESE PEOPLE WERE PART OF A KIEV COLLABORATION GROUP, WORKING WITH THE PARADEMONS.
THEY WERE PLANNING A TERRORIST ATTACK ON MOSCOW.
THEY WOULD'VE KILLED THOUSANDS. MORE. HE SAYS THE TEAM HAD A RESPONSIBILITY TO ACT.
THAT DARING YOUNG MAN ON THE FLYING TRAPEZE
HE THANKED US FOR HELPING. FOR TAKING ON THE DEMONS WHILE THE OTHER TEAM WENT IN AND...TOOK CARE OF THIS GROUP.
HIS MOVEMENTS WERE GRACEFUL, ALL THE GIRLS HE DID PLEASE
THE BEAST OF THE EAST SAID HE COULDN'T HAVE DONE IT WITHOUT US.
AND MY LOVE HE HAS STOLEN AWAY

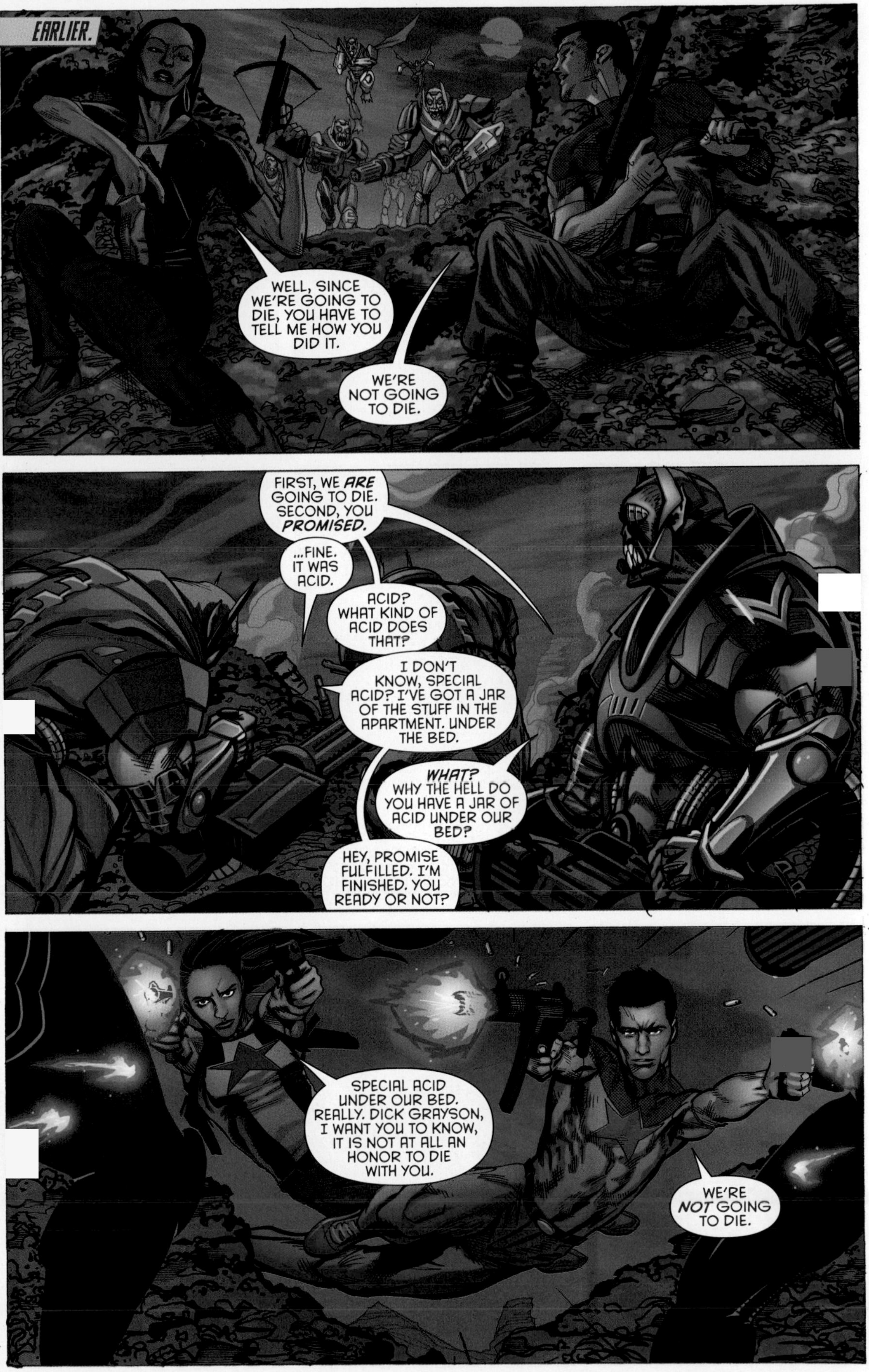
EARLIER.
WELL, SINCE WE'RE GOING TO DIE, YOU HAVE TO TELL ME HOW YOU DID IT.
WE'RE NOT GOING TO DIE.
FIRST, WE *ARE* GOING TO DIE. SECOND, YOU *PROMISED.*
...FINE. IT WAS ACID.
ACID? WHAT KIND OF ACID DOES THAT?
I DON'T KNOW, SPECIAL ACID? I'VE GOT A JAR OF THE STUFF IN THE APARTMENT. UNDER THE BED.
WHAT? WHY THE HELL DO YOU HAVE A JAR OF ACID UNDER OUR BED?
HEY, PROMISE FULFILLED. I'M FINISHED. YOU READY OR NOT?
SPECIAL ACID UNDER OUR BED. REALLY. DICK GRAYSON, I WANT YOU TO KNOW, IT IS NOT AT ALL AN HONOR TO DIE WITH YOU.
WE'RE *NOT* GOING TO DIE.

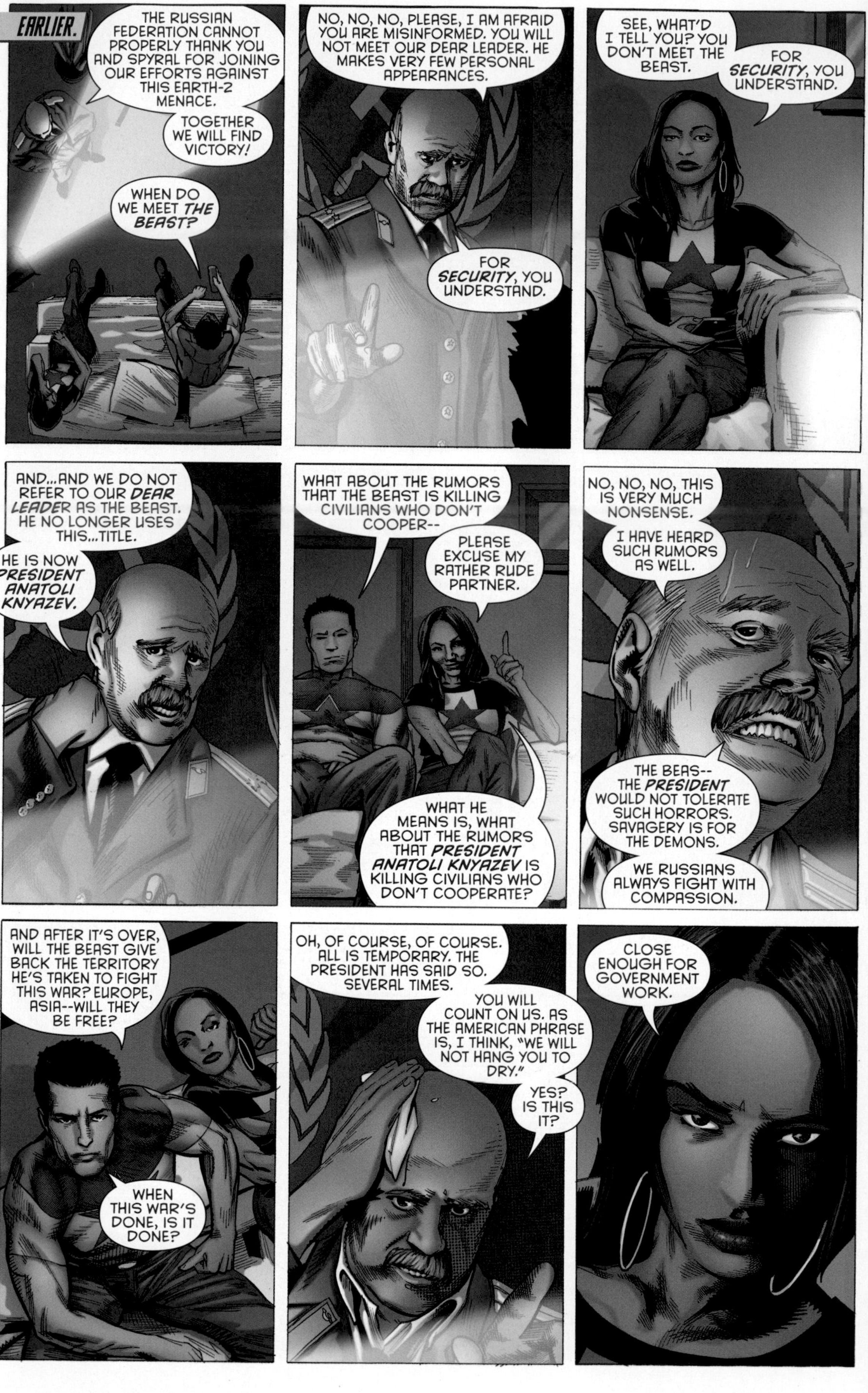
EARLIER.
THE RUSSIAN FEDERATION CANNOT PROPERLY THANK YOU AND SPYRAL FOR JOINING OUR EFFORTS AGAINST THIS EARTH-2 MENACE.
TOGETHER WE WILL FIND VICTORY!
WHEN DO WE MEET THE BEAST?
NO, NO, NO, PLEASE, I AM AFRAID YOU ARE MISINFORMED. YOU WILL NOT MEET OUR DEAR LEADER. HE MAKES VERY FEW PERSONAL APPEARANCES.
FOR SECURITY, YOU UNDERSTAND.
SEE, WHAT'D I TELL YOU? YOU DON'T MEET THE BEAST.
FOR SECURITY, YOU UNDERSTAND.
AND...AND WE DO NOT REFER TO OUR DEAR LEADER AS THE BEAST. HE NO LONGER USES THIS...TITLE.
HE IS NOW PRESIDENT ANATOLI KNYAZEV.
WHAT ABOUT THE RUMORS THAT THE BEAST IS KILLING CIVILIANS WHO DON'T COOPER--
PLEASE EXCUSE MY RATHER RUDE PARTNER.
WHAT HE MEANS IS, WHAT ABOUT THE RUMORS THAT PRESIDENT ANATOLI KNYAZEV IS KILLING CIVILIANS WHO DON'T COOPERATE?
NO, NO, NO, THIS IS VERY MUCH NONSENSE.
I HAVE HEARD SUCH RUMORS AS WELL.
THE BEAS-- THE PRESIDENT WOULD NOT TOLERATE SUCH HORRORS. SAVAGERY IS FOR THE DEMONS.
WE RUSSIANS ALWAYS FIGHT WITH COMPASSION.
AND AFTER IT'S OVER, WILL THE BEAST GIVE BACK THE TERRITORY HE'S TAKEN TO FIGHT THIS WAR? EUROPE, ASIA--WILL THEY BE FREE?
WHEN THIS WAR'S DONE, IS IT DONE?
OH, OF COURSE, OF COURSE. ALL IS TEMPORARY. THE PRESIDENT HAS SAID SO. SEVERAL TIMES.
YOU WILL COUNT ON US. AS THE AMERICAN PHRASE IS, I THINK, "WE WILL NOT HANG YOU TO DRY."
YES? IS THIS IT?
CLOSE ENOUGH FOR GOVERNMENT WORK.

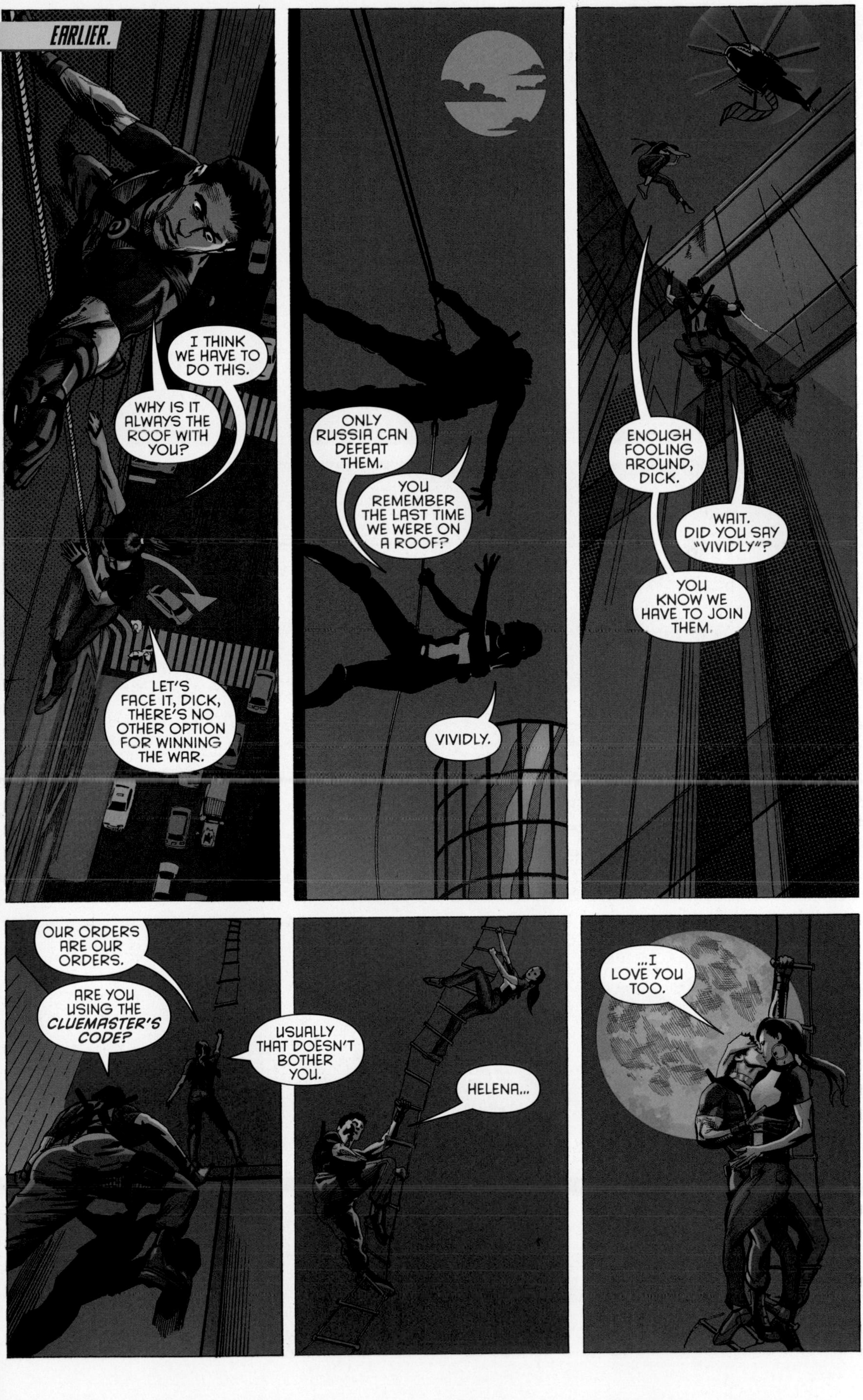
EARLIER.
I THINK WE HAVE TO DO THIS.
WHY IS IT ALWAYS THE ROOF WITH YOU?
LET'S FACE IT, DICK, THERE'S NO OTHER OPTION FOR WINNING THE WAR.
ONLY RUSSIA CAN DEFEAT THEM.
YOU REMEMBER THE LAST TIME WE WERE ON A ROOF?
VIVIDLY.
ENOUGH FOOLING AROUND, DICK.
WAIT. DID YOU SAY "VIVIDLY"?
YOU KNOW WE HAVE TO JOIN THEM.
OUR ORDERS ARE OUR ORDERS.
ARE YOU USING THE *CLUEMASTER'S CODE?*
USUALLY THAT DOESN'T BOTHER YOU.
HELENA...
...I LOVE YOU TOO.

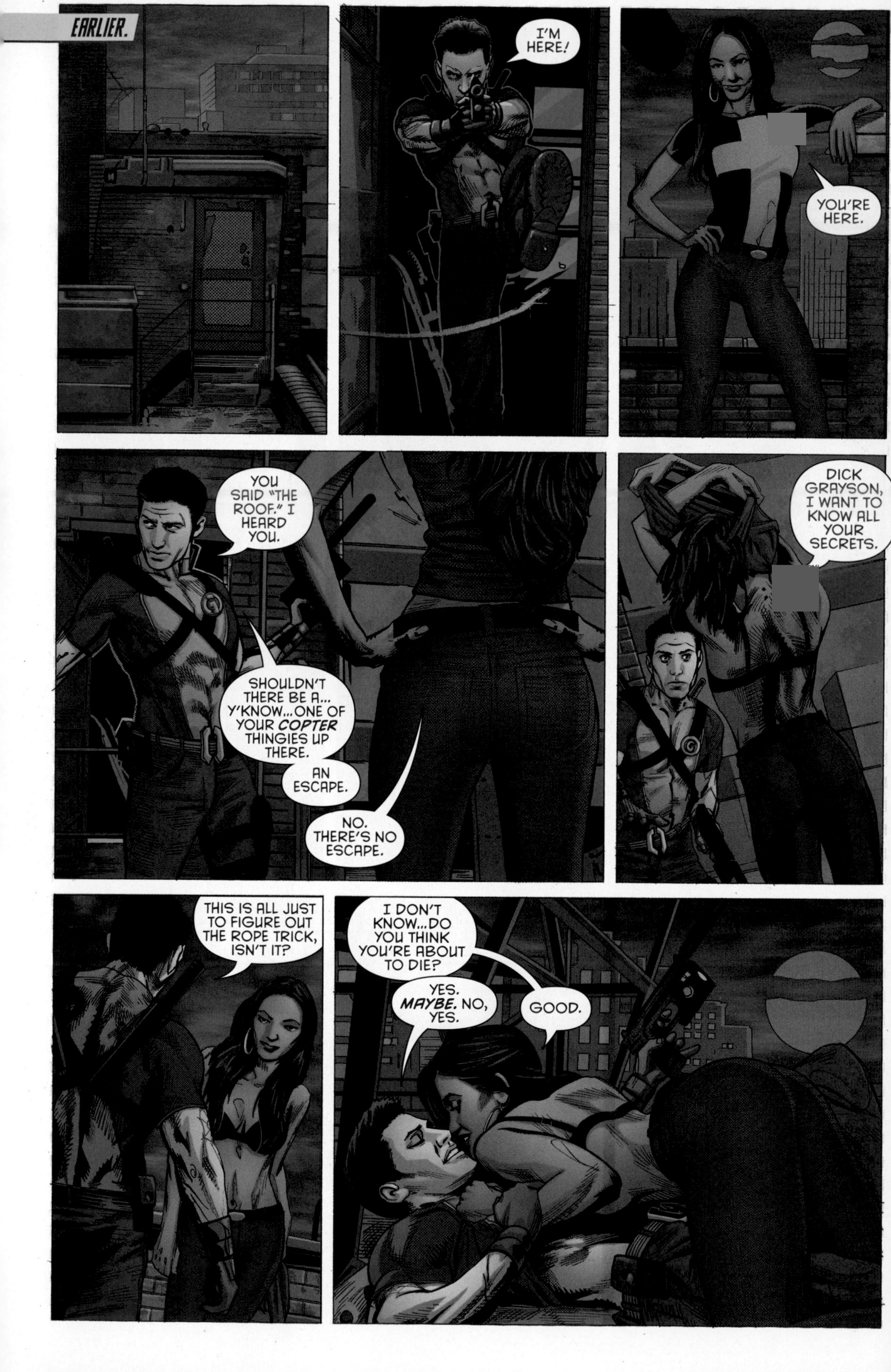
EARLIER.
I'M HERE!
YOU'RE HERE.
YOU SAID "THE ROOF." I HEARD YOU.
SHOULDN'T THERE BE A... Y'KNOW...ONE OF YOUR COPTER THINGIES UP THERE.
AN ESCAPE.
NO. THERE'S NO ESCAPE.
DICK GRAYSON, I WANT TO KNOW ALL YOUR SECRETS.
THIS IS ALL JUST TO FIGURE OUT THE ROPE TRICK, ISN'T IT?
I DON'T KNOW...DO YOU THINK YOU'RE ABOUT TO DIE?
YES. MAYBE. NO, YES.
GOOD.

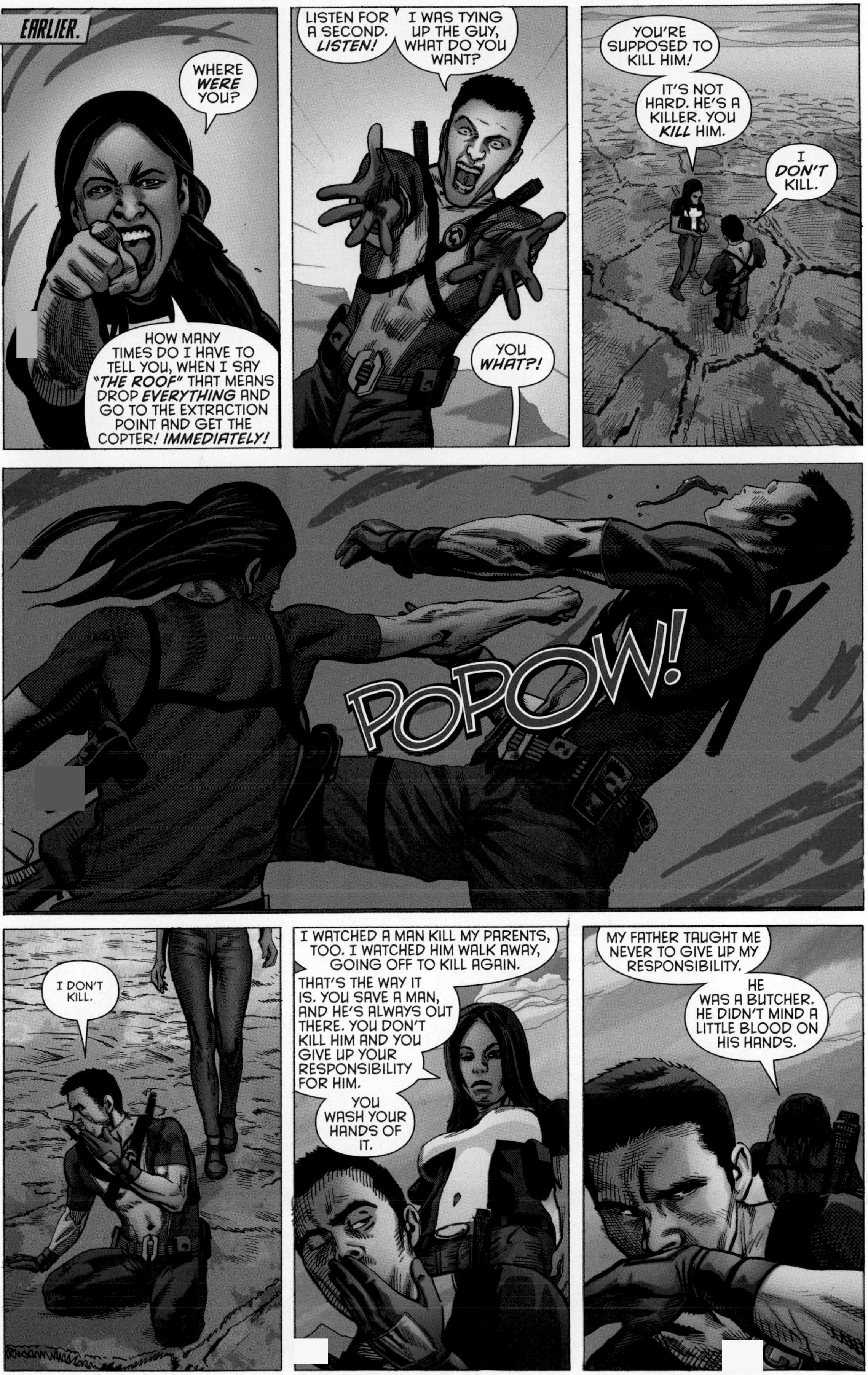
EARLIER.
WHERE WERE YOU?
HOW MANY TIMES DO I HAVE TO TELL YOU, WHEN I SAY "THE ROOF" THAT MEANS DROP EVERYTHING AND GO TO THE EXTRACTION POINT AND GET THE COPTER! IMMEDIATELY!
LISTEN FOR A SECOND. LISTEN!
I WAS TYING UP THE GUY, WHAT DO YOU WANT?
YOU WHAT?!
YOU'RE SUPPOSED TO KILL HIM!
IT'S NOT HARD. HE'S A KILLER. YOU KILL HIM.
I DON'T KILL.
POPOW!
I DON'T KILL.
I WATCHED A MAN KILL MY PARENTS, TOO. I WATCHED HIM WALK AWAY, GOING OFF TO KILL AGAIN.
THAT'S THE WAY IT IS. YOU SAVE A MAN, AND HE'S ALWAYS OUT THERE. YOU DON'T KILL HIM AND YOU GIVE UP YOUR RESPONSIBILITY FOR HIM.
YOU WASH YOUR HANDS OF IT.
MY FATHER TAUGHT ME NEVER TO GIVE UP MY RESPONSIBILITY.
HE WAS A BUTCHER. HE DIDN'T MIND A LITTLE BLOOD ON HIS HANDS.

TATTOO PARLOR

THIS IS CRAZY. WHY WOULD A SPY GET A TATTOO?

WHEN THEY CAPTURE ME WITH THIS, THEY'LL KNOW WHO I AM.

NO, THAT'S NOT QUITE RIGHT.

WHEN THEY CAPTURE YOU WITH THAT, THEY'LL KNOW WHO YOU ARE, AND THEY'LL KILL YOU.

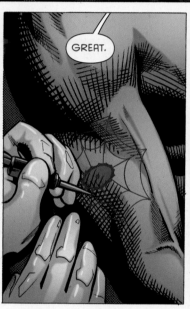

GREAT.

THAT'S WHY YOU HAVE IT.

SO YOU DON'T GET CAPTURED.

HAHAHA!

WHAT'S SO FUNNY?

NOTHING. JUST YOU REMIND ME OF SOMEONE.

SOMEONE I LOVED. IT'S FUNNY IF YOU THINK ABOUT IT.

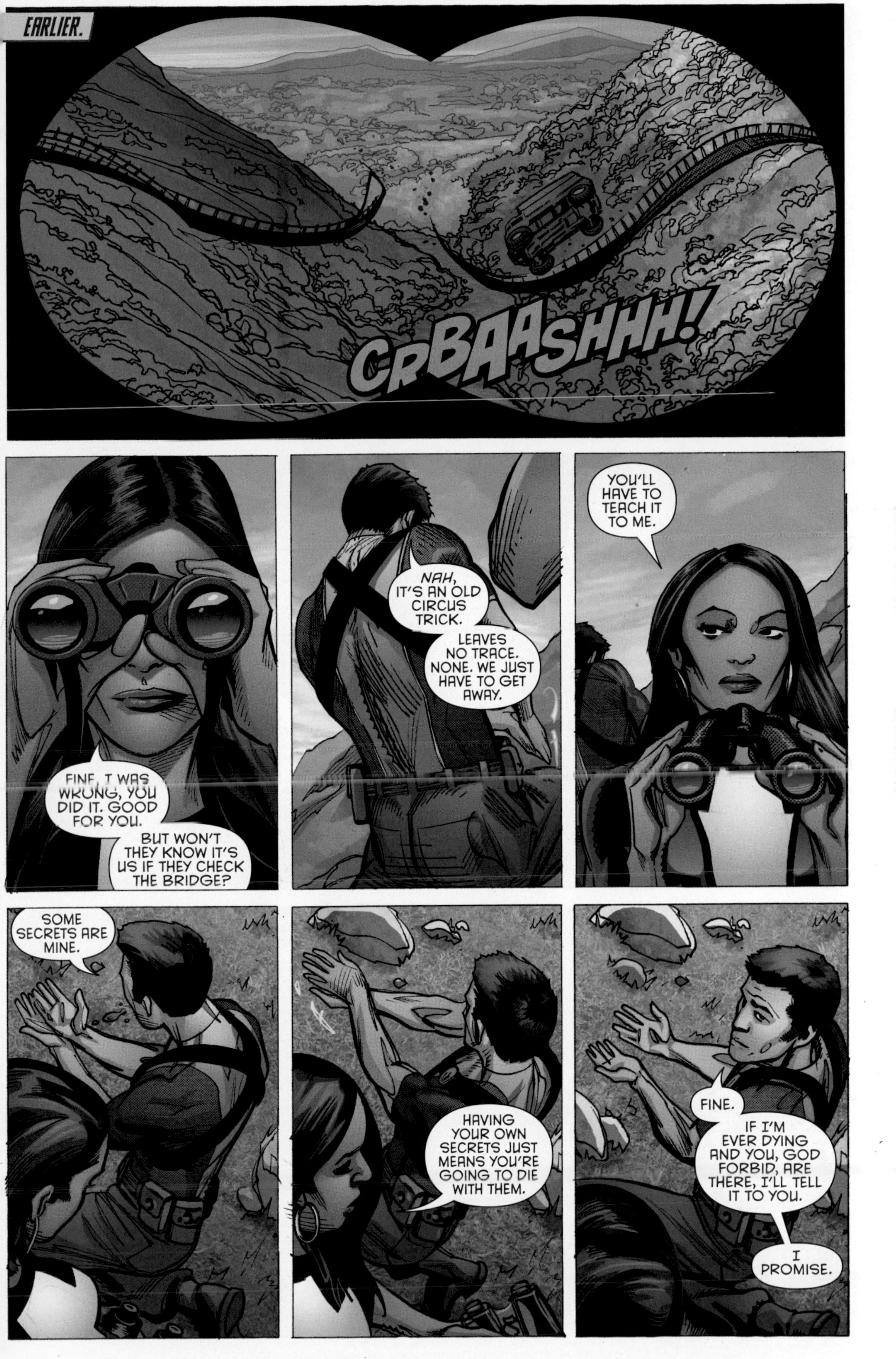
EARLIER.
CRBAASHHH!
FINE, I WAS WRONG, YOU DID IT. GOOD FOR YOU.
BUT WON'T THEY KNOW IT'S US IF THEY CHECK THE BRIDGE?
NAH, IT'S AN OLD CIRCUS TRICK.
LEAVES NO TRACE. NONE. WE JUST HAVE TO GET AWAY.
YOU'LL HAVE TO TEACH IT TO ME.
SOME SECRETS ARE MINE.
HAVING YOUR OWN SECRETS JUST MEANS YOU'RE GOING TO DIE WITH THEM.
FINE.
IF I'M EVER DYING AND YOU, GOD FORBID, ARE THERE, I'LL TELL IT TO YOU.
I PROMISE.

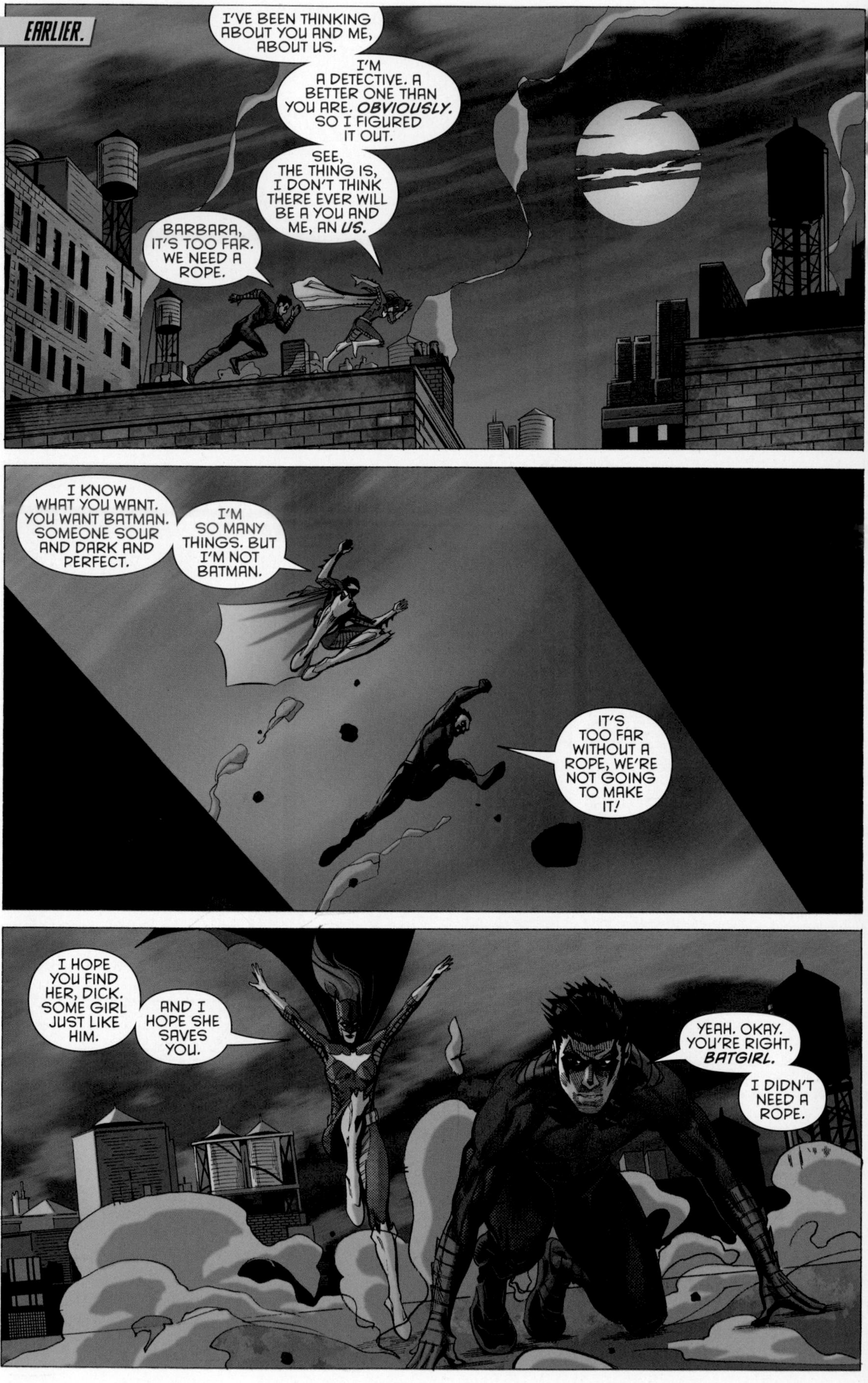
EARLIER.
I'VE BEEN THINKING ABOUT YOU AND ME, ABOUT US.
I'M A DETECTIVE. A BETTER ONE THAN YOU ARE. OBVIOUSLY. SO I FIGURED IT OUT.
SEE, THE THING IS, I DON'T THINK THERE EVER WILL BE A YOU AND ME, AN US.
BARBARA, IT'S TOO FAR. WE NEED A ROPE.
I KNOW WHAT YOU WANT. YOU WANT BATMAN. SOMEONE SOUR AND DARK AND PERFECT.
I'M SO MANY THINGS. BUT I'M NOT BATMAN.
IT'S TOO FAR WITHOUT A ROPE, WE'RE NOT GOING TO MAKE IT!
I HOPE YOU FIND HER, DICK. SOME GIRL JUST LIKE HIM.
AND I HOPE SHE SAVES YOU.
YEAH. OKAY. YOU'RE RIGHT, BATGIRL.
I DIDN'T NEED A ROPE.

SO, YOU THINK YOU CAN FIND ME?

PERHAPS YOU WILL.

REALLY, IT'S NOT SO HARD.

ANSWERS ARE RIGHT IN FRONT OF YOU.

NOTHING COULD BE EASIER.

GOOD LUCK!

WHAT IS IN FRONT OF US, ROBIN?

THE SCREEN? THE MAN? THE CLUE?

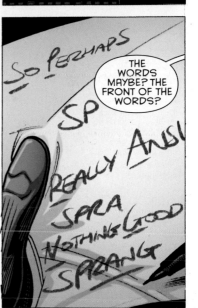

THE WORDS MAYBE? THE FRONT OF THE WORDS?

I'VE GOT IT! *THE CLUEMASTER'S CODE!* IT'S RIGHT THERE. FIRST LETTER OF EVERY SENTENCE HE SAYS--IT SPELLS SOMETHING.

S-P-R-A-N-G. HE'S AT THE SPRANG BRIDGE!

BATMOBILE. NOW!

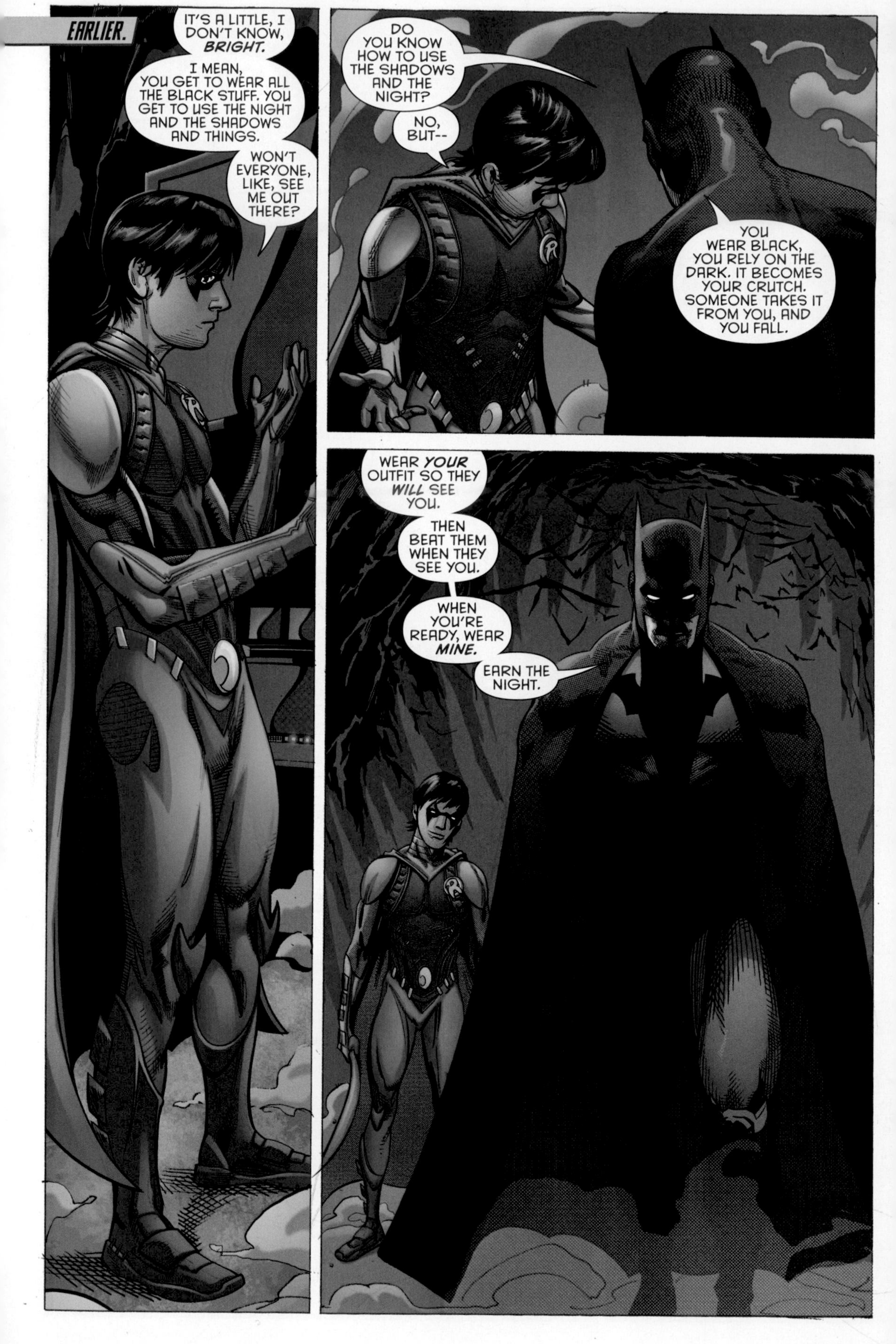
EARLIER.
IT'S A LITTLE, I DON'T KNOW, BRIGHT.
I MEAN, YOU GET TO WEAR ALL THE BLACK STUFF. YOU GET TO USE THE NIGHT AND THE SHADOWS AND THINGS.
WON'T EVERYONE, LIKE, SEE ME OUT THERE?
DO YOU KNOW HOW TO USE THE SHADOWS AND THE NIGHT?
NO, BUT--
YOU WEAR BLACK, YOU RELY ON THE DARK. IT BECOMES YOUR CRUTCH. SOMEONE TAKES IT FROM YOU, AND YOU FALL.
WEAR YOUR OUTFIT SO THEY WILL SEE YOU.
THEN BEAT THEM WHEN THEY SEE YOU.
WHEN YOU'RE READY, WEAR MINE.
EARN THE NIGHT.

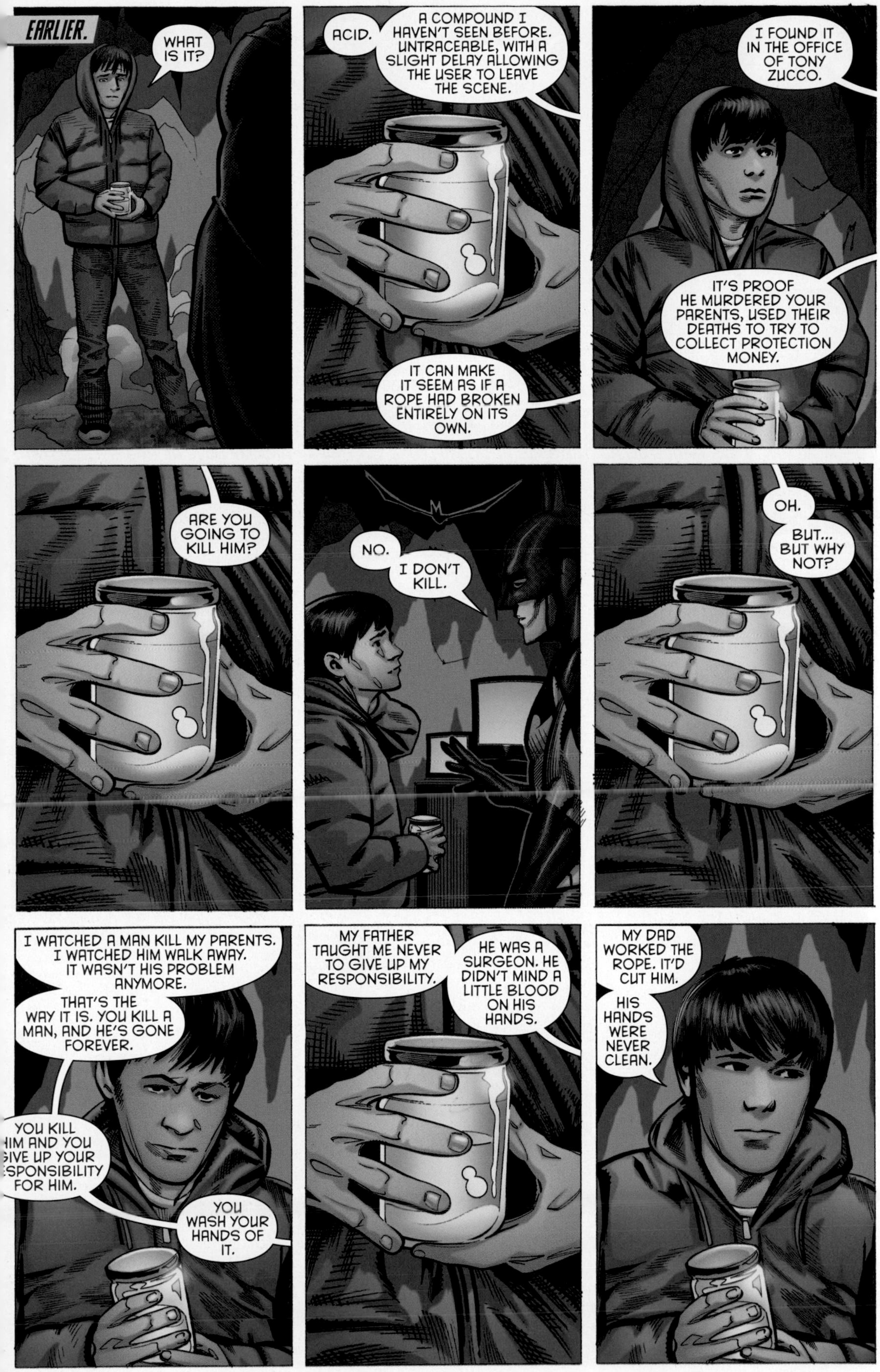
EARLIER.
WHAT IS IT?
ACID.
A COMPOUND I HAVEN'T SEEN BEFORE. UNTRACEABLE, WITH A SLIGHT DELAY ALLOWING THE USER TO LEAVE THE SCENE.
IT CAN MAKE IT SEEM AS IF A ROPE HAD BROKEN ENTIRELY ON ITS OWN.
I FOUND IT IN THE OFFICE OF TONY ZUCCO.
IT'S PROOF HE MURDERED YOUR PARENTS, USED THEIR DEATHS TO TRY TO COLLECT PROTECTION MONEY.
ARE YOU GOING TO KILL HIM?
NO.
I DON'T KILL.
OH.
BUT... BUT WHY NOT?
I WATCHED A MAN KILL MY PARENTS. I WATCHED HIM WALK AWAY. IT WASN'T HIS PROBLEM ANYMORE.
THAT'S THE WAY IT IS. YOU KILL A MAN, AND HE'S GONE FOREVER.
YOU KILL HIM AND YOU GIVE UP YOUR RESPONSIBILITY FOR HIM.
YOU WASH YOUR HANDS OF IT.
MY FATHER TAUGHT ME NEVER TO GIVE UP MY RESPONSIBILITY.
HE WAS A SURGEON. HE DIDN'T MIND A LITTLE BLOOD ON HIS HANDS.
MY DAD WORKED THE ROPE. IT'D CUT HIM.
HIS HANDS WERE NEVER CLEAN.

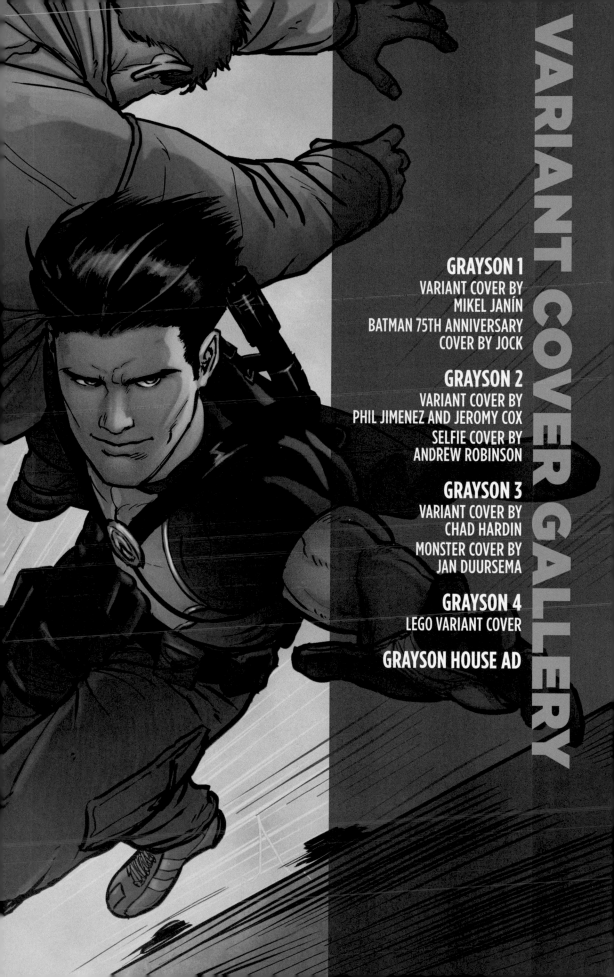

VARIANT COVER GALLERY

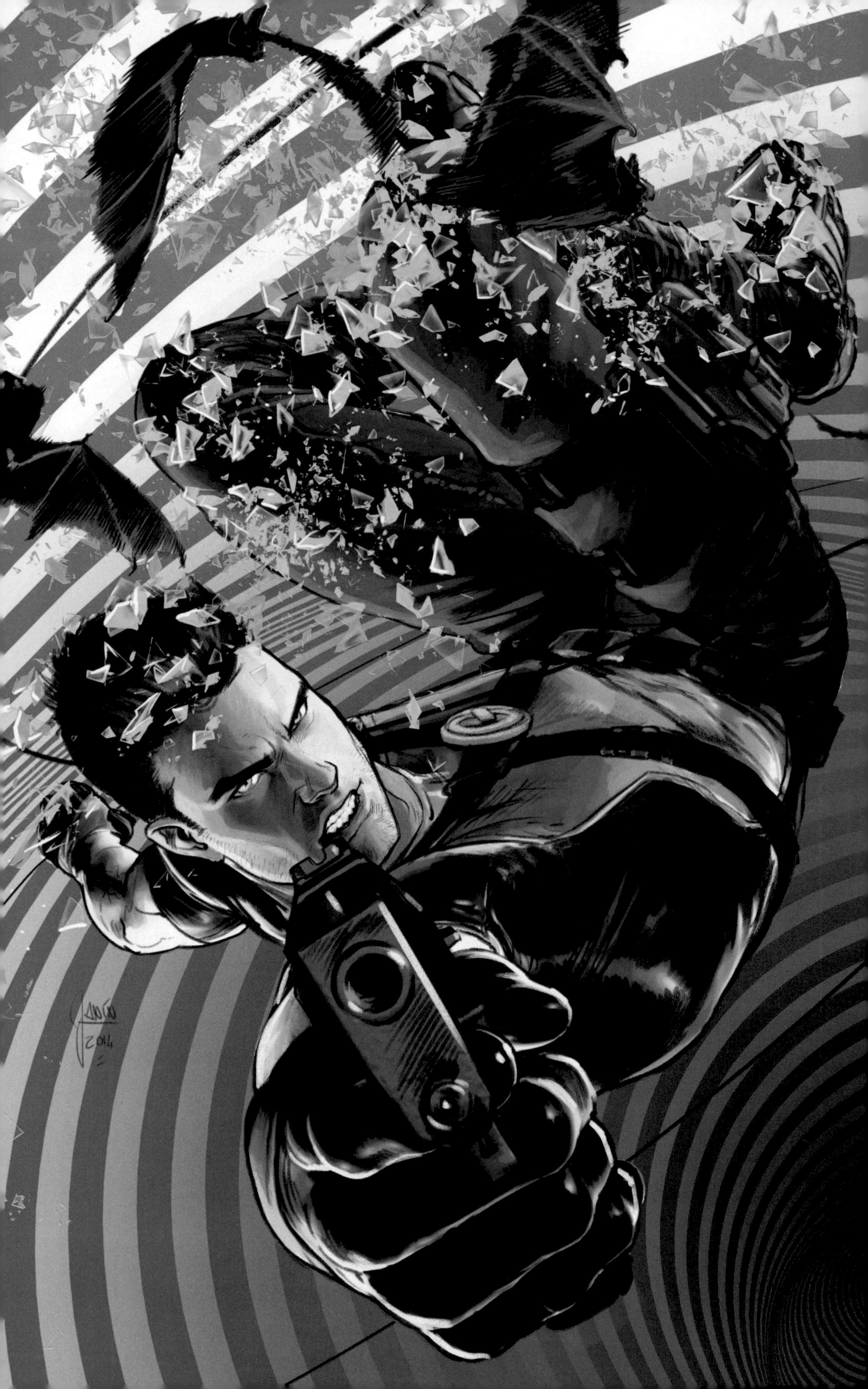

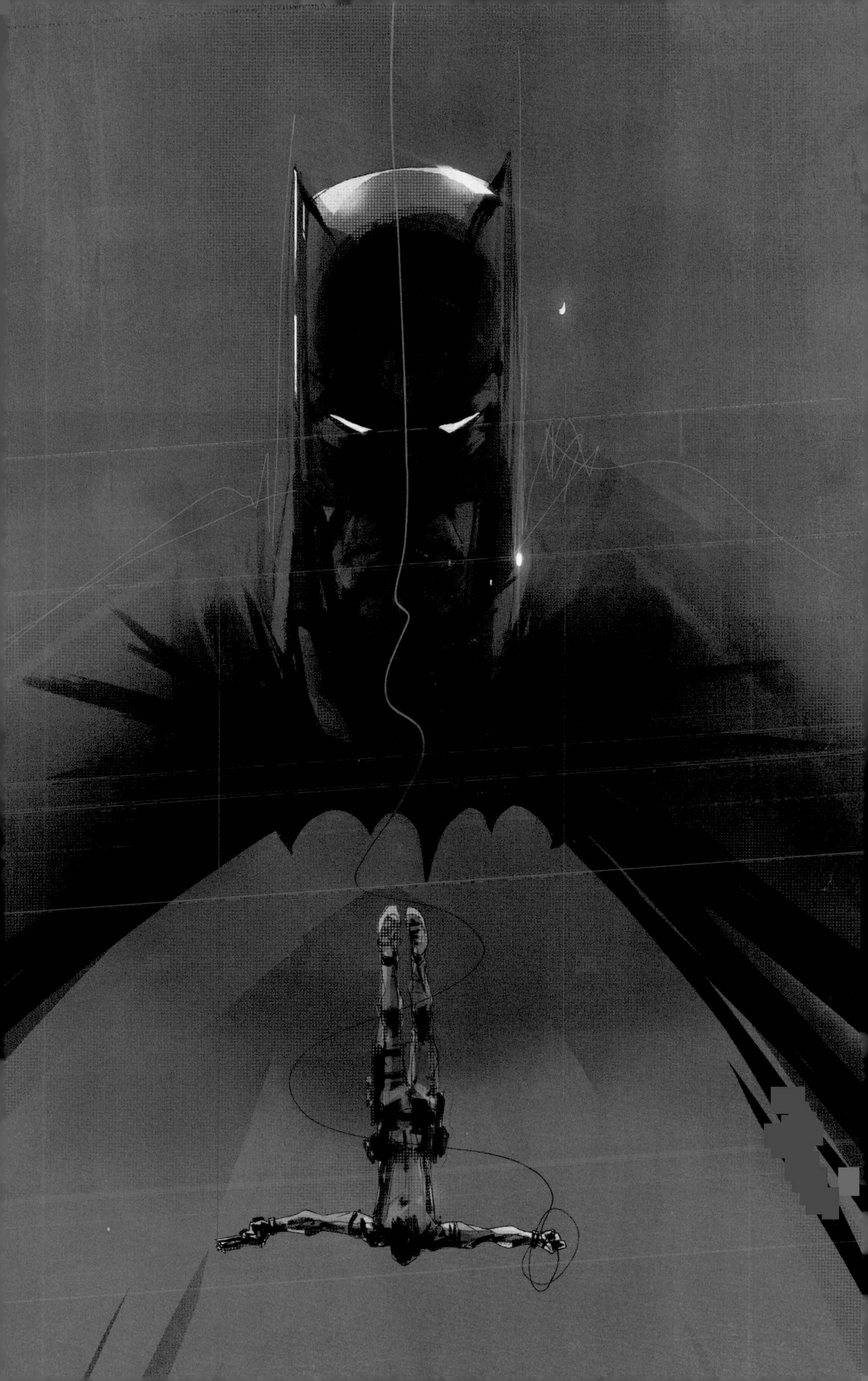

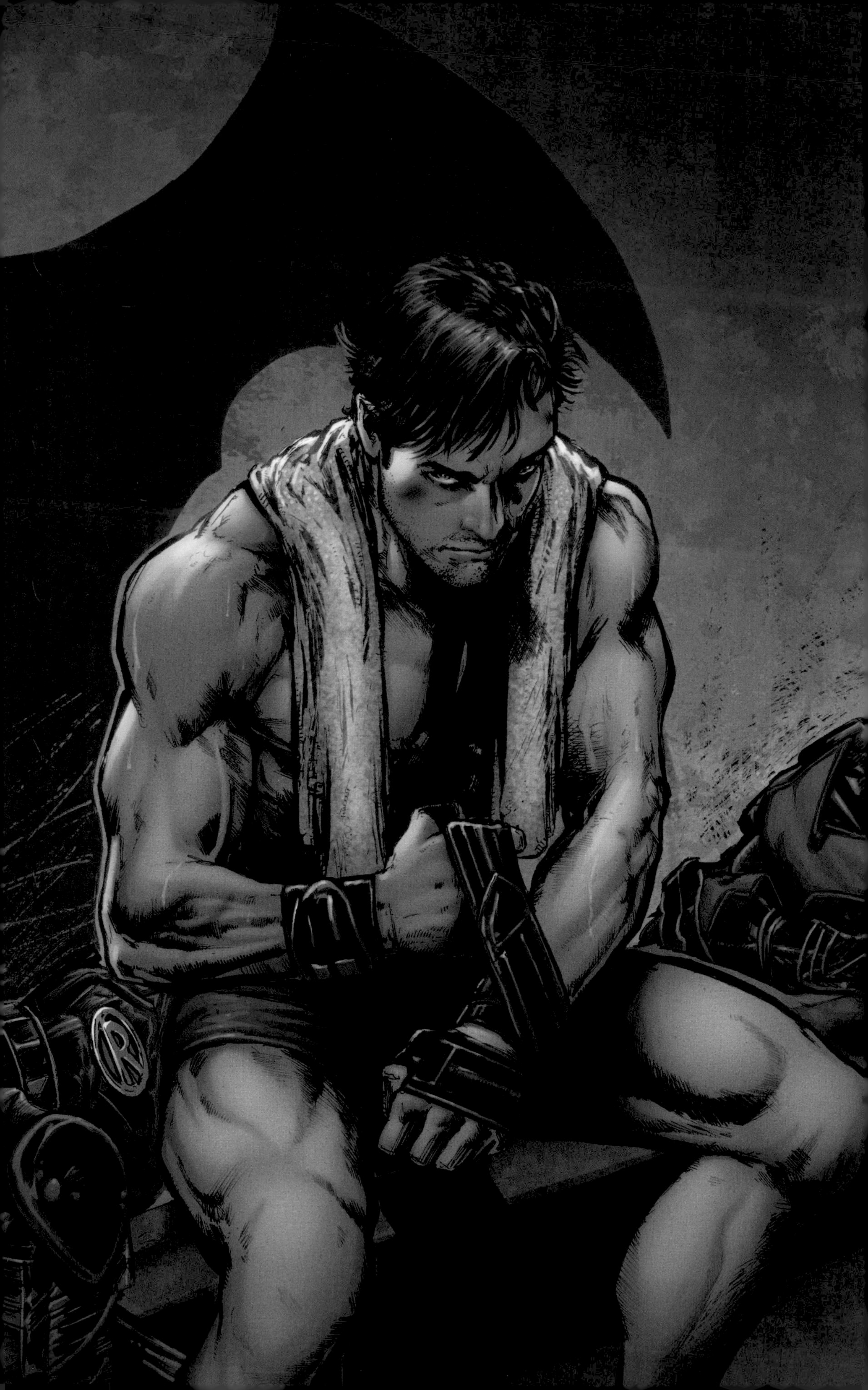

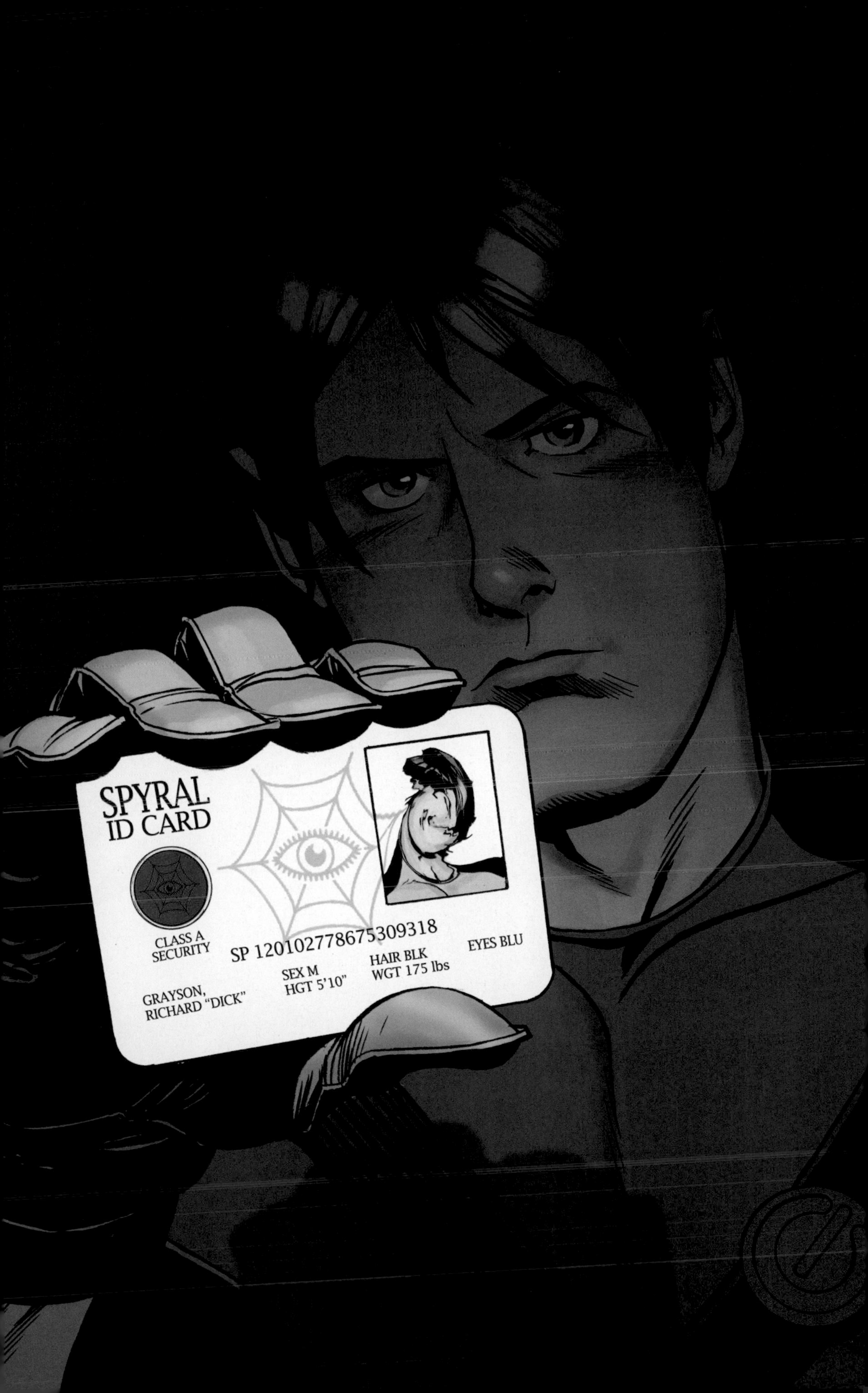
SPYRAL ID CARD
CLASS A SECURITY
SP 1201027786753093l8
EYES BLU
HAIR BLK
WGT 175 lbs
SEX M
HGT 5'10"
GRAYSON, RICHARD "DICK"

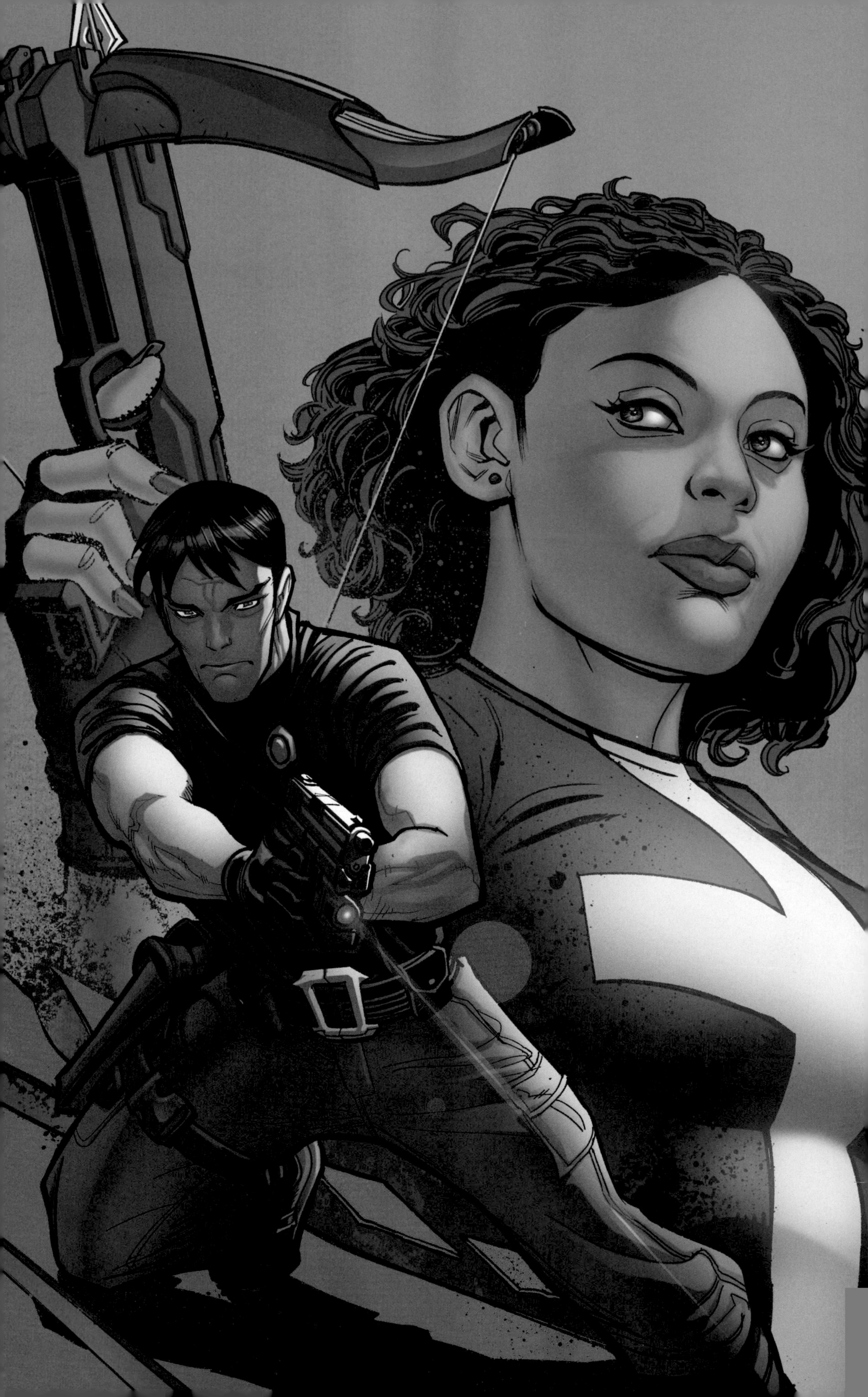

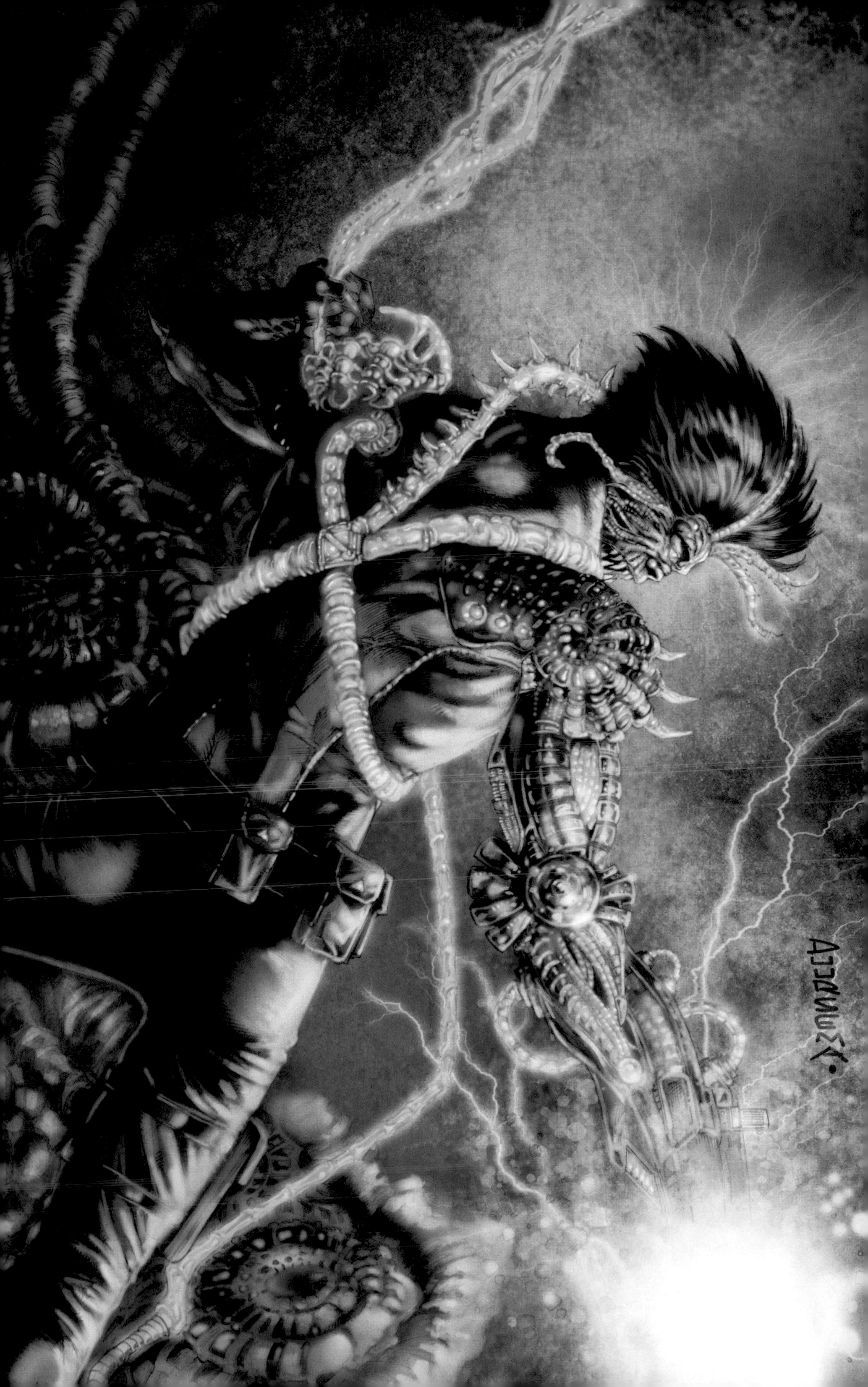

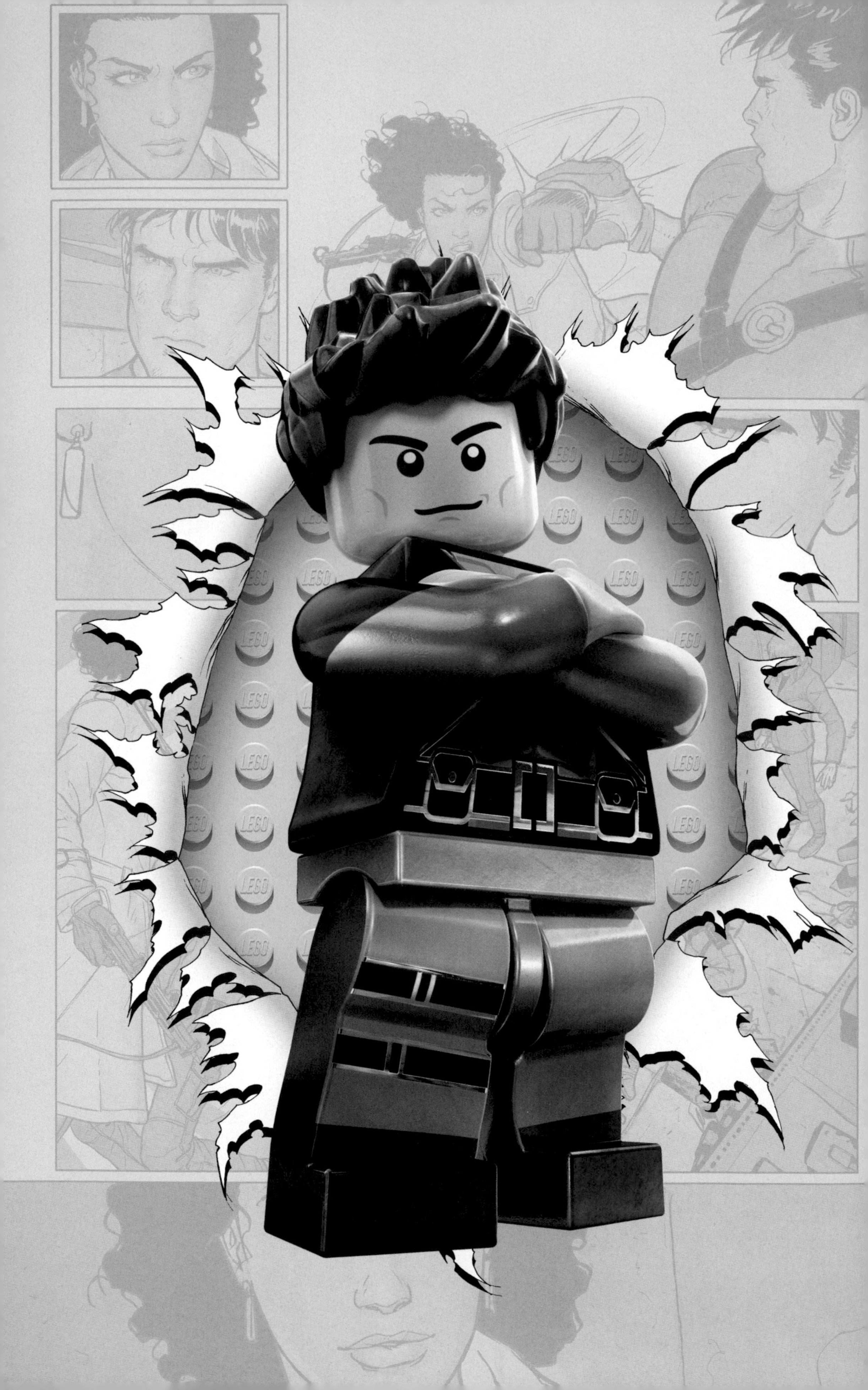

YOU THINK YOU KNOW NIGHTWING...
YOU DON'T KNOW DICK

A New Monthly Series

Tim Seeley

Tom King

Mikel Janin

July 2014

THIS IS GRAYSON

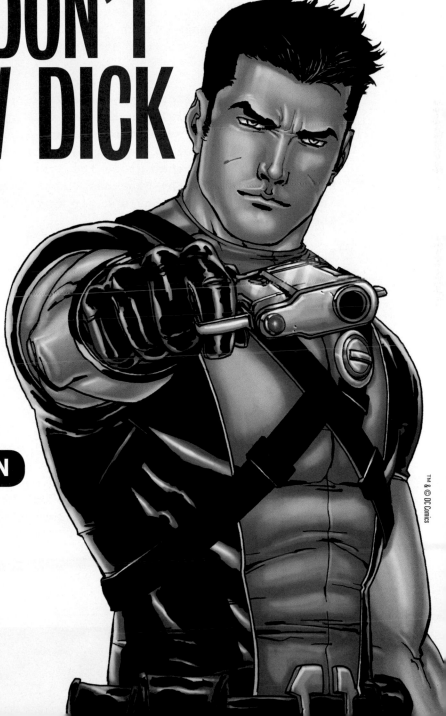

DC COMICS™

THE NEW 52!

GRAYSON
series pitch
by Tim Seeley
2-14-2014

DICK GRAYSON. Former sidekick. Former superhero.
His identity revealed to the world. Believed dead by
everyone, save his mentor, Batman, Dick is man who
does not exist.

SPYRAL. An international spy organization run
by Kathy Kane. Specializes in mind erosion,
brainwashing and misdirection. Tasked with keeping
an unblinking eye on all emerging superhumans,
and trapping those that cross the line in their
sticky threads. Kathy Kane has given Batman clear
instructions that he should never try to find Spyral.
They do not exist.

Batman has never listened particularly well to
instructions.

Now, clandestinely funded and backed by Batman,
Dick Grayson will infiltrate SPYRAL, a spy for them,
and a spy on them. He will navigate the shadowy,
morally grey world of international superhuman
espionage. He will battle great evils, and be asked
to commit them.

And with every decision he makes, Dick will ask
himself if it came of his own freewill or because
the insidious mind tricks employed by his beautiful
and seductive boss, Kathy Kane. Is Dick the hero
he spent his young life training to be? Or is he
someone new? When Dick Grayson no longer exists,
who is Dick Grayson?

EARLY CHARACTER DESIGNS BY
TIM SEELEY

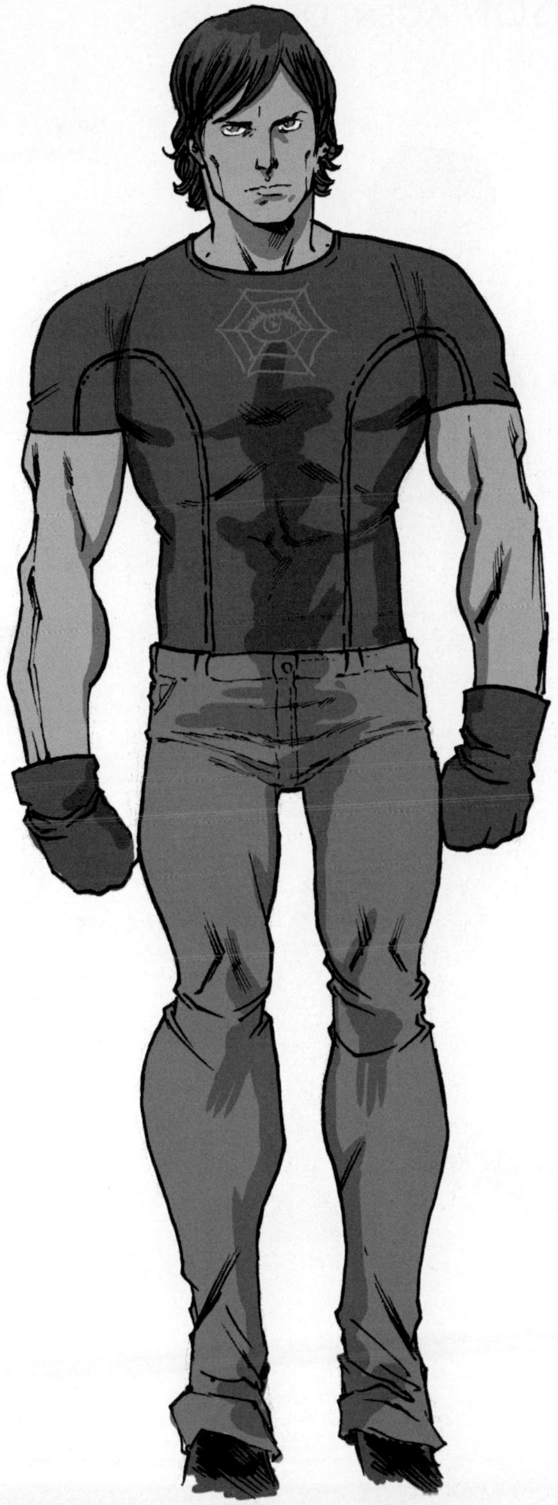

DICK GRAYSON AGENT OF SPYRAL

"SPYRAL SPECIALIZES IN MIND EROSION, BRAINWASHING, AND MISDIRECTION..."

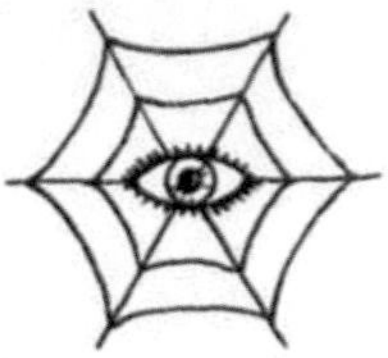

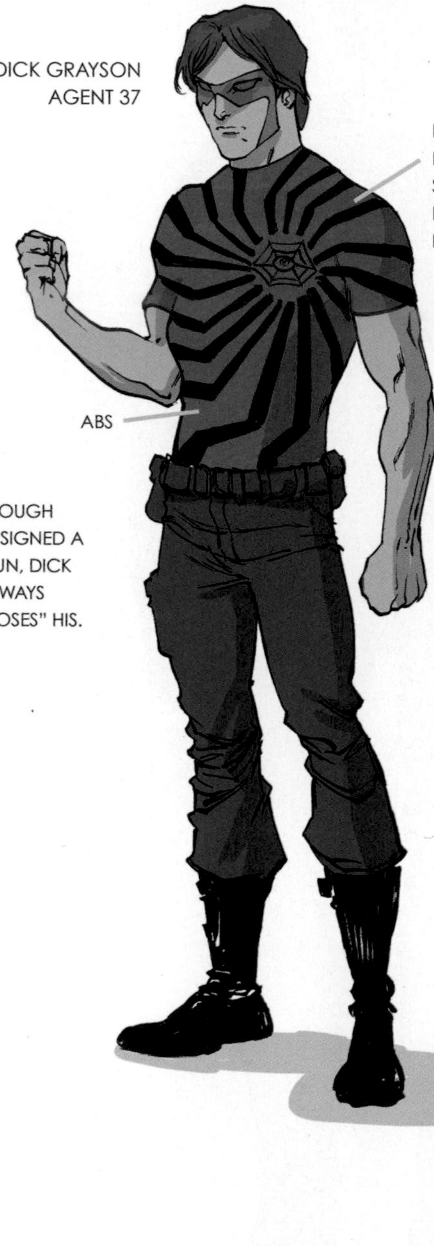
DICK GRAYSON AGENT 37
HYPNOS SUIT HYPNOTIC SUGGESTION SHIRT, APPEARS AS PREPROGRAMMED DISGUISE
ABS
THOUGH ASSIGNED A GUN, DICK ALWAYS "LOSES" HIS.

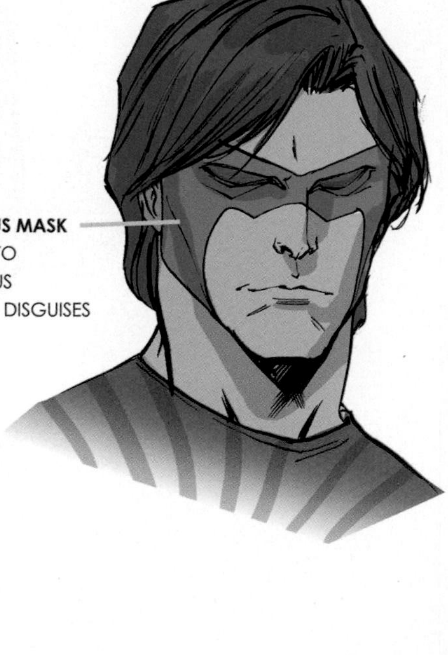
PROTEUS MASK SHIFTS TO VARIOUS FACIAL DISGUISES

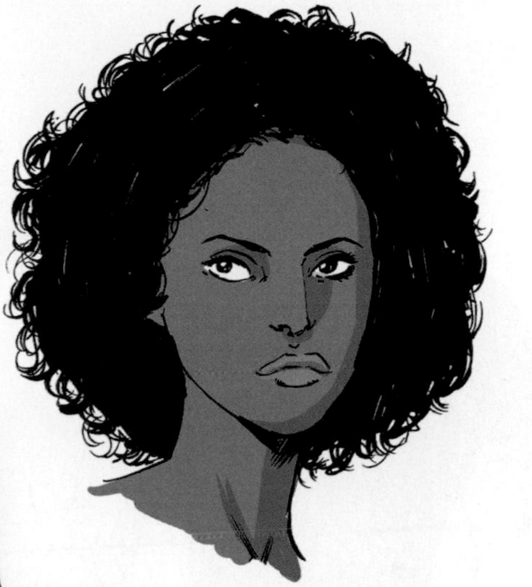

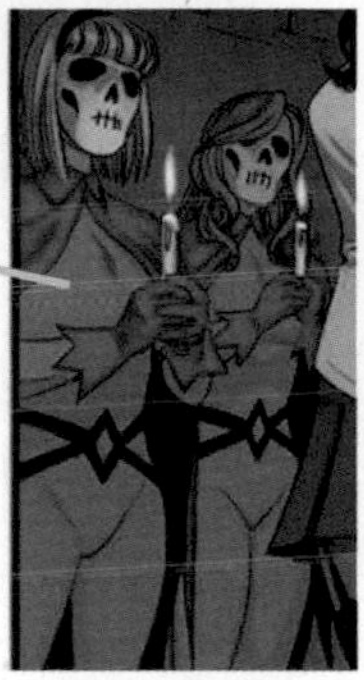

DERIVED
FROM
SPYRAL
AGENTS FROM
"FINISHING
SCHOOL."

COLOR
INDICATES
RANK.

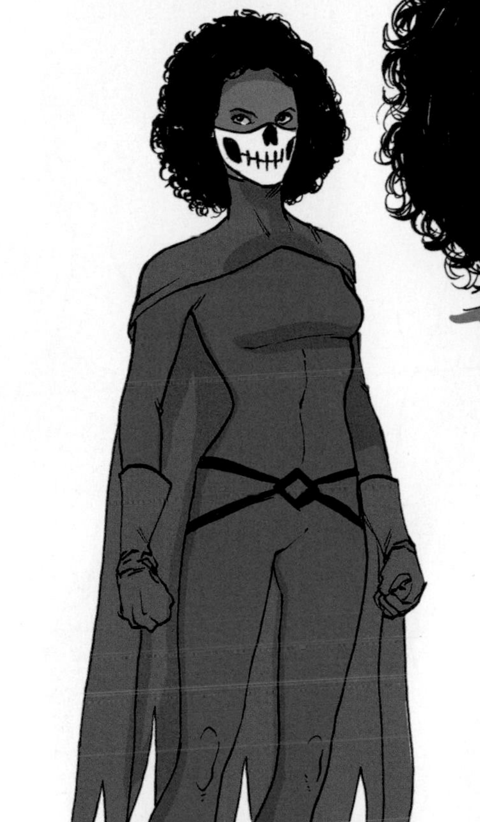

HELENA BERTINELLI
MATRON 1

CHARACTER DESIGNS BY
MIKEL JANÍN

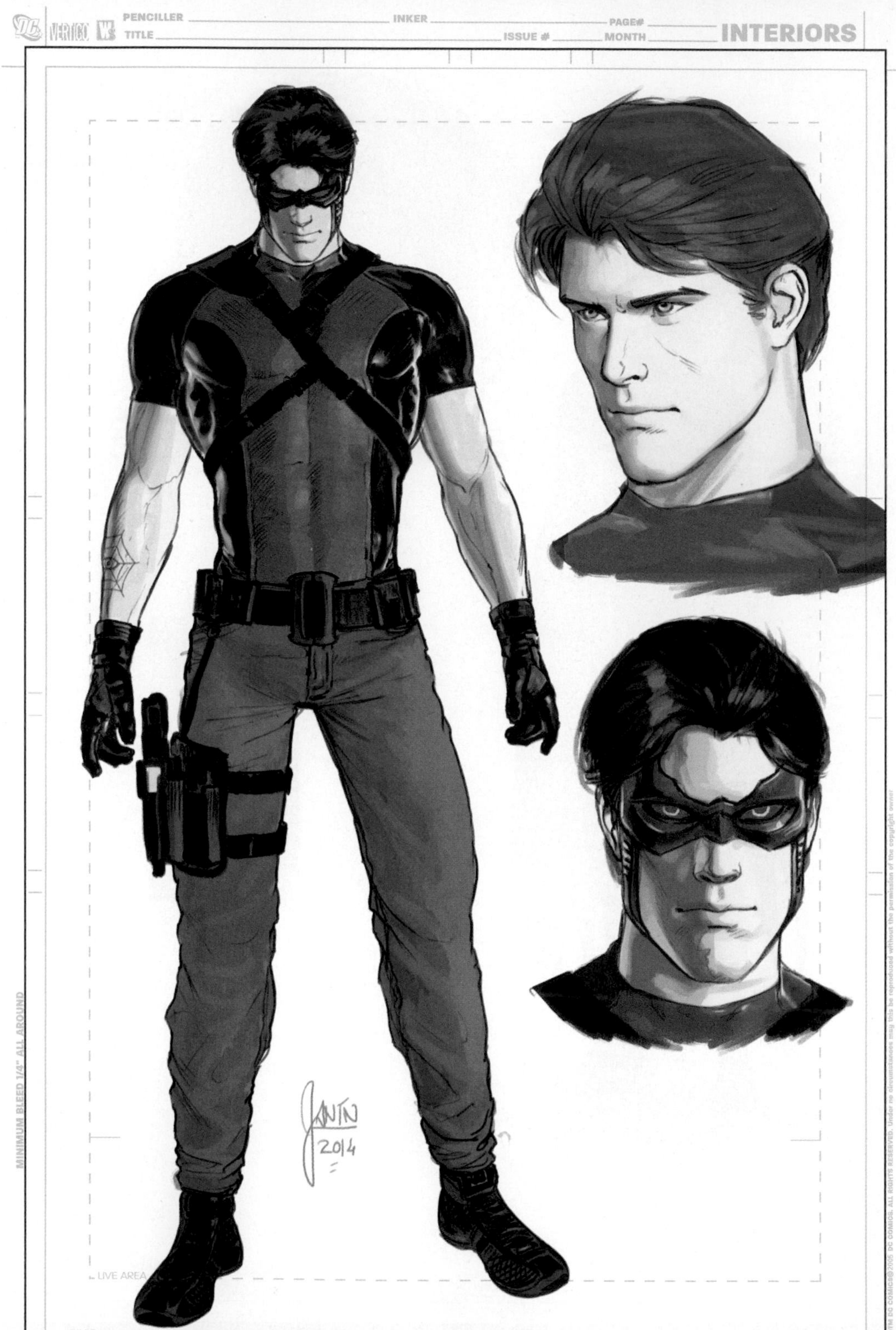
PENCILLER
INKER
PAGE#
TITLE
ISSUE #
MONTH
INTERIORS
MINIMUM BLEED 1/4" ALL AROUND
LIVE AREA
CROP
BLEED
JANÍN 2014
CUT RIGHT-HAND PAGE AT THIS LINE
DOUBLE PAGE SPREAD: CUT AS SHOWN, ABUT PAGE EDGES, TAPE ON BACK, DO NOT OVERLAP
CUT LEFT HAND PAGE AT THIS LINE

PENCILLER _____ INKER _____ PAGE# _____ **INTERIORS**

TITLE _____ ISSUE # _____ MONTH _____

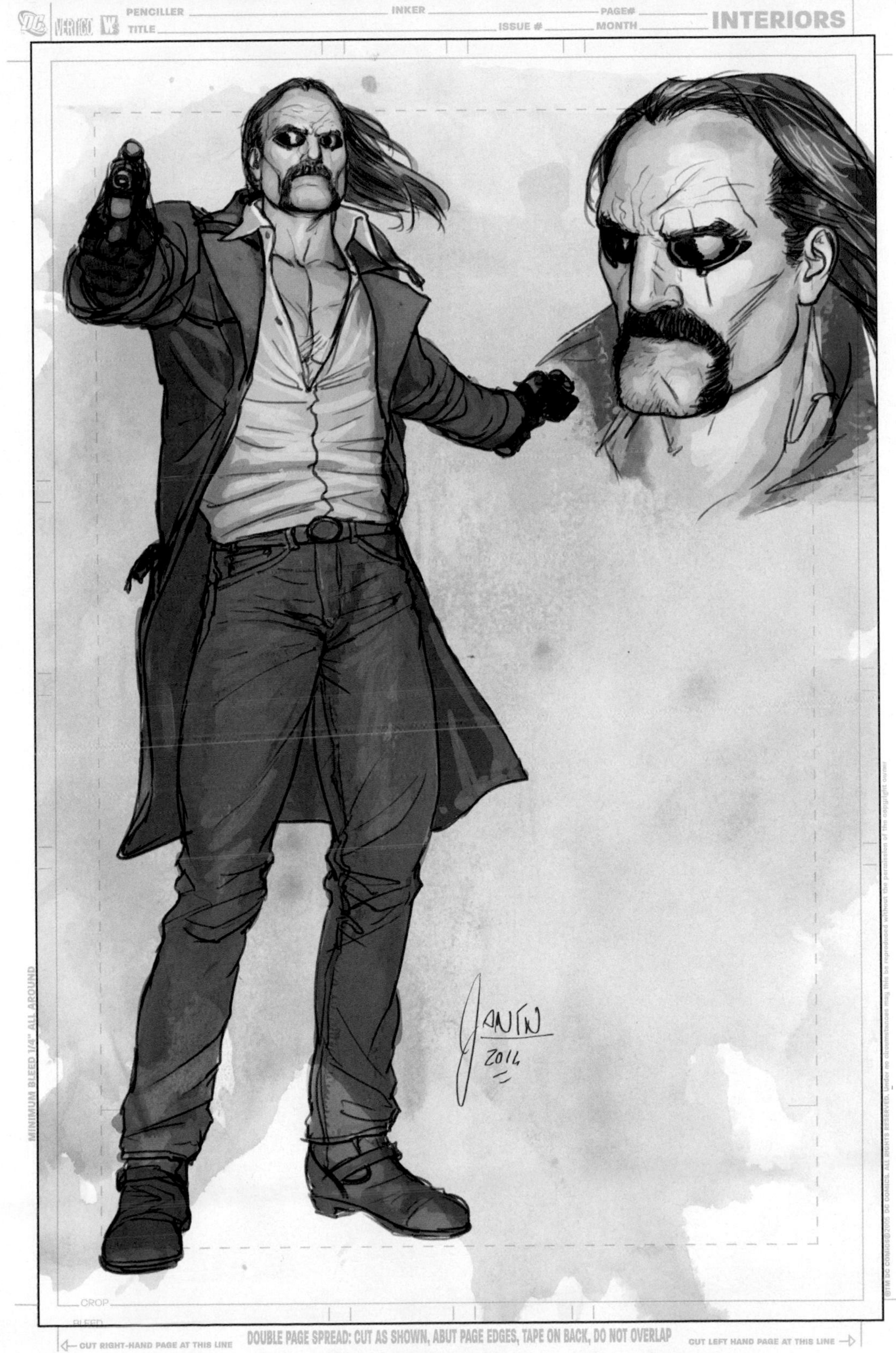
PENCILLER
INKER
PAGE#
TITLE
ISSUE #
MONTH
INTERIORS
CROP
MINIMUM BLEED 1/4" ALL AROUND
CUT RIGHT-HAND PAGE AT THIS LINE
DOUBLE PAGE SPREAD: CUT AS SHOWN, ABUT PAGE EDGES, TAPE ON BACK, DO NOT OVERLAP
CUT LEFT HAND PAGE AT THIS LINE

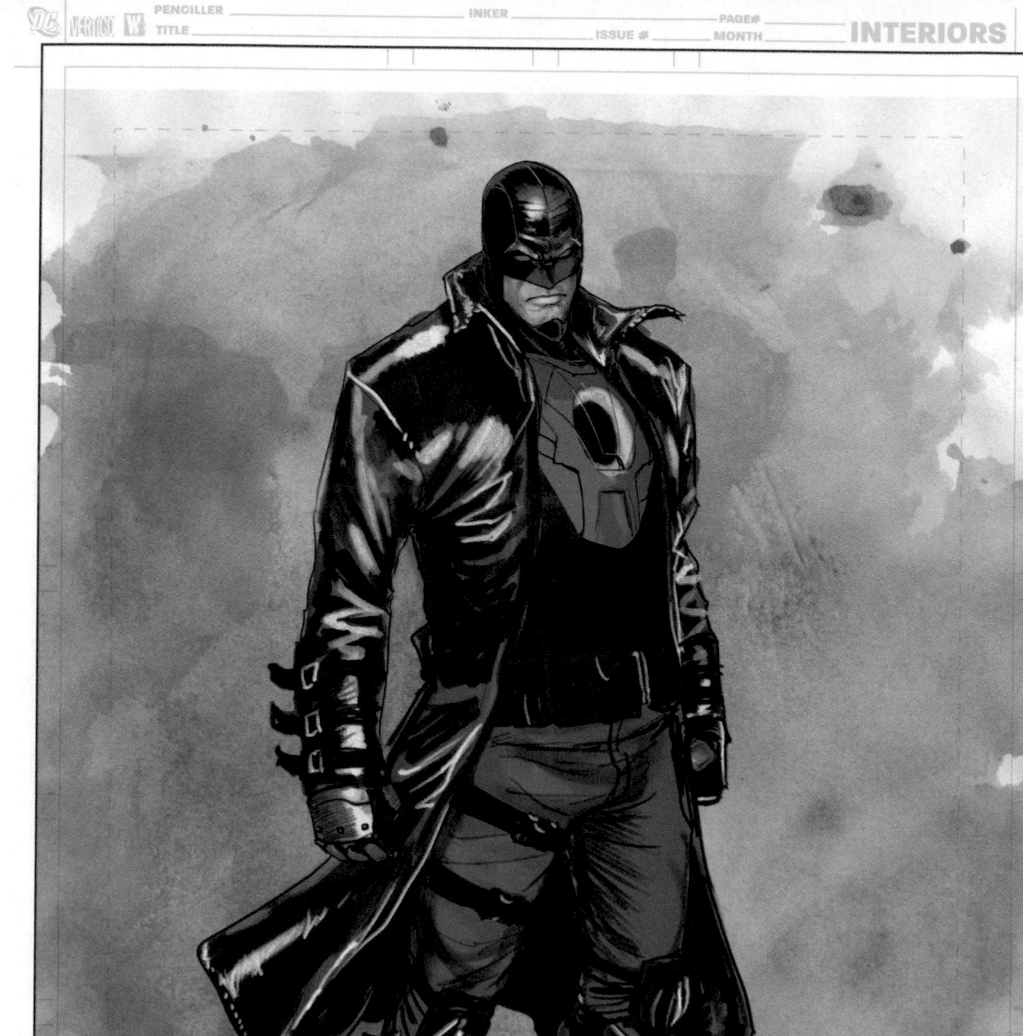
PENCILLER
INKER
PAGE#
TITLE
ISSUE #
MONTH
INTERIORS
JANÍN
2014
CUT RIGHT-HAND PAGE AT THIS LINE
DOUBLE PAGE SPREAD: CUT AS SHOWN, ABUT PAGE EDGES, TAPE ON BACK, DO NOT OVERLAP
CUT LEFT HAND PAGE AT THIS LINE

GRAYSON PENCIL STUDY BY
STEPHEN MOONEY

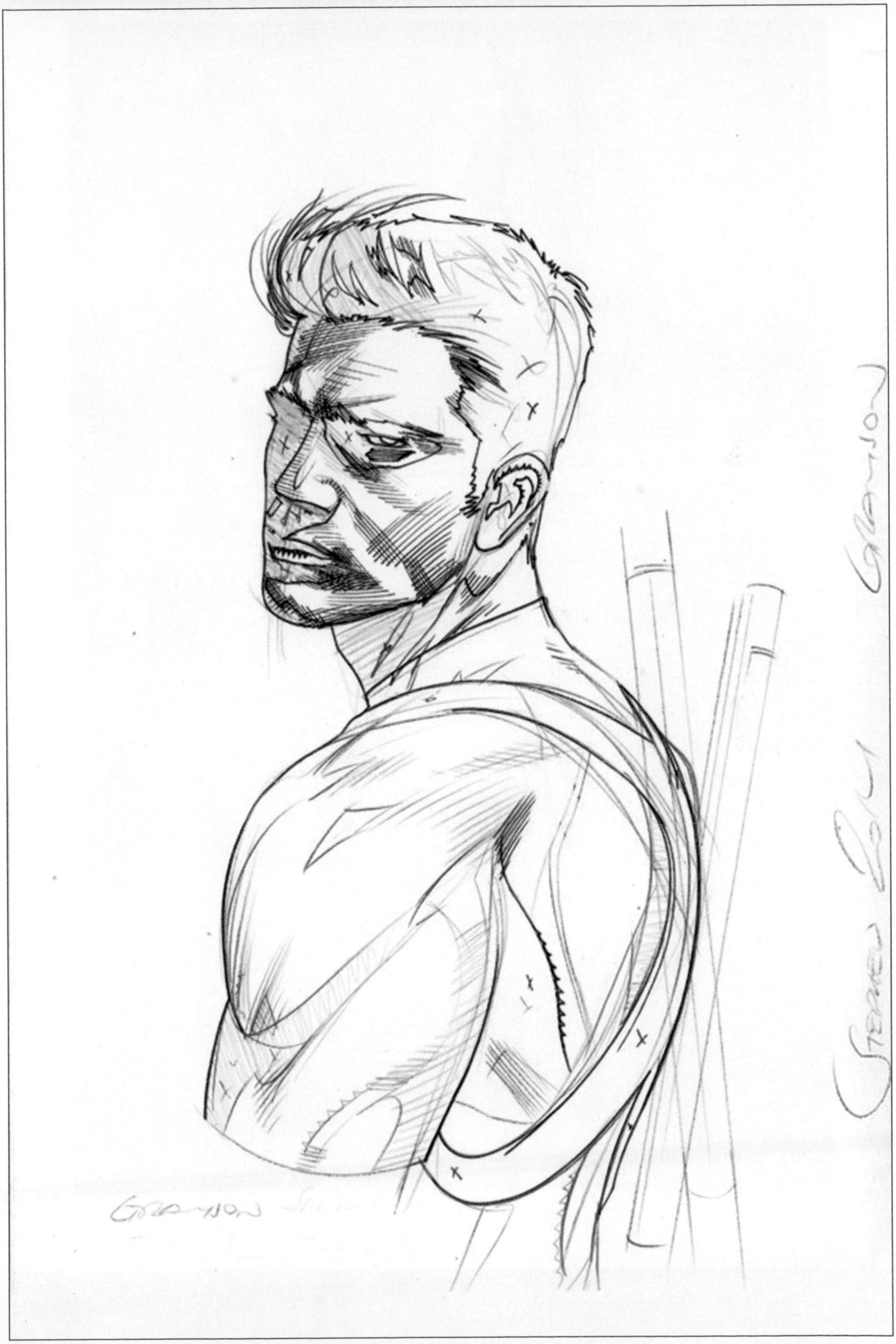

GRAYSON: FUTURES END #1
TEASER BY STEPHEN MOONEY

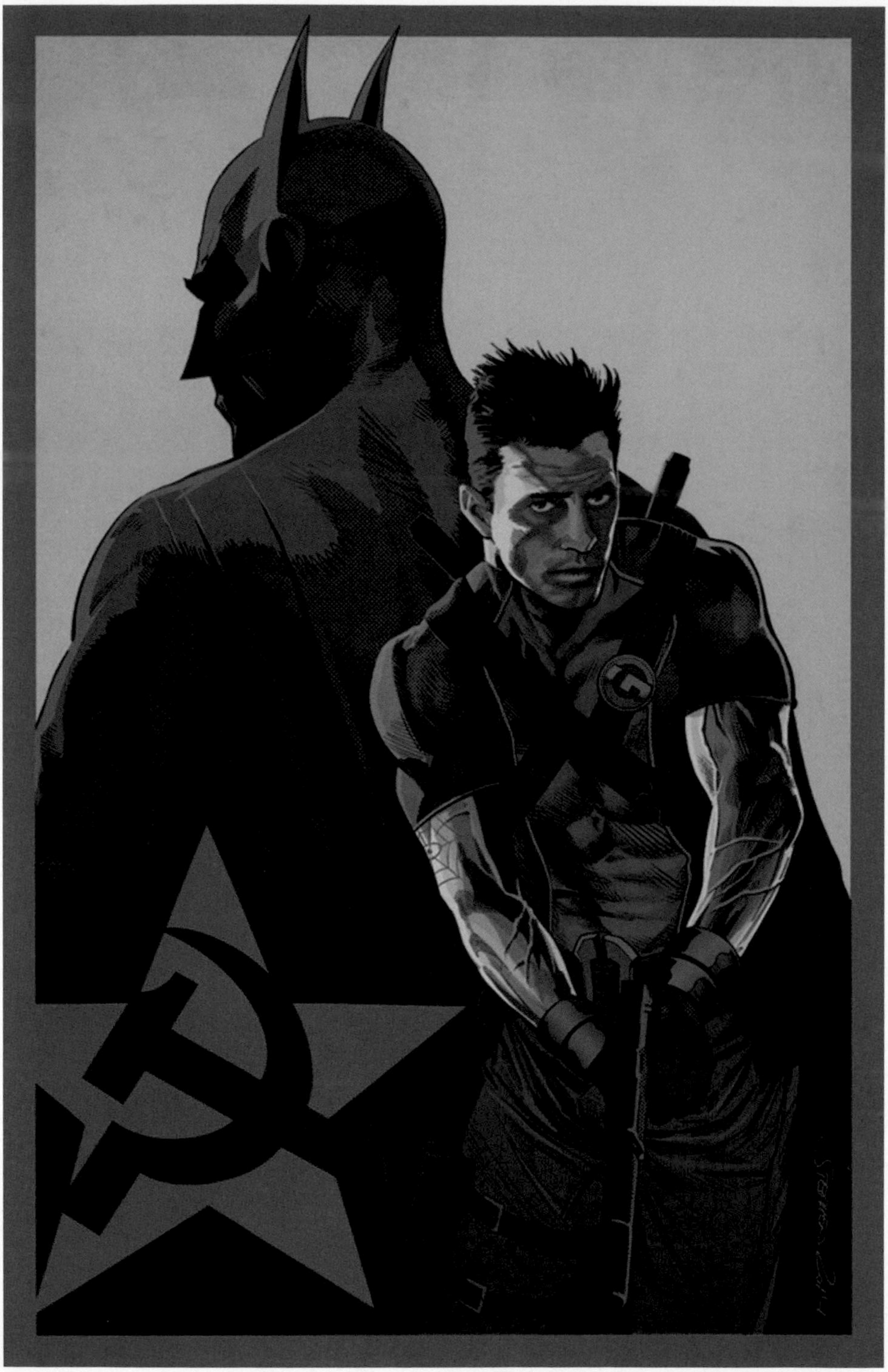

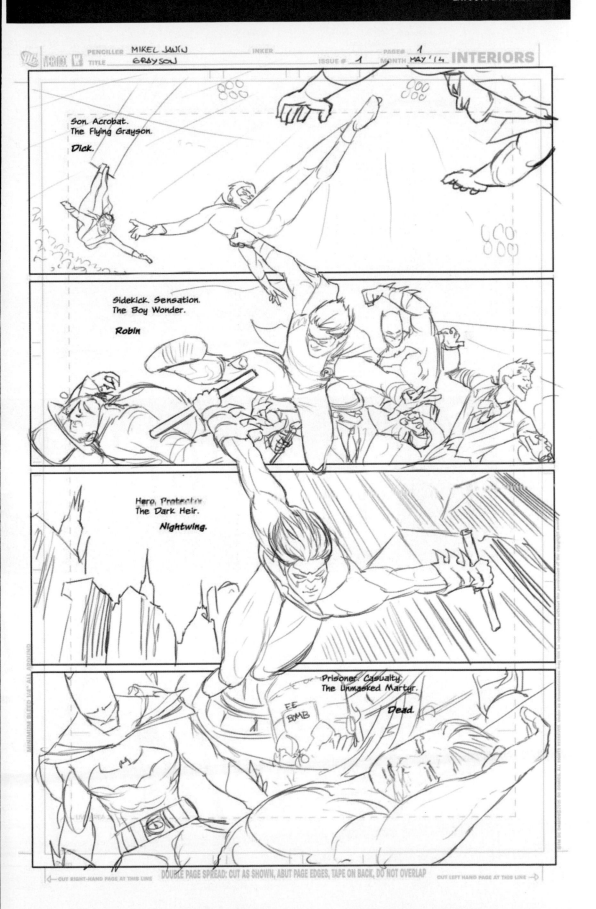

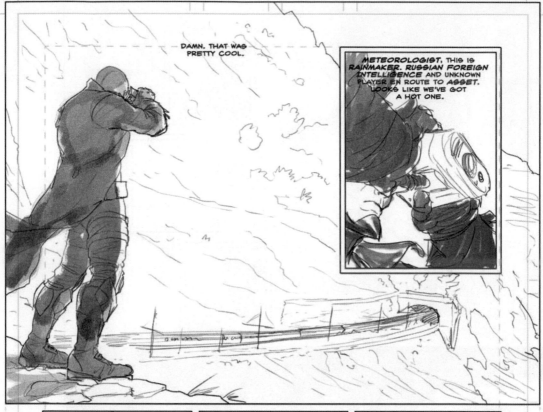

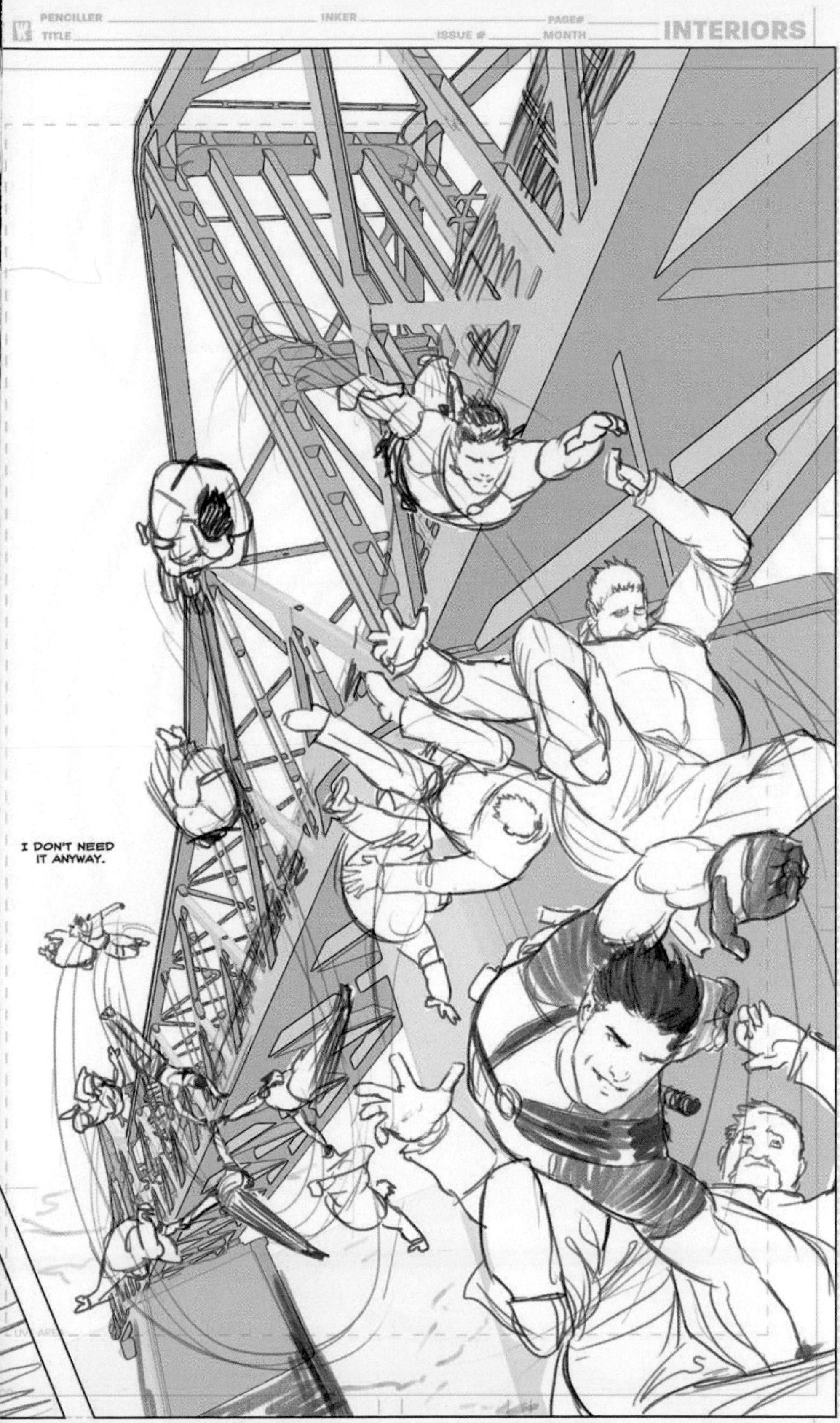
PENCILLER
INKER
PAGE#
TITLE
ISSUE #
MONTH
INTERIORS
I DON'T NEED IT ANYWAY.
RIGHT-HAND PAGE AT THIS LINE
DOUBLE PAGE SPREAD: CUT AS SHOWN, ABUT PAGE EDGES, TAPE ON BACK, DO NOT OVERLAP
CUT LEFT HAND PAGE AT THIS LINE

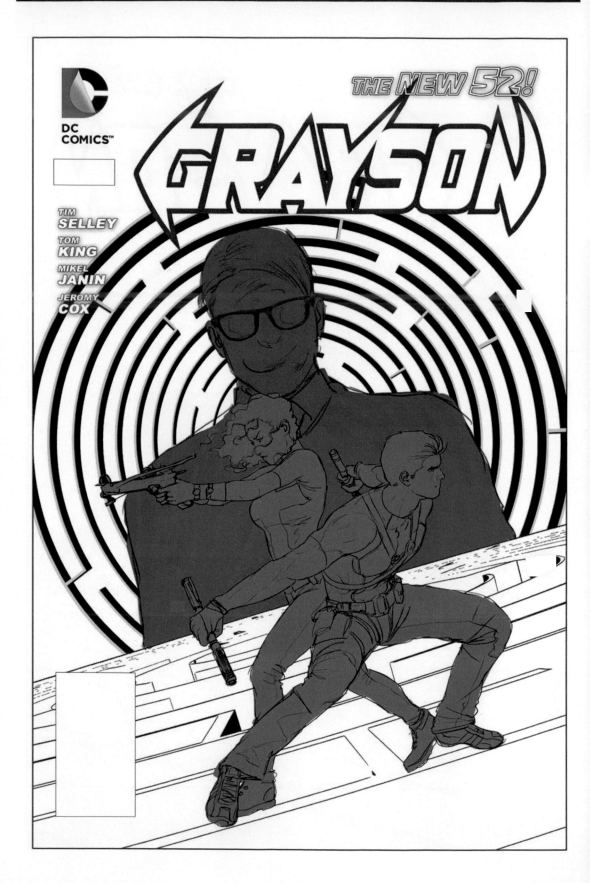